THE AFRICAN POLICIES OF GABRIEL HANOTAUX 1894–1898

Alf Andrew Heggoy

University of Georgia Press ❧ *Athens*

Library of Congress Catalog Card Number: 78–145888
International Standard Book Number: 0–8203–0272–4

The University of Georgia Press, Athens 30601

Printed in the United States of America
by The TJM Corporation
Baton Rouge, Louisiana 70806

*The African
Policies
Of Gabriel Hanotaux
1894–1898*

Contents

Preface

In the historiography of French colonialism there are few studies of the men who shaped France's colonial policies during the last decade of the nineteenth century. The heirs and successors of Jules Ferry—Théophile Delcassé, Eugène Étienne, and Gabriel Hanotaux—were energetic promoters and directors of French colonial destinies. Gabriel Hanotaux, probably the most important French colonialist of the 1890s, is the subject for this study. His tenure at the Quai d'Orsay spanned the period from the end of May 1894 to the middle of June 1898 and was broken only once, by an absence of less than six months. During the four years that he directed the foreign and colonial policies of France, Hanotaux completed the work of earlier colonialists. He excluded non-French powers from the protectorates of Madagascar and Tunisia. He found a formula which prevented a premature settlement of the Moroccan question and thereby allowed the French government time to work out its own solution. He completed West African territorial delimitations, leaving all foreign holdings in the area, except Nigeria, as mere enclaves in a French vastness. Only in the Sudan was he unable to effect a settlement by the time he was ousted from the Quai d'Orsay.

While dealing with African problems, Hanotaux never forgot the European situation upon which advances in Africa depended. He was a convinced proponent of the Franco-Russian alliance which permitted France momentarily to turn her eyes from her eastern border with Germany. Opposed by the British on nearly every African question, Hanotaux made only those concessions which were absolutely necessary. He usually took advantage of whatever diplomatic help he could secure, occasionally acting in concert with the German government too. This did not, however, imply germanophile and anglophobe attitudes on his part, as has been asserted. Hanotaux was not anti-British; he was an ardent French nationalist. Beyond this, he was quite willing to settle all Franco-British differences. Indeed, from 1894 to 1898, he did all he could to eliminate problems that troubled Anglo-French relations.

The conclusions presented in this study were reached after working first with the printed sources of French colonial history, including the many official yellow books on African questions and the *Documents diplomatiques français* for the years 1894–1898. The story that would have emerged from using only the printed sources would have been incomplete. Too many dispatches revealing slight changes of policy, for example, were never printed. The author therefore spent seven months in Paris doing research at the *Archives Nationales,* the *Archives de l'Ancien Ministère d'Outre-Mer,* and the *Archives Diplomatiques.* The *Archives de l'Ex-Gouvernement général de l'Algérie* at Aix-en-Provence and the *Archives du Ministère de la Guerre* at the chateau de Vincennes near Paris were also used, but only on a sampling basis to cross-check information found in other depositories. The research in the manuscript sources of French colonial history permitted the confirmation of the general theses already reached. It also made possible a more careful presentation of the events covered. Research was carried on in London as well, where materials about the Congo, Madagascar, Nigeria, and Tunisia were examined.

In conclusion, the author wishes to thank the many persons who have helped him in the preparation of this study. I am especially thankful for the constant encouragement given me by Professor Joel Colton and Professor Harold T. Parker of Duke University, both of whom read various drafts of this study and made many helpful suggestions. Mr. Robert Kubicek, a fellow graduate student, then a professor at the University of British Columbia, criticized the chapters on West Africa and kindly let me see notes he had taken while doing research in the *Joseph Chamberlain Papers* at the University of Birmingham. A debt of gratitude is owed the staff of the Duke Library in Durham, N.C., of the *Archives Nationales, Archives de l'Ancien Ministère d'Outre-Mer,* and *Archives Diplomatiques* in Paris, of the Public Records Office in London, and of the other depositories mentioned above. The Duke Research Council, the Southern Fellowship Fund, and the Institute of International Education supported the research of Gabriel Hanotaux's African policies. Several colleagues at the University of Georgia helped by reading various chapters as I revised the original manuscript. Dr. Joseph R. Berrigan, Dr. Lee Kennett, Dr. Roger Nichols, Dr. Ronald R. Rader and Dr. Lester Stephens took time to read portions of the final draft and extended useful criticisms. Last but not least, my wife Carol assisted by giving moral support, typing early drafts of revisions, and unhesitatingly questioning the content and the form of this narrative.

A.A.H.

Gabriel Hanotaux: French Historian, Diplomat and Colonialist

Chapter 1

In 1928, in a revealing introduction to Albert Duchêne's *La politique coloniale de la France*, Gabriel Hanotaux drew upon his personal experience at the Quai d'Orsay. He described the visit of one of France's colonial heroes and presented his own thoughts on colonialism:

> I have seen Savorgnan de Brazza, just back from his first trip to Gabon; his eyes filled with enthusiasm, he described in his motley tongue, half French, half Italian, the magnificent flow of the Congo across Africa, the river highway from the western coast to the great lakes, and the tempestuous cataracts. He inflamed us all. The majestic plateau in the center of Chad, link between the Niger and North Africa, all this was vividly presented in his idyllic description. One listened to him because he was *a man*. Marchand inspired his troops toward the Nile.
>
> At first then, there is a man. But how does the dream of a man become an empire? Adventures must become enterprises; enterprises, administration. Colonial administration is an end. (pp. ix-x)

Hanotaux went on to say that no country bordering on the sea can remain without a navy, and a navy inevitably leads to colonization. Colonization, he continued, is not a bad occupation in itself since to colonize is a way of national expression, "une façon d'être." He was obviously excited about this national way of life.

Hanotaux and de Brazza were an interesting pair. The former had not yet made his mark, although he would soon lead France to diplomatic achievements in colonial enterprises. The latter had already earned renown as an explorer who claimed vast areas of Africa for the French. De Brazza, with his Roman nose, deep-set and piercing eyes, full beard and not overly long hair parted on the left, was an impressive soldier and officer. In the mid-eighties, Hanotaux was very much a young, academically inclined bourgeois whose pince-nez with oval lenses, short sideburns and a wavy or even bushy shock of hair gave him a distinctly civilian appearance. He too wore a mustache and a beard, but these were neatly trimmed to surround his mouth but not to cover his face. Both men were provincials and each encountered difficulty with Parisian French. De Brazza spoke with a heavy trace of Italian while Hanotaux's Picardy accent induced him to change early career plans. He had hoped to pursue law as a vocation but abandoned this idea when a friend pointed out the disadvantage of arguing cases in an amusing idiom. Such were the physical and personal attributes of two colonial leaders of France's "New Imperialism." [1]

The meeting between the two men probably took place during the 1880s during Hanotaux's apprenticeship in the craft of diplomacy. In 1879 he had joined the staff at the Quai d'Orsay as an unpaid *attaché* of the Department of the Archives. On this occasion, as once before when he had transferred to the Ecole des Chartes, Hanotaux received assistance from an uncle, Henri Martin. An established scholar and historian, Martin was able to secure the position for his young relative. Fortunately the ambitious and energetic Hanotaux was well prepared. He had earned a degree as archivist in paleography and he had a great deal of ambition. The archives of the Quai d'Orsay were closed to all but a few carefully screened scholars, such as Albert Sorel, whom Hanotaux met during his first day of work in the ministry. [2] The young historian and archivist was getting a good start.

At the Quai d'Orsay Hanotaux had familiarized himself with many details of French diplomatic history while only occasionally participating in diplomatic negotiations. In his four volume memoirs, *Mon Temps* (1933) he proudly announced that he was a historian and added, "history brought him to politics and politics gave him back to history" (II, 1). Actually, he never separated the two vocations, believing his work in history as important as that in politics. [3] An able negotiator, Hanotaux advanced in the French civil service, taking charge of the Quai d'Orsay in 1894. His diplomatic masters, the foreign ministers of the 1880s and of the early 1890s, were Jules Ferry, Charles de Freycinet, and Léon Gambetta—all of whom were convinced imperialists.

Ferry, Freycinet, and Gambetta all advocated French imperialism at a time when their nation was suffering from what might aptly be called a national inferiority complex. During the 1880s most Frenchmen thought their nation too weak to exert strength outside Europe. At the same time many demanded an impossible war of *revanche* against Germany. The effect of defeatism and the pressures of the *revanchards* were keenly felt by the officials at the Foreign Ministry in Paris. Freycinet was ousted from the government for openly advocating colonialism, for such a policy would have diverted attention from the Vosges. Ferry was overthrown for adding

Tunisia and then Indo-China to the French empire. Gambetta, who was not an imperialist until Ferry induced him to change his views, was defeated by the Chamber of Deputies for advocating a strong stand against the British in Egypt in 1882. Imperialism, then, was not a popular cause in the France of Ferry, Freycinet, and Gambetta.[4] But public opinion changes. Their policies were to find fulfillment during the 1890s when such men as Théophile Delcassé, Eugène Etienne, and Gabriel Hanotaux steered the nation through a period of unprecedented colonial advancement.

These "young men" were the heirs of Ferry, Freycinet, and Gambetta; [5] they had been trained in the early imperialistic school. In the 1890s, they carried out the policies of their masters: Etienne as an able speaker in the Chamber of Deputies, Delcassé as Minister of Colonies—a ministry that was not created until February 1894—and Hanotaux as master of the Quai d'Orsay and originator of the new French colonial policy. These men had the backing of a rejuvenated and energetic France, a prestige-conscious country intent on assuming once more its rightful place among the powers of Europe. Support came not only from colleagues in the government and in the legislature, but increasingly from a growing number of organizations outside the government. These were the active and often quite effective "colonialists." [6]

In 1881 Hanotaux was promoted to assistant in the cabinet of Foreign Minister Léon Gambetta, a burly one-eyed lawyer and devout republican who was also the leader of the so-called Grand Ministry (August 1882–January 1883). According to André Siegfried, a contemporary of Hanotaux, the latter wrote a series of historical articles in *Le Temps* and in *La République Française* that so impressed Gambetta that he talked the young author into abandoning the musty profession of archivist and historian to pursue a political career. Although Gambetta left, Hanotaux stayed at the Quai d'Orsay to serve as *chef de cabinet* under Paul Challemel-Lacour, the foreign minister in the second Jules Ferry government (February 1883–April 1885).[7] For a time Hanotaux pursued three careers at the same time, serving at the French Foreign Office, teaching, and studying and writing history. It was during these years that Hanotaux found time to make a detailed study of Cardinal Richelieu. The first volume of this work appeared in 1893; the second, which obtained the "Grand Prix Gobert" at the *Academie Française,* was not published until 1896,[8] when Hanotaux had already been Minister for foreign affairs for almost two years. The award was the highest tribute for historical publications ever granted by the Academy. Before he became foreign minister Hanotaux had also published a biography of his uncle, Henri Martin in 1885 and two books entitled

Etudes historiques sur le xvie et xviie siècle en France (1880) and *Instructions données par les Rois de France à leurs Ambassadeurs à Rome* (1888). In recognition of his scholarship, Hanotaux was voted membership into the Academy in 1897—a crowning event for a man who had also accomplished so much in the service of his country.

Before his election to the Academy and before his appointment as Foreign Minister, Hanotaux completed his diplomatic and political training at the Quai d'Orsay, in the Chamber of Deputies and abroad. He won an election in 1886 and was deputy for the department of Aisne. During his term he sat on the left in a house that still had enough monarchists and ultraconservative republicans to fill the benches to the right. His voting record, however, was only moderately liberal by the standards of his own days. A member of the Moderate party, he intervened in debates only twice, once in defense of compulsory military service and once, in 1888, to question the wisdom of maintaining a French "spiritual protectorate" over Roman Catholics in the Near East. He opposed the anti-republican Ligue des Patriotes and was in favor of stripping parliamentary immunity from deputies of like convictions. He also thought criminal charges should be brought against General Georges Boulanger. While he did not oppose limited state interference in matters of general welfare, he believed strongly in the sanctity of private property. At the same time, he had little sympathy for land speculators. Although he occasionally voted with the Radicals, he shared his own party's distrust of the masses.[9] Hanotaux was, in short, a conservative bourgeois with strong republican convictions. In 1889 in the midst of the Boulanger crisis, he lost his seat in the Chamber of Deputies and returned to the Quai d'Orsay. Serving first as deputy director of protectorates, he then moved to the more prestigious job of director of consular and commercial affairs. Finally, he fulfilled a diplomatic assignment in the Middle East and in the Balkans, filling such posts as counselor, then as charge d' affaires at Pera with the French diplomatic mission to the Ottoman Empire.

Hanotaux returned to France where, late in 1893, Moderates from the department of Aisne asked him to run for the Senate. But Hanotaux felt attached to another candidate, William Waddington, a man who had been his chief at the Quai d'Orsay between December 1877 and February 1879. Hanotaux refused to run against the former foreign minister although he was undoubtedly tempted to do so. Election to the Senate would have given him a good sinecure and more time to devote to his history of the Richelieu era. Jean Casimir-Perier, the premier and foreign minister between April and December 1893, wanted Hanotaux to stay on as director of consular and commercial affairs.[10] The young man followed the advice of his party's most prominent leader. Even in early 1894, few could have guessed that within a few short months, Hanotaux would take over in his chief's old position. But on May 30, 1894, Hanotaux was appointed foreign minister of France. He was already well prepared for his new position, although he was one of the few politicians of the Third Republic to hold a ministerial post while he did not sit in either the Chamber of Deputies or the Senate.

Hanotaux held office at the Ministry of Foreign Affairs during the most crucial years of the new imperialism. Unlike Jules Ferry, his master in colonial matters, Hanotaux was more persistently successful in applying his teacher's ideas, partly because anti-colonialism was not as strong after 1894 as before. He also had more time in which to make Ferry's program of colonial expansion work. Only forty-one when he became foreign minister Hanotaux was, to that time, the youngest man ever to hold that office. An excellent diplomat, he came to have to his credit one of the longest tenures at the important post: from May 30, 1894, to November 1, 1895, and again, from April 2, 1896, to June 28, 1898, for a total of forty-four months. His great skill in diplomatic affairs (which was generally recognized by his own contemporaries) and his relatively long tenure enabled Hanotaux to provide France with an unprecedented continuity of policy.

Trained as a "Chartiste" at the "Ecole des Chartes," Hanotaux became an admirable official. On the staff at the Quai d'Orsay, he had learned to search documents for the smallest details and the imperceptible changes in any given negotiation which might help to establish a claim and solve in a manner favorable to France the diplomatic impasse of the moment. Hanotaux's thoroughness and comprehension of often microscopic facts rendered him invaluable to his superiors. Hanotaux earned the nickname "the professor" by invariably lecturing the chambers whenever he was called upon to defend his policies. On such occasions he would lean over carefully prepared texts, read them in a dull voice, and rarely answer parliamentary taunts. Yet to intimate friends, Hanotaux was a brilliant conversationalist, a man whose mind was open to "large and elevated considerations," always *"sympathique,* gracious, and attractive." [11] As a minister, Hanotaux was to continue in his old accustomed manner, never advancing boldly, but always basing his action on the record of past treaties and diplomatic notes. This method of work and thought enabled him to face his opponents with undeniable truths which shifted responsibility for refutation to their shoulders. "The very defect of this favorite of fortune," wrote a political observer in 1898, "had become the most precious qualities." [12]

A self-made man, Hanotaux was an aristocrat by taste. He was a bourgeois republican of the Moderate party in an age in which conservative middle-class values dominated French politics. Nothing in his person suggested traits of a "parvenu," for he lived simply, preferring to wear a simple black coat though his high office entitled him to a brilliant uniform and numerous decorations. In his personal relations he was a steadfast friend, though he did not marry until his sixtieth year when he married Mademoiselle Marie de la Crompe de la Boissière who was less than half his age.[13] Until then, he had had several mistresses. His most serious affair was with Géronime Negadelle who had two children by him; Hanotaux adopted a third child, Mlle. Negadelle's eldest daughter. Since his mistress was somewhat older than he, Hanotaux soon began to seek pleasure elsewhere although he did not marry until seven years after her death. He found diversion with the beautiful and talented actress Mlle. Valentine Verlaine but ended the relationship in 1899 when she proved to be too jealous. Hanotaux's affairs did not affect his public life for as one author has written, the minister was too intelligent to let sensuality destroy him. But Mlle. Verlaine, probably with assistance from Hanotaux's enemies in the *Action Française*, took revenge by privately publishing an unflattering account of her former lover's life after hours, *La faux du Ministre*.

In politics Hanotaux believed strongly that European peace was a necessity; he was therefore more interested in preserving the existing equilibrium than in risking a clash. Hanotaux was also a patriot who, while working to avoid armed conflict, wished to strengthen France. He was therefore a partisan of the Franco-Russian alliance which had been concluded shortly before he became Minister of Foreign Affairs. It is not surprising that he followed in colonial affairs the lines established by Léon Gambetta and Jules Ferry. Basically, Hanotaux believed, as had his two predecessors, that in becoming a great colonial power, France would increase her resources and thereby become stronger. Hanotaux set out to carry through the active colonial policies of Gambetta and of Ferry, the imperial program which France had pursued down to 1885. In colonial affairs, there had followed a period of withdrawal as France lived through the Boulangist crisis, then through various scandals such as the Panama Bubble. There had been a consequent waning of interest in colonies, which Hanotaux consciously and in cooperation with colonialist groups and politicians sought to revive.

Prestige was perhaps the most important element in the new expansionist drive. Some of Hanotaux's own books written partially as apologia for his own colonial policies give strong evidence about this motivation. *Pour l'empire colonial* was a clear example of this; so was *La paix latine* which also advanced the ideal of inheriting the Roman empire, an obvious attempt to give France reflected glory. While Hanotaux was Foreign Minister, the arguments used to convince deputies to approve the credits needed for active penetration all over Africa included the old economic, military, and political arguments. The calls to the "mission civilisatrice" of France, the French version of the "white man's burden," continued to be stressed. But prestige was certainly more important. Hanotaux's Moroccan policy, for example, was directed squarely at keeping anyone from taking over the country and toward gaining French predominance. In West Africa, French missions raced into marshes and into semi-arid areas with more forethought to gaining glory than to securing economically sound territorial acquisitions. As often as not, advances into African hinterland were made to foil the designs of other powers. This was certainly so in the case of the French reaction to the Anglo-Congolese treaty of 1894 and of the policies that preceded the agreement between London and Brussels. Later the French developed the Fashoda plan to foil British advances into the region of the Upper Nile from Uganda.[14] In 1894 the scramble for Africa degenerated into a mad race which did not peak until Hanotaux's tenure came to an end, although he himself tended to moderate the programs of his fellow colonialists.

By 1894 only two areas were still open for expansion—North and Central Africa—and in both these areas French advances meant inevitable friction with England. In his first days in office, Hanotaux tried to find a way to make England annul the Anglo-Congolese treaty of May 5, 1894, which, if in effect and recognized as legal, would thwart French designs in Central Africa. As Hanotaux further explained in 1909 when he published *Fachoda,* he did not oppose the British because of Anglophobe opinions. He was appointed to lead the Quai d'Orsay after Charles Dupuy, the prime minister of the first cabinet in which Hanotaux served, decided that Delcassé, who was first considered for the position, was too closely identified with the colonialist faction in the Chamber of Deputies. He was not anti-British, but, as he put it in his memoirs, he would not let "Britain get, for all future times, the rivers and territories over which France had an equal right to settle and trade." (II, 233) Like his predecessors, Gambetta and Ferry especially, Hanotaux believed France would be strengthened by acquiring a colonial empire. Searching in history for the precepts of his own political system, Hanotaux concluded that "France must not be chosen; she must choose." [15]

Chef de cabinet at the Foreign Ministry under both Gambetta and Ferry, Hanotaux in his work as Foreign Minister synthesized the thoughts and ideas of these two remarkable statesmen of the Third Republic. From Ferry, Hanotaux adopted his special understanding of colonialism. From Gambetta, Hanotaux inherited "opportunism." The "opportunists" were the republicans grouped around Gambetta and "opportunism" was just another word for politics. The name describes rather well a group of politicians who believed in getting things done, who were disposed to allow their policies to be shaped by circumstances. They were mostly pragmatic leaders who practiced their own brand of *Realpolitik*. "Opportunism" was their method as well as their philosophical approach to politics. With Hanotaux this method became an approach to politics on a world scale during the period of greatest imperialistic activity for France and other European nations. Judged on the basis of results achieved during Hanotaux's long tenure at the Quai d'Orsay, the method was quite successful. Hanotaux's pragmatic approach to political and diplomatic problems assured him of a chance to apply Ferry's ideas far better than the master ever managed. But his method has also been called "pin-pricking" because he often created a problem deliberately in the hope that he could gain something for France. He himself claimed the "pin-pricking" was done by his opponents.

Opportunism, as Hanotaux's method, was applied to the resurgent French imperialism of the 1890s. The desire for a colonial empire had become an active one; Hanotaux set out to gratify it. Advancing in fields of previously uncontested British imperialism and energetically competing with Britain for the remaining areas open to colonization, France met opposition. As one French scholar put it: "On the high road of colonial conquest we encountered the British at Tunis, in Madagascar, on Lake Chad, in the Congo and at the headwaters of the Nile as well as in Indo-China and the islands of the Pacific." [16]

In this growing dispute, which found the two powers even on the brink of war in 1898–99 over the Fashoda incident, Hanotaux accepted what diplomatic support he could, including that of Germany. This policy led many of Hanotaux's contemporaries, as well as scholars of more recent times, to blame him for being too much of a Germanophile and too much of an Anglophobe.[17] Charles Maurras, in *De la paix de Francfort à la conférence d'Algesiras* (1909), even suggested that the former foreign minister had too much admiration for German culture. Five years later, Ernest

Dimnet in *France Herself Again* no longer argued, but simply reported as fact the same allegation. More careful historical interpretations, however, hinted that Hanotaux may have been too much involved in a search for "compensation" for the defeat of 1870. Allied to this argument was one that was already being addressed to Hanotaux while he was the master of the Quai d'Orsay and which was more carefully explored by Pierre Renouvin in 1948 in his *Revue Historique* article on the origins of the Fashoda crisis. This theory was that Hanotaux did not really seek cooperation with Germany, but that he followed France's new-found ally, Russia, into cooperation with Germany. French participation in the inauguration of the Kiel Canal in 1895, and the Gallic position on the Greek question in 1897 are the usual illustrations for this Russian-German thesis. A contemporary cartoon, for example, showed Hanotaux with an overly-long nose, the end of which was tucked in the belt of a Russian canoneer. Next to Hanotaux was another soldier whose gun, which was pointed at a Greek nationalist, was clearly labeled *Allemagne*. When cooperation with Germany led to daring challenges of the British in Africa or in other colonial areas, Hanotaux did run very high risks as German help was never sure. Thus, criticism of Hanotaux on this ground is not easily countered by apologists for the former foreign minister.[18]

To suppose that Hanotaux wanted an alliance with Germany would be incongruous—as much so as to suppose that Ferry, a native of Lorraine, would have wanted such an attachment. Both men, master and disciple, were faced by the same problem. They were both convinced proponents of French imperialism and saw clearly that England was the great obstacle to any colonial advance. Germany had a similar problem. Cooperation, therefore, seemed logical and desirable.

This does not imply that Ferry or Hanotaux ignored the problem of the lost provinces or rejected the *revanche*. Hanotaux himself had felt the full impact of the war of 1870 which occurred when he was sixteen. In his memoirs he told with pride about his part in the capture of a few German prisoners at the border town of St. Quentin. Ferry realized that "the dream of recovering Alsace-Lorraine could not, for a long time at least, be translated into practice." He had therefore come to believe "that the wisest thing to do would be to cooperate with Germany for the attainment of certain specified colonial aims, while reserving the larger and more knotty problem for the future." [19] This conclusion, this flexibility, was accepted by Hanotaux who, backed by a changed French public opinion about imperialism, was capable of carrying imperialist policies to profitable ends. Again, the acceptance of German diplomatic help in colonial matters did not imply an acceptance of the status quo in Alsace-Lorraine. It was an application of Gambetta's maxim always to think but never to speak of the severed provinces. The grave problem was reserved for the future while France turned to practical policies. For the time being, thoughts turned to imperialism.

Hanotaux has explained the African policies of France during the 1890s. This explanation can be found in two works, both personal and largely documentary books, *L'Affaire de Madagascar,* published in 1896 while he was temporarily out of office and its complement, *Fachoda* which did not appear until 1909. To effect the consolidation of all French holdings in Africa was the core of Hanotaux's policy, a policy that was not *consciously* anti-British. The politician-historian looked to history and to geography for his politics. Here he found that France had many "footholds" on the black continent—Senegal, the Ivory Coast, and Gabon in the West, Algeria and Tunis in the North, Obock (Somaliland) in the East. These footholds, he easily concluded, were but so many bases of operation. By a simultaneous exploration from the various centers of French control, by a vigorous and sustained penetration of the continent, all of France's African holdings would be linked.[20] The point of junction was the Chad which became one of Hanotaux's tactical objectives. France did get to Lake Chad in 1897, thereby largely completing her ambitious plan: only Obock in East Africa remained isolated.

In implementing his plan for Africa, Hanotaux inevitably ran into British opposition. By luck or by design, he believed, the British had seized the best portions of Africa. France had to move quickly and energetically simply to protect her own imperial future. Jules Ferry had initiated a rush for colonial conquests that Hanotaux continued even as he moderated Delcassé and other extremists in his own colonialist circles. Long unchallenged in colonial endeavors, Britain quickly noticed the rejuvenated French imperialism at an early stage. Said Lord Rosebery in a speech at Leeds during the year 1888: "The other powers are beginning a career of colonial aggrandisement." The other powers were, indeed, entering the imperial contest and in less than a decade, all but Morocco, Abyssinia, and Liberia had been claimed. In the "saturation" of Africa, France and Germany were Britain's closest competitors. That these two powers should have cooperated on specific issues in colonial matters seems, in retrospect, almost unavoidable. But they combined against Britain on specific issues only; the Franco-German cooperation was never more than a case-by-case affair. Britain, though already in possession of a huge empire, continued to expand during the years of Hanotaux's deliberate colonial expansion.

The British policy was one of "pegging out claims for the future" as Lord Rosebery put it in 1893. Everyone was aggressive and conflicts arose as each nation sought to follow its own interests. If Hanotaux worked with Germany, then so did Salisbury. In this, France was at a distinct disadvantage. Whatever she did, wherever she engaged her energies, France always had to think in terms of Europe. She could strive for a large share of Africa, but not at the price of a war with England, nor at the risk of leaving Germany dominant on the continent. Britain, in her "isolation," could work with Germany without fear. But for France this was impossible.[21]

Hanotaux's policies were carefully balanced. Even while occasionally working with the Wilhelmstrasse, he remained a strong protagonist of the Franco-Russian alliance. The fact that this pact was to last as long as Germany's Triple Alliance brings out its essential meaning: it was directed against Germany. Also, Hanotaux accepted or rejected German advances according to the gains possible for France. There was an effort made to arrive at an equilibrium: France, under Hanotaux, maintained Russia against Germany, Germany against England—though he would not have committed himself to a permanent arrangement with the Germans—and maybe England against Germany. It was a dangerous game which reveals Hanotaux as an audacious thinker. He would not commit France to either Britain or Germany. When he became Foreign Minister, Delcassé was disposed to ignore German advances. In contrast, Hanotaux listened to proposals for cooperation while he consistently pushed French claims as far as possible without, however, risking permanent alienation or war with Britain.[22]

No two nations had as many outstanding conflicts as France and Britain, and between these two nations, no problem was as important as that of Egypt. Ever since the British had occupied this area, France had stood for a policy diametrically opposed to that of Britain. Though this was the greatest problem between the two, it was by no means the only one. Indeed, republican France never held ambitions about Africa as conspicuous as those which she proclaimed during those years when Hanotaux was in charge of the Quai d'Orsay. In those years, "Great Britain and France found themselves at odds in every part of the globe where their colonial interests were neighboring." [23] In 1925, in his memoirs, *Twenty-Five Years, 1892–1916*, Edward Grey, an undersecretary at Downing Street during the 1890s remarked:

> It was in West Africa that incidents most frequently occurred. British officials explored the country and made treaties with native chiefs on which we

based our rights. French officials would overlap ours in their exploration and treaties; hence claims and counter-claims and confusion. It was sometimes possible to argue that a treaty had been made with a native chief who was not independent but subordinate, and that the treaty was therefore valueless. (I, 16)

France had come late into West Africa, and the Congo territories and Nigeria, the areas that promised to become economically rewarding, had already been claimed. Sierra Leone which offered good harbors for coaling stations had also been staked. There remained only abandoned strips of coast between profitable sections. And it was on these steamy tropical points of the coastline, usually damned with arid hinterlands merging into deserts, that France founded her bases of operations.

From these bases, France, starved for prestige and needing an economic justification for the high cost of what West African holdings she had acquired, launched an attack on all of West Africa. And all but Nigeria became little more than enclaves in a French African vastness. Gambia, Sierra Leone, Liberia, Togo, and other synthetic political divisions in West Africa, lost what was potentially their hinterland. The French expanded around established areas in an attempt to drain more trade through their own poor harbors.

Sooner or later the diplomats had to intervene, and it was Hanotaux who directed French diplomacy through the negotiations that followed the French rush on Africa. Hanotaux also had to settle many of the disputes that arose from actual clashes between French and British, and French and German explorers and treaty-makers. To secure a claim to given African territory, or to challenge the claim of another power, Hanotaux sometimes deliberately created or sanctioned colonialist activities that would create Franco-British or Franco-German problems in West Africa. Expeditions that went into the Bahr-el-Ghazal or on the left bank of the Niger are clear examples of this kind of challenge to imperial competitors. These maneuvers clearly reflect the manner of someone quite sure of himself.

Knowing his own capabilities as a negotiator Hanotaux would first create a problem. He then offered to negotiate the "new" problem and any other outstanding issue. He always knew the details of the problem—the treaties, the geography, and the history of the disputed areas. Usually he managed to achieve his own aim, some specific colonial gain for France. He was a man willing to take risks and at the same time able to manage with great care the feelings of his opponents, a man playing with "l'équilibre entre les forces européennes." [24]

Even while seeking to satisfy French colonial desires, Hanotaux worked
for an entente with Great Britain. He was apparently one of the few officials in either France or Great Britain who sincerely wanted such an entente, although he did not feel that an entente was urgently needed.[25] He
worked for agreement with the British only insofar as it could be reached
without great sacrifices in colonial matters. He was both sanguine in his
imperial demands and sincere in his work for the establishment of a French
and British entente. During his four years at the Quai d'Orsay, Hanotaux
was caught in this strange dilemma. His experience as a civil servant and
as an academician occasionally limited his ability to make clear-cut decisions. This characteristic was sometimes reflected in his official acts and in
his policies.

Thus, when his colleagues in January 1895 refused to accept a convention about West and Central Africa which Hanotaux had personally negotiated with Great Britain, he was sincerely disappointed.[26] He thought
this convention would have put an end to the divisive problems in these
areas. His policy rebuked, Hanotaux wished to resign, but France was going
through the first throes of the Dreyfus affair and an appeal to his patrio-
tism kept him at the Quai d'Orsay. The Dreyfus affair started in 1894 and
in January 1895 led to heated diplomatic discussions between France and
Germany. Hanotaux handled these talks as he also resumed Anglo-French
talks about Africa. He stubbornly worked to overcome imperial differences
which kept London and Paris from a political entente.[27]

Hanotaux's solutions of the Madagascar problem in 1895 and the Tunisian capitulations question in 1897 put an end to uncertain political situations. Though the British were not pleased, the arguments about Madagascar and Tunis were brought to an end, and it was the Convention which
Hanotaux signed on June 15, 1898, just a few hours before the Chamber
of Deputies overthrew the Jules Méline government of which he was a
member, that made possible the creation of the Anglo-French Entente of
1904.[28] Delcassé naturally reaped credit for this important achievement of
French diplomacy. It was he who was foreign minister when the entente
came to life, and he managed the final and difficult negotiations. But talks
could not have begun if Delcassé's advice had been followed in 1894. Indeed, he was probably more directly responsible for the Fashoda crisis than
Hanotaux, although the latter lost his position at the Quai d'Orsay because
of this problem. It was under Minister for Colonies Delcassé that the Marchand expedition which led ultimately to the Fashoda crisis, became a detailed plan of action. Hanotaux delayed the execution of the plan long
enough to solve practically all other outstanding imperial differences be-

tween Paris and London. In the end, he laid the foundation for Delcassé's entente, a diplomatic institution that might have been scuttled by the latter's earlier colonial aims.

In 1894 Delcassé was first considered for the position which was given to Hanotaux. Hanotaux, with the historian's awareness that his political notes might one day be used by other scholars, wrote that Delcassé had been unacceptable for the Quai d'Orsay position because of his "insufficient experience ... and close affiliation with the colonial party whose interference during the delicate Anglo-Congolese negotiations could be embarrassing." [29] These words in his "Carnets" clearly show that Hanotaux was aware of his role as a historical figure, a role he sometimes embellished in official diplomatic documents as well.[30] Throughout his ministry at the Quai d'Orsay, he labored to rid Anglo-French relations of mutual antagonisms. One of the first issues on which the Quai d'Orsay and the Foreign Office found it possible to cooperate was that involving Morocco in 1894.

Morocco, 1894

Chapter 2

Gabriel Hanotaux was foreign minister of France but a few days when Mouley Hassan, the sultan of Morocco, unexpectedly died on June 6, 1894. The Sultan's death was kept secret for several days and it was not until the 10th that the French resident in Tangiers reported the event to the Quai d'Orsay.[1] Hassan's realm which was precarious in his lifetime now fell into near anarchy as chancelleries throughout Europe reacted with a flurry of diplomatic activity. Hanotaux, first as Director of Commercial and Consular Affairs, then as foreign minister, was already involved in difficult negotiations about King Leopold's Congo and British claims in the Sudan and Upper Nile regions. In the Moroccan situation, however, he faced a new problem that he did not inherit. How Hanotaux handled this difficulty revealed a great deal about his colonial attitudes, his working habits, and his character.

Besides Abyssinia, the valley of the upper Nile and Liberia, Morocco was the last independent territory open to colonial expansion. A sovereign state, Liberia was controlled by a small percentage of its population, by the Afro-Americans who had colonized the area during the nineteenth century. But it was not a colony and it enjoyed relative freedom from European interference. Perhaps the fact that Liberia had no natural harbors or that it had been created by the United States which, however, did not control it, indirectly assured the country's sovereignty. There was, in any case, nothing like the European competition for predominance that weighed so heavily on Abyssinia or on Morocco. North of the Sahara, European rivalries were undermining the political structure of the Sheriffian Empire. The powers seemed bent on fostering the social and political unrest which threatened to lead to a "breakup" of this Muslim state. In Morocco, the dissolution of central authority and anarchic political conditions were not new in 1894, but when Hassan died, imperialists thought the final crisis could be precipitated.

In 1894 the interested European powers were not ready to accept an imperial solution for the Moroccan problem. Germany's position was perhaps typical. As a latecomer in the scramble for Africa, Germany feigned disinterest, and worked for the preservation of the status quo.[2] Logically enough, the Wilhelmstrasse considered that it had nothing to gain from a quick settlement of the question: German interests in the Sultanate were still negligible. But in time, Germany could be expected to improve its Moroccan position. Other powers, Italy for example, expected compensations in Morocco or the Sheriffian Empire as it is also known, for colonial losses suffered elsewhere. But Italy was too much committed in East Africa. So Rome joined others in seeking to avoid change. So did France.

The common desire for the maintenance of the status quo was complicated by a universal distrust of all interested powers towards their competitors. As in most of Africa, the chief antagonists were Downing Street and the Quai d'Orsay. The Moroccan interests of Great Britain were considerable. In 1902 just a few years later, British share of Morocco's foreign trade was 41 percent, while France accounted for 31 percent and Germany for only 8 percent.[3] British policy, however, was strongly influenced by concepts of Mediterranean strategy: Her Majesty's Government did not wish to see a major European power facing it across the straits of Gibraltar.[4] In spite of this, the British were not interested in taking Morocco themselves, although the French Resident in Tangiers continually reported about the "péril anglais." [5]

In their negative policy, the British Government was usually supported by the Italians who were already preoccupied with their Abyssinian problems and were perhaps hoping their Mediterranean ally would help them in East Africa. Crispi, the leader of the Italian Government, would have liked compensation for the "loss" of Tunis in Morocco. Short of this, he was combatting French influence in North Africa with all the means available to him. The apparent entente between London and Rome led to suspicions in Paris and in Madrid that there existed an intrigue to turn the new Sultan against them. And Crispi worried lest England should reach a workable solution with the French.[6]

France and Spain each considered itself the logical successor to the political order they were quietly undermining, for they had long enjoyed a predominant position in the Moroccan government. This advantage was partly due to geographical factors which both Paris and Madrid were quick to exploit in imperial arguments. But they were not yet ready in 1894 to assume control over the sultanate. Hassan's sudden death left the major nations unprepared to meet the crisis that followed. No one, the French Minister for Foreign Affairs included, seemed to have a decided Moroccan policy. The powers did fear that other nations would try to intrigue for predominance in Morocco. Hanotaux meant to keep ahead of all competitors.

Although he was an African specialist at the Quai d'Orsay before he
became foreign minister,[7] Hanotaux did not know all the intricacies of
the Moroccan situation. He immediately began to collect the information
upon which to base his Moroccan policy. After learning of Mouley Hassan's
death, Hanotaux telegraphed d'Aubigny, his representative in Tangiers,
for further information about Abd el Aziz, the successor-designate. The
heir apparent was a fourteen-year-old boy. Would not one of Abd el Aziz's
two older brothers challenge the inheritance? The ruling house of Morocco
did not have a tradition of primogeniture. Since a successor had been des-
ignated, the transition of power should occur without difficulties. But the
French foreign minister was dubious. He directed d'Aubigny to report
on the reactions of his European colleagues. Clearly, the thoughts and actions of foreign representatives in Morocco were just as important as those
of the Moroccans themselves.[8]

While still seeking reliable information the French foreign minister
called the ambassador of Spain to the Quai d'Orsay, where promises were
exchanged: Paris and Madrid would continue to exchange information
about Morocco and, when possible, consult each other in an attempt to act
in common accord in the Sheriffian Empire. This cooperation with Spain
on North African questions was simply a continuation of a policy evolved
during the 1880s by Hanotaux's former masters in colonial matters. A parallel diplomatic discussion was taking place in Madrid where Sigismond
Moret, the Spanish Foreign Minister, had called to his office the French
chargé d'affaires, Theodore Roustan, in order to show him a telegram announcing the death of the sultan. In a second interview, the French diplomat dutifully reported on June 12, Moret insisted that all the powers involved in Morocco act in accord on the succession problem, and recognize
Abd el Aziz with the shortest possible delay.[9]

Still another diplomatic discussion started when Lord Dufferin, the
British ambassador in Paris, approached Hanotaux on the 11th of June.
The Spanish Government had asked the British Foreign Office about its
intentions with respect to the Moroccan succession. Dufferin wished to
know if the French intended to recognize Abd el Aziz immediately, or
whether they would prefer to wait and see.[10] Hanotaux, pleading incomplete intelligence reports, asked for a delay. The two men parted on the
promise to continue the cooperation in Sheriffian affairs started earlier in
the year at the time of the Melilla crisis.[11] Spain had nearly gone to war
against the Sultan when the latter's Government failed to meet indemnity
payments due in accordance with earlier diplomatic agreements. The Span-
ish-Moroccan crisis was solved when the Sheriffian government agreed to

pay Madrid stipulated indemnities, these terms having been reached largely because of French cooperation.

While he was gathering his information from his representatives in Tangiers and in Madrid as well as from the ambassadors who came to his office, Hanotaux was learning what the intended policies of other governments were, and was preparing the ground for the diplomatic discussion which would temporarily settle the Moroccan question. Indeed, the discussion was already engaged. But as far as the French were concerned, France would eventually gain control over most of the sultanate. Hanotaux certainly expected the Sheriffian Empire, or a large portion of its territories, to fall within the African Empire of France.[12] The diplomatic talks aimed at the preservation of a Moroccan status quo were but a holding action.

For the moment, the maintenance of an independent Morocco would best serve French colonial ambitions.[13] The Chamber of Deputies had recently opened a large credit for political and military action in Central Africa. That the prestige of France was involved in the Congo had been an important determinant in the financial and colonial debate. Usually shy about imperial ventures, the deputies could not be expected to accept still another exceptional budget to cover possible colonialist action in Morocco. Paul Leroy-Beaulieu, a leading French colonialist, had complained in 1886 about the anti-colonial reaction of France to the imperial policies of Jules Ferry.[14] In 1894 the French were about to engage in new colonial ventures. But there was still a determined opposition to colonial advances in both the Chamber of Deputies and in the Senate. In Morocco itself, the objections of other powers to a French solution had yet to be circumvented. Until such internal as well as external objections to a French take-over in the sultanate could be met, only one policy appeared likely to meet any success. Briefly explained, this would be a policy of "conservation." Hanotaux would work for the maintenance of the status quo so as to assure the preservation of the relative preponderance of France in Moroccan politics until the time came to apply the ultimate solution to the problem, unhindered French rule in the sultanate.[15] Only Great Britain had more trade in Morocco than France. The French position was further strengthened by unchallenged control in Algeria, all along the eastern frontier of Morocco. But for the moment, the diplomatic situation in Europe dictated a cautious policy in North Africa.

Even an advance plan for the penetration of certain oases in the Sahara, all close to the undetermined Moroccan border, and all claimed by the Sheriffian Government, had to be put off.[16] The danger of interna-

tional complications was too great. To have made the proposed advance
would certainly have brought France into conflict with some Moroccan
tribes and their allies, dissident Algerians who had taken refuge in the
contested areas. Other European powers, of course, would have interpreted the French move as an attempt to overrun the Sheriffian Empire
itself. In 1895 a rumor about a French advance on Tuat led Italy to that
very conclusion. Germany "recognized" the same problem and planned to
call an international conference if the Moroccan government turned to
Italy for help.[17]

In order to explain French policy Hanotaux summoned Jules Cambon,
the Governor General of Algeria to his office on June 11.[18] Cambon had
become an accomplished and highly respected diplomat though he had
prepared for a career in administration. He was an aristocrat, quite the
opposite of his interlocutor, a respectable bourgeois.[19] The interview between Jules Cambon and Gabriel Hanotaux must have been interesting.
During his residence in Algiers and his long official tours along the thou-
sand kilometers of the Algerian-Moroccan border, Cambon had seen Moroccan developments first hand. In a way, he had been in competition with
the Sultan, repeatedly attempting to enforce claims on Gouarra, Tidikelt,
and Tuat, three Saharan oases South of Algeria. Hassan had been in the
Tafilelt, near the disputed areas, when a revolt in his northern provinces
had suddenly called him away on the expedition during which he died.[20]

Coming to his administrative position in Algiers shortly after the signing of the Anglo-French agreement of August 1890, Cambon from the start
had been very much a partisan of colonial expansion. The 1890 agreement
had recognized as a French sphere of influence the area lying south of Algeria to a line drawn from Say to Barrowa in the hinterland of the territories assigned to the Niger Company, a British concern. Year after year,
Cambon had advocated the implementation of this concession. The conception of many of the plans was grand, envisaging the junction of French
holdings on the Mediterranean with those on the Atlantic in West Africa.
A first step would involve the penetration of the Sahara.[21] This expansion,
incidentally, would have put France in a better position to intervene in
Morocco when the appropriate moment arrived. Meanwhile, the French
apparently intended to take advantage of Moroccan weakness to conquer
uncontrolled areas south of Morocco and to assign the same to Algeria.

The Algerian-Moroccan border was largely undetermined. Agreement
and delimitation had not gone beyond Teniet el Sassi, and it was French
policy to refuse negotiations to delimit farther south. This policy, based
on the calculation that time was on the side of France which would be free

to reserve for itself vast areas south of Algeria and of Morocco, worked towards the disintegration of the sultanate. As France grew stronger in Algeria, the Sheriffian Empire was falling apart.[22] The French applied, simultaneously, two apparently contradictory policies. The Quai d'Orsay worked to preserve the Moroccan status quo even as the Ministry of the Interior, in control of Algeria, pushed for more and more expeditions into the Sahara. Some of these advances were directed at oases claimed by the Sheriffian autorities but over which the Sultan was unable to exercise any semblance of control. The French were careful not to move against un-contested Moroccan areas, whether effectively ruled or not. The activist policy was perhaps unnecessary. The French leaders certainly expected most of Morocco to fall to French imperial expansion. But they could not be sure. So the Third Republic hedged on its Moroccan bet by seizing ter-ritories south of that country and assigning these areas to Algeria. Mean-while, the rest of the Sultan's realm was protected from other would-be colonial masters by the Quai d'Orsay's effective work for the maintenance of a very special kind of status quo that favored France. Cambon was one of many leaders who wished to push the French conquest of the Sahara from Algeria to West Africa.

Hanotaux, convinced that the greatness of France required an active colonial policy, shared Cambon's view that the object of French policy should be the joining of all its African holdings near Lake Chad. That this junction was in fact a result of negotiations over which he presided, and through the organ of an Anglo-French convention which he signed just a few hours before he was overthrown with the Méline cabinet in 1898, was in later years Hanotaux's proudest memory.

In 1894 the Morocco question was not ready for a French solution. France needed time in which to prepare its diplomatic backing. This was what Hanotaux had to tell Cambon. No doubt Cambon understood, all the while presenting his own views and assuring himself of the coopera-tion of the Quai d'Orsay in solving Algerian-Moroccan differences. The undetermined borders, Cambon thought, should be definitely delimited. Damages caused by Moroccans should be quickly settled. And the Sahara should be penetrated and dominated by France. Only then could trade develop in southwestern Algeria, and only then would France be fulfilling her *mission civilisatrice* in North Africa. Cambon must certainly have given Hanotaux much detailed information about Algeria, Morocco, and the relations between the two countries. And he must have answered questions about the measures he had taken for the defense of Algeria. Hanotaux has written that he did ask about the defense of Algeria and that he gave

Cambon some advice on this subject. Trouble in Morocco could easily spread to Algeria.[23]

The problem was real enough because dissident Algerians had sought sanctuary along the whole length of the Moroccan border, just out of reach of the French authorities. Some Moroccan tribes even crossed the border to till fields that the French claimed were under their jurisdiction. The next season these same Moroccans left, going back into what even the French recognized as territories of the Sultan. But the unpaid taxes, and oftentimes the murders committed against Algerians, protégés of the French, remained unsettled. Perhaps there was a *razzia,* a quick raid across the border during which camels or sheep would be stolen.[24] With no effective central authority in the sultanate, the likelihood of repeated raids was even greater. There was also the notorious Bou Amama. An Algerian dissident, he was usually found close to Algeria, attempting to provoke other dissidents and related Moroccan tribes against the French.[25]

Jules Cambon was fully aware of the seriousness of the problem created by Hassan's death. The security of Algeria was threatened, and if Morocco could not be taken, France should at least make the Makhzen, or ruling house of Morocco, understand that France had the might to punish the transgressions of the Sultan's subjects. The Makhzen, of course, was held responsible for the misdemeanors of Moroccans whom it tenuously controlled.

In view of the chaotic political situation in Morocco, the Algerian government fortified the western portion of the province of Oran. And while the French in Algeria were effecting a military buildup to check the spread of Moroccan political disorder into their colony, the nations of Europe interested in the sultanate were coming to an agreement about whether or not to recognize Abd el Aziz. Roustan reported that Moret, the Spanish foreign minister, was becoming "neurotic" about the succession problem, fearing no doubt that the arrears on indemnity payments due Spain by the government of Morocco would not be paid. On June 14 Roustan wrote that the blame for Moret's excited state of mind should probably be placed on the interim chief of the Spanish delegation in Tangiers who was trying to pull off a big diplomatic coup. D'Aubigny himself was advising the Quai d'Orsay to wait and see. Nothing could be gained through recognition of Abd el Aziz before his own subjects had proclaimed him. Indeed, such action would probably turn the Moroccans against the new ruler.[26]

While Ba Ahmed, the Negro Grand Vizir and in fact the power behind the fourteen-year-old Sultan, had his young master proclaimed in city after city, a policy was evolved in Paris and in London. Briefly, it was decided that recognition would be withheld until the European legations in Tangiers had been notified of the accession of Abd el Aziz. France and England combined to reassure Moret and to bring Spain around to a less alarmist position. A common answer would be drawn up and sent in reply to the succession notification.[27] Only Germany, perhaps to impress on the British that it was not advisable to follow an anti-German policy in Africa, was slow to join the other powers. Germany's partner in the Triple Alliance, Italy, was disturbed by the Anglo-German difference which, Crispi thought, might make possible an Anglo-French accord in Morocco. Indeed, the Italian government found itself supporting England. France, Italy's North African antagonist who had felt cheated when, in 1882, the French had conquered Tunisia, was also in perfect agreement with the British.[28]

The Moroccan foreign minister, Si Mohammed Gharnit, sent the notification of the accession of Abd el Aziz in the form of a circular to all the foreign legations in Tangiers. The answer to this circular, drawn up by the French, British, and Spanish delegates, extended felicitations to the new Sultan and went on to suggest that, "if His Sheriffian Majesty is agreeable," they would go "in person to bring these (felicitations) to him in Rabat." Most delegates were opposed to the latter part of the letter thinking a visit by Christians to the holy city of Rabat would undermine the authority of the young ruler. But the proposal was retained because of Spanish insistence and because of the support it received from the French and the British as well.[29]

With a very few exceptions, outsiders had not been permitted inland. The French military mission, one of the outstanding exceptions, was with the Makhzen at all times. Traditionally, European missions had been permitted to call on the Sultan in Fez to pay homage and to negotiate outstanding problems. But though these missions had grown more and more frequent throughout the nineteenth century, they were still, in the 1890s required to obtain advance permission from the Makhzen and had to be escorted by troops furnished by the Moroccan government. Now the French proposed to install a consular official in Fez permanently. The change seemed revolutionary to the Grand Vizir; he was fighting the last battle to halt the penetration of Morocco by Europeans. When Ba Ahmed died and Abd el Aziz took the helm, the strong hand was lost.

To the common answers and felicitations of the Christian powers, the officials of the Muslim state replied with a circular expressing gratitude for the good wishes extended the new sultan and a curt, though polite, refusal to receive the suggested visits in Rabat.[30] All the foreign powers had acted together, calculating that this unity would impress the Moroccan Government and keep it from attempting to cancel any acquired concessions within the realm. Ba Ahmed, who was the real successor of Moulay Hassan, answered in a way which clearly indicated that nothing had changed and that the penetration by foreigners of the Sheriffian Empire would be resisted. Acting for Abd el Aziz, Ba Ahmed also complained specifically about the establishment of a French vice-consul in Fez and generally about the difficulties created for the Makhzen by foreigners traveling during very unsettled times. Missions to the sultan could go only to centers where established custom would permit. The sultan had never received European delegations in Rabat. For the moment, the Grand Vizir begged the powers to delay their missions to the traditional center of Fez, where the Sultan might grant audiences. He justified his request by explaining the impossibility of guaranteeing the safety of Europeans outside the walls of ports traditionally open to outsiders. Fez was inland, and the trip from port cities to Fez, Ba Ahmed claimed, would be too dangerous.[31]

Although Abd el Aziz had been recognized peacefully and the feared breakup of the sultanate did not occur in 1894, the country remained in a state of anarchy which the central government of Morocco had neither the power nor the financial resources to control. The foreign powers were no help, seeing in Ba Ahmed's warning a challenge to established rights that must be defended.[32] Therefore, European governments reacted by sending cruisers and other naval ships to Moroccan ports, while continuing to intrigue for larger shares of influence and control. They bickered about the least concession made and if one were granted, demanded equivalent compensation. The most important questions of the decade preceding the death of Moulay Hassan—contraband of arms and abuses of extraterritorial jurisdiction or capitulations rights—again came into the forefront in the European negotiations about Moroccan affairs.

The problem of contraband shipment of arms was, of course, worsened by the anarchy which accompanied the accession of the new Sultan and of his Negro Regent, Ba Ahmed. Some of the latter's enemies tried to play on the fact that he was a Negro but got very little response. Islam doesn't readily lend itself to racism.[33] While the representatives of the various powers jealously guarded rights acquired by their respective governments and suspiciously scrutinized all new proposals, discussion about means and legislation for contraband control began on the basis of a Spanish proposal.[34] A discussion among European representatives, heated in the days preceding Hassan's death, was reactivated.

The Spanish proposal would give Spain the right to exercise surveillance on the Moroccan coast and to visit and search ships suspected of carrying contraband weapons. Consuls of all nations would be permitted, exceptionally, to visit the houses of all suspects and would gather as a judicial body for judgment on implicated persons. The necessary legal authority would be obtained from the Sultan as a concession.[35]

Satow, the British consul in Tangiers, and d'Aubigny answered the proposal of the Spaniard Potestad in much the same vein. A preponderant position for Spain could not be recognized by the powers most interested. D'Aubigny's other colleagues agreed that no arrangement could be reached on the contraband problem without the approval of France and Great Britain, but lacked authority from their home governments to conclude an agreement. That the French representative had no specific orders reflected Hanotaux's policy toward the Moroccan question. He was waiting to see how the other interested powers would react. Momentarily, the problem seemed insoluble until all governments had sent to their representatives in Tangiers identical and formal orders prescribing a policy directed toward helping the Makhzen control war contraband. Meanwhile, travel between Moroccan cities such as Marakesh and Mazagan became hazardous for Europeans, and the Sultan had to ask accredited consuls and other representatives to forbid their nationals from travel in the interior of his empire. Discussion of the contraband problem begun in Tangiers continued in Madrid, but no quick solution could be found.[36]

Meanwhile, Hanotaux and his staff turned the Quai d'Orsay into a clearing house for French information and policy decisions about the Moroccan question. When Europeans seemed threatened by the political upheavals of Morocco, Hanotaux had portions of his Tangier representative's report sent to the Minister for the Marine, M. Faure. The texts transmitted formed the basis for negotiations about the number of naval ships to be sent to Moroccan waters to "protect" French life and property. As often as not, ships were sent in order to keep up with other European powers demonstrating in Sheriffian ports. Intimidating the Sultan in such a fashion was a well established practice. Not to have demonstrated when the British, Spaniards, or some other people were displaying their armed strength would have been a slight to French prestige. *"Notre agent me parait s'être un peu endormi par les assurances de son collègue d'Angleterre,"* was Hanotaux's specific marginal reaction. This was done in a period when France and Great Britain were cooperating on Sheriffian affairs. To win his case with the Marine Ministry, Hanotaux sometimes used subterfuge. In one case he omitted a paragraph in a letter from Souhart to be communicated to the Marine. The paragraph omitted assured the master of the Quai d'Orsay that, though anarchy was complete in the countryside, Europeans were safe behind the "impregnable" walls of Moroccan cities.[37]

Governor General Jules Cambon was also kept well informed of Moroccan developments. His reactions to communiqués from the Quai d'Orsay, and his advice based on information gathered in Algeria, often influenced Hanotaux's decisions and policies. The Spanish proposal for contraband control, for example, alarmed M. Cambon. Sharing this information with his representatives in Tangiers and in Madrid, Hanotaux instructed them to stand firmly on "our traditions and our principles of right." [38] In short, Spain should not be allowed to gain surveillance and search rights on the Riff coast. There were and continued to be many instances of direct cooperation between Hanotaux at the Foreign Ministry and Cambon, whose orders and authority emanated from the Ministry of the Interior.

Anarchy and political upheaval in Morocco, as expected, led to a certain amount of popular agitation in Algeria. Moroccan tribesmen attacked an Algerian caravan in the Sahara and a Riff tribe crossed into Algerian territory where it plowed and seeded fields that it did not legally own.[39] Like so many other claims of the Algerian Government against the Sheriffian Empire, the indemnities demanded were added to an already long list. But the border delimitations which might have solved the problem were put off indefinitely. Hanotaux's innovation was, apparently, to insist that the Algerian indemnities question was the most important one the French Resident in Tangiers would have to negotiate during his next mission to the Sultan's court in Fez.[40] Cambon, meanwhile, was permitted to proceed with a military demonstration along the Moroccan border calculated to frighten the squatters and to alarm the Makhzen, thereby forcing the Moroccan Government into an agreement with Algeria.[41]

In his dealings with the European powers on problems relating to Morocco, Hanotaux usually worked in cooperation with Spain and Great Britain. Hanotaux frequently made marginal comments on Souhart's, d'Aubigny's, and Monbel's letters, and the following question was typical: "Is his trust in the English agent not somewhat excessive?" [42] While working with London and Madrid, Hanotaux accepted arguments against letting French representatives visit Fez, the capital of Morocco, at the same time as the consuls from the two "allied" powers. Dr. Linarès, one of Hanotaux's principal advisers on Moroccan affairs, had argued that it would be detrimental to French prestige to be too closely allied to Great Britain and Spain.[43] Hanotaux translated this suggestion into policy. On taking office in Tangiers, Monbel excused himself from presenting his credentials by alleging that he had many files to read before he could talk to the Sultan.[44]

The mainstay of Franco-Spanish relations in Morocco was talks and agreements reached in a meeting between Hanotaux and Moret in the summer of 1894.[45] Reference was frequently made to this meeting, but only to bring Spain into line with the French understanding of what was meant by maintenance of the status quo. Hanotaux continued to use every means at his disposal to further his own aims in Morocco. Dr. Linarès, a former member of the French military mission at the Sultan's court, the only doctor ever permitted to inspect Hassan's harem, and an unofficial French agent, was asked to use his influence. He opposed Moret, for example, on a plan to reinstate a Spanish military mission in the Makhzen, a mission that had been withdrawn at the time of the Melilla crisis.

While the powers were discussing the timing and procedure to be followed in recognizing Abd el Aziz, Hanotaux had the Cherif of Ouazzan, a Sheriffian tribe settled near the Algerian border, pledge allegiance to the new Sultan. The Ouazzani were French proteges and, no doubt, their rallying to the cause of Abd el Aziz was calculated to create good feeling toward France at the court. In fact, Ba Ahmed tried to force the Cherif to deal with the Makhzen directly, rather than through the French. The Ouazzan tribe, which had been persecuted by Hassan for their Francophile sympathies, remained, however, tools of French diplomacy in the Sheriffian empire.[46]

While attempting to create good Franco-Moroccan feeling, Hanotaux, after considerable hesitation, ordered the establishment of a French vice-consulate in Fez. The Moroccan government did not want this innovation. But the French felt they could affect the balance of power within Morocco if they gained representation not afforded other European states. The gain would probably be only temporary as the other powers could be expected to force the Sheriffian authority to extend the French privilege to themselves. The right of France to establish a diplomatic official had been won in a concession from Moulay Hassan. But it was never a popular concession from the point of view of the North African government. Traditionally, only ports had been open to Europeans. Since Fez was inland as well as a holy city, there was considerable fear in the Makhzen that the Muslims would rise in revolt against a government that allowed Christian infidels into a sacred center of Islam.[47]

In 1894 Hanotaux sent a career diplomat, de Marcilly, to Fez. De Marcilly replaced an Algerian who had served as a French agent and thus upset the status quo for which France was ostensibly working. An Algerian, pre-

sumably a Muslim, was easily accepted. But a French agent would be a
Christian. The presence of an infidel in Fez was distasteful as well as un-
usual for Moroccans. While the Makhzen protested and pleaded,[48] the
diplomatic corps in Tangiers took positions. Most Europeans were in favor
of the French move, including the Francophobe Italian consul who was
ready to move his whole legation from Tangiers to Fez.[49] The British representative who had a diplomat-trader as agent in Fez approved the French
insistence on sending a career diplomat; he thought this move, if followed
by the other powers, might end a diplomatic abuse in which private persons with official functions used their positions for personal advantage.
"In all contraband affairs," d'Aubigny had complained, "at least one European is involved." The situation was aggravated by certain irresponsible
consuls who habitually extended and even sold consular protection to Moroccans who were often partners in the crime of contraband.[50]

That the French sent a professional diplomat to fill the position of vice-
consul in Fez was neither good nor bad for the Makhzen. The precedent,
however, started a new discussion among the foreign representatives in
Tangiers and their governments and led to some improvements in the capitulations system practiced in Morocco. At the same time, the presence of
a non-Muslim official in Fez tended to undermine the Makhzen whose authority depended in part on certain religious attributes of the Sultan. Other
powers, of course, soon followed the example of France and sent their own
vice-consuls to Fez.

In 1894 Hanotaux's Moroccan policy helped to maintain a status quo
which was, from the beginning, to the advantage of France. But he also
tinkered with consular representation since he forced the Moroccans to
accept a new diplomatic representative inland, in Fez. Only ports had been
open to foreigners. Hanotaux also watched the actions of other powers
carefully, fearing that they might gain concessions and positions France
could not acquire. He therefore opposed the Spanish plan for contraband
control. He carefully maintained the French military mission at the Makhzen, repeatedly ordering the members not to let themselves be separated.
At the same time, he used what influence he could muster in Morocco to
foil a Spanish plan to re-establish a military mission of their own. Hanotaux kept up with all naval demonstrations in Moroccan waters and was
once annoyed when a French ship ordered to Moroccan ports did not visit
there. Cannon shots for "traditional" salvos had been insufficient and to
have gone into port without noisily saluting would have been a slight to
French prestige. Though he forced a postponement of French advance
south of Algeria into the Sahara, Hanotaux did change the Moroccan sit-

uation by ordering Consul M. de Marcilly to Fez. The policy was one of maintenance of a status quo until France was ready to act. It was perhaps inevitable that having taken Tunisia from Algerian bases, France should turn to Morocco. In 1894 however, there were more pressing problems. The political situation in Madagascar was quickly reaching a breaking point as Malagasy subjects sought to rid their country of foreign control. Another difficulty involved the Belgians in the Congo who were threatening to close French access to the Valley of the Upper Nile. And already the Italians were circulating a rumor about French advances on Tuat. But Rome's alarm did not change the basic situation. The imperceptible disintegration of the Moroccan status quo continued. France remained poised to profit from this political deterioration even as Hanotaux turned his attention to other African problems.[51]

The Anglo-Congolese Treaty
of May 12, 1894

Chapter 3

On May 12, 1894, an amazing agreement in the history of colonial bargaining was signed between England and the Congo Free State. Disregarding earlier treaties affecting the area of the Upper Nile between Lake Albert and Fashoda, these two states agreed to trade territories. In exchange for a lease on a strip of land 25 kilometers wide along the border between Lake Albert-Edward and Lake Tanganyika, the British offered King Leopold II of the Belgians, personal ruler of the Free States, a life lease on the so-called Bahr-el-Ghazal, a large district on the left bank of the Nile. This agreement broke several earlier treaties and threatened the plans of several colonial powers not involved in the agreement but vitally interested in the Upper Nile regions. When the contents of this Anglo-Congolese treaty became known in the capitals of the other colonial powers, official protests were lodged in London and Brussels. Germany, and especially France, would not accept the new order in Central Africa.

France and Great Britain had both engaged in talks with King Leopold early in 1894. Both powers had decided to negotiate when faced with reports of Belgian advances into regions that each considered strategically important in their African calculations.[1] The British, besides wanting to regulate the settlement of Congo officials and merchants in the Bahr-el-Ghazal, an area Britain considered her own sphere of influence, were well aware of French designs on the Upper Nile. In concluding the Anglo-Congolese treaty, the British had clearly attempted to block a potential French advance on Fashoda.[2]

While the Anglo-Congolese negotiation succeeded, Franco-Congolese talks in Brussels yielded no positive results, but King Leopold was obviously speculating on Anglo-French rivalry. Hanotaux, not yet Minister for Foreign Affairs, was one of the French delegates assigned to confer with representatives of King Leopold in March 1894. The failure of the talks may well explain the rigid attitude Hanotaux adopted a few months later when he was foreign minister. In June 1894 after the Anglo-Congolese treaty had been signed, France voted a large sum of money for the military occupation of the Upper Ubangi territory, and possibly, even for the occupation or policing of the Bahr-el-Ghazal. France had decided to answer occupation with occupation.[3]

In May 1894 the news of the Anglo-Congolese treaty had caught France in one of her recurrent ministerial crises. An ironic set of circumstances had led to the overthrow of the Casimir-Périer government on May 22, 1894. Interpellated on a question of labor legislation, the Casimir-Périer cabinet had already been defeated when reports of the new Anglo-Congolese treaty reached Paris. Casimir-Périer, the foreign minister in his own toppled cabinet, did not wish to bind his successor and had limited his action on the matter to an official protest dispatched, for communication to the respective governments, to his ambassadors in London and Brussels.[4]

The change in government had been brought about by the strong opposition of the Radical party which wanted power for itself. For a week France had no government while the leaders of the Radical party, Léon Bourgeois, then Paul Peytral, turned down presidential requests to organize a new cabinet. Strong enough to bring down a cabinet, the Radicals were not strong enough to rule. They realized, no doubt, that to hope for a parliamentary majority would be pure temerity. In the end, the same party which had been in office before the May 22 crisis, the Moderate Republicans, returned to power. The personnel was new, but the policies which the new government proposed to follow were, on the whole, the same as those of the cabinet which had been overthrown.[5]

The continuity of program and policy was especially stressed with respect to foreign affairs. In his inaugural address on May 31 Charles Dupuy, the new prime minister, stated: "With respect to foreign policy, we have at heart the maintenance of that continuity of view and of relations (among parties) which, in spite of political rivalry, has permitted our nation to recover among the nations, a place worthy of its name and of its history." [6] The new ministry, strengthened by the support of the Chamber of Deputies, Dupuy continued, would at all times be the guardian of the interests of France in the world and the defender of her rights. At the ministry of Foreign Affairs would be M. Gabriel Hanotaux, the only member of the new government who did not have an elected position and apparently the last such official in the history of the Third Republic.[7]

By the time he was appointed Minister of Foreign Affairs in the Dupuy government, Hanotaux had become Comptroller of Commercial and Consular Affairs, near the top of the permanent officialdom at the Quai d'Orsay. Hanotaux's position had brought no political glory, and with the exception of a few professional diplomats, historians and archivists, no one knew who Hanotaux was. In spite of his obscurity, he soon won general confidence.[8] The new minister knew how to safeguard the interests of his nation, as he soon proved when he carried on the protest of his precedessor with great vigor as well as caution.

When first asked to take the ministerial position, Hanotaux hesitated long enough to consult with friends and colleagues. He sought out the advice of leading Moderates, of people such as Jean Casimir-Périer, Alexandre Ribot and others. The latter expressed indifference, apparently because he had expected Dupuy's assignment to form a new government for himself. Hanotaux's former chief at the Quai d'Orsay, Casimir-Périer, counseled the young historian and civil administrator to refuse the commission. He simply thought Hanotaux would lack authority. But Sadi Carnot and Dupuy quickly overcame hesitations based on this judgment by promising their full support. When Nisard, the Director of the Bureau of Political Affairs at the Foreign Ministry, encouraged his young colleague from the Commercial and Consular section of the Quai d'Orsay, Hanotaux accepted power. Once in office he had no difficulty imposing himself upon the staff. All the professional civil servants to the Ministry respected him because, unlike many of his predecessors, he knew his job well.[9]

The wisdom of Hanotaux's decision might be questioned. He was a civil servant who took a political appointment. Another professional diplomat, Paul Cambon, was also offered the ministerial position in 1894. But he turned it down reasoning that he could serve France better, in the long run, by staying in the diplomatic service. Ministerial tenure in the Third Republic was always unsure and usually very short. But Hanotaux, already familiar with the outstanding current diplomatic difficulty about the Anglo-Congolese treaty of May 1894, reasoned that even in a few months he could win the case for France and thereby render "a service to my country." [10]

By examining documents Hanotaux found the grounds for his protest of the Anglo-Congolese treaty. Hanotaux supported the French right of pre-emption to any territory which the Congo Free State wished to alienate. He further insisted that the Congo Free State, a neutral whose borders were guaranteed by European powers at the Berlin Congress of 1885, could not change its territorial borders and still remain a neutral state. On the other side, the British could see no reason why the Congo Free State should not be allowed to expand.[11]

A more realistic reason for the French protest of the treaty is that the French wanted to reopen the Egyptian question. To no avail they had repeatedly protested the British occupation of Egypt. Unwilling to brave the danger that would follow a direct challenge of British occupation of

Egypt, France hit on an alternative plan. By occupying the Upper Nile Valley and presenting England with a *fait accompli,* the French hoped to force England out of Egypt or retain the region their own troops would occupy; some sort of a "quid pro quo" would lead to a solution. This plan of action was obviously threatened by the Anglo-Congolese treaty which would interject between the region of the Upper Nile and the French colony of Gabon a large district of Belgian territory. The approach to the coveted region in the Anglo-Egyptian Sudan would be closed.[12] The details of this policy could, of course, not be revealed in public debate.

A plan for the occupation by French contingents of some point on the Upper Nile had actually been mapped in 1893. Faced with a British advance from Uganda and into the coveted area, M. Delcassé, then Undersecretary for Colonies at the Marine Ministry, had called Monteil, an able officer in the Colonial Army, to his office. Together, and apparently with the wholehearted approval of President S. Carnot, they drafted a plan to plant a French flag "at or near Fashoda." [13] It was at that time that Gabon, on the Atlantic coast of Central Africa, had been selected as the probable base of operations for the projected penetration.

When the news of the Anglo-Congolese treaty was released, Monteil reacted with a caustic letter to the new Minister for Colonies, Delcassé. Monteil wanted to know why the Fashoda plan had not yet been implemented.[14] Delcassé probably agreed with Monteil, but he had to reckon with Hanotaux who, though a colonialist, was too much aware of the dangers involved in brazenly challenging Great Britain. Delcassé's wish and his anglophobe reputation would provoke Great Britain at a time when conciliation was necessary with crises flaring in the Bahr-el-Ghazal, in East Africa, and elsewhere all at once.[15]

Consultations between Delcassé at the Colonial Ministry and Hanotaux at the Quai d'Orsay led to a plan which, in appearance, challenged only the agents of King Leopold's Congo. Already in 1893 France had begun to organize the Upper Ubangi region, partly to protect what she considered her own sphere of influence in the area and partly to keep open the route to Fashoda. Delcassé and Hanotaux, reacting to the implications of the Anglo-Congolese treaty of May 12, agreed that the Upper Ubangi should be effectively occupied. In 1894 they pushed the policy decided upon in the previous year and presuaded the Chamber of Deputies to vote the necessary credit.[16] As a result, an invasion of the Bahr-el-Ghazal remained a distinct probability although it was put off. Hanotaux argued that since the Upper Ubangi was contiguous to the Bahr-el-Ghazal, occupation of the Upper Ubangi would make an advance on Fashoda a possibility.[17] The

Upper Ubangi was not claimed by the British who did claim the Bahr-el-Ghazal, though France did not recognize that claim. In June of 1894 Hanotaux was not ready to challenge the British; he reserved his strongest words for King Leopold II.

On June 1 M. Albert Decrais, French ambassador in London, sent Hanotaux a telegram announcing the British response to Casimir-Périer's official protest of May 26: the British could see no reason why the Congo Free State should not be allowed to expand.[18] Hanotaux had already found the basis for the Republic's objections. In an "unofficial" talk with Lord Dufferin, the British ambassador in Paris, Hanotaux expressed the French objection to the Anglo-Congolese treaty in the following terms: "We are complaining not about this or that point alone, but about the convention as a whole and about the manner in which it was concluded." [19] He asked Lord Dufferin if the British government were inclined to talk and if so, if a communication could be made as soon as possible, preferably before he had to answer an interpellation. Hanotaux was being pressed and, much to his regret, he told E. C. H. Phipps, Dufferin's chief assistant at the British embassy, his first act would have to be rather strong and against the British, although he would like to have gained an anglophile reputation.[20]

Dufferin was not as well disposed toward Hanotaux as was Phipps, the African specialist at the British embassy.[21] An early exponent of British imperialism, Dufferin's connections were with India. He knew little of African affairs and certainly did not want serious differences to arise between France and Great Britain during his ambassadorial tenure.[22] In answer to Hanotaux's objections to the Anglo-Congolese treaty, Lord Dufferin noted that the troublesome treaty had already been signed and that it would be difficult to withdraw it. Hanotaux interjected that the treaty had been poorly made and it would have to be renounced. In any case, some basis for negotiations should be found and some settlement should be reached as quickly as possible, for French public opinion was incensed and running at a high pitch. It was generally felt, in France, that England had given away a territory which was not hers to give. The Bahr-el-Ghazal was an Egyptian province, not English property.[23]

At the Congress of Berlin, European powers that gained control of coastal territories were guaranteed, subject to certain conditions, the hinterland of such settlements. The conditions included the requirement to notify other signatory powers of annexations whether acquired or taken by military might. Other powers, of course, could then protest such changes. Another condition that Hanotaux chose to stress involved the necessity of maintaining an authority sufficient to enforce respect of acquired rights over annexed territories.[24] The so-called Anglo-Egyptian Sudan had been abandoned in 1885 following the defeat of General Charles G. Gordon. The French, consequently, decided to consider the Bahr-el-Ghazal, a province of what became the Anglo-Egyptian Sudan, *terra nullius*. This interpretation became an important part of Hanotaux's answer to his first interpellation in the French Chamber of Deputies.

On June 7 Hanotaux was questioned on the Anglo-Congolese treaty. Eugène Etienne, a leading colonialist, presented the interpellation in a long speech giving a virtual history of British "wrongdoings" that time and again had thwarted the colonial ambitions of France. Colonial development was what Etienne and the colonialists wanted for France. Moreover, the alliance recently concluded with Russia enabled the French leaders to be more energetic in colonial matters.[25] Not that Russia usually backed France in Africa or anywhere else, but French leaders felt that the eastern flank of France was secure and therefore dared turn their eyes in another direction.

In answer to the interpellation Hanotaux explained his policy in a speech to the Chamber.[26] Not wishing to repeat Etienne's speech, the foreign minister presented his objections to the treaty as a whole. Central to Hanotaux's protest was the Berlin treaty of 1885 and the acts which had been added to this treaty in the years that followed. Here lay the foundation of the "international association of the Congo" whose successor was the Congo Free State, signatory of the troublesome treaty of May 12. The Congo, in its conception, Hanotaux continued, had been made a ward of Europe, European powers having guaranteed the integrity of this African state *"as that territory was delineated when the guarantee was made."* Bounds within which the Congo State was to spread had been determined at that time. In return for the guarantees extended to the "international association of the Congo," and, consequently, to its successor, Europe had laid down certain conditions within which the created state was to operate. These conditions included guarantees of commercial liberty and of equality of treatment to all nationals of the signatory nations within the boundaries of the created state. The Gabon, Hanotaux explained, because of its location had been meant to expand into the territory then set aside for the "international association of the Congo." This, in brief, was the basis of the special rights of France over the area in question. Also, because France sacrificed some real "rights" and because the new state was the immediate neighbor of her own colony, the Gabon, France had obtained an option on all territory which the new state might choose to alienate from its allotted territory. As Dufferin explained in a long report on his own discussion with Hanotaux, the French thought the narrow strip of land leased to the British and stretching along the probable limit between Leopold's property and German East Africa should have been offered to France.[27]

Hanotaux found the Anglo-Congolese treaty to be a breach of French and European "international rights." The Congo Free State proposed in the document signed on May 12 to alienate some of her allotted territory without consulting France, which had a definite right of pre-emption over said territory. In exchange for a strip of land between Lake Tanganyika and Lake Albert-Edward, the Congo State proposed to advance into the Bahr-el-Ghazal. This, Hanotaux maintained, would be a breach of the Congo's neutrality and of a Franco-Congolese arrangement which limited the advance of the Congo State to the 4th parallel and to the south of the Ubangi River. The proposed advance would also involve a rejection of the European guarantee of the integrity of the Ottoman Empire, made at Paris in 1856.

A second basic objection to the Anglo-Congolese treaty could be drawn from this violation of territory belonging to the Ottoman Empire. That the Bahr-el-Ghazal was a province of Egypt, itself a state whose suzerain was the Sultan in Constantinople, was an established fact. Logical as the argument based on Ottoman rights might have been, it sounded false. Monteil and Delcassé had already planned an expedition to Fashoda. Hanotaux held the mission back in 1894 and 1895. When Marchand was ordered to proceed with this penetration in 1895, Hanotaux was temporarily out of office. But Hanotaux did not recall that mission in 1895–96 when he came back to the Quai d'Orsay. He was clearly inclined to seek diplomatic solutions. Yet in public, Hanotaux took a strong position. In closing his address of June 7, 1894, he promised to pursue a vigorous policy of protest on the grounds he had enumerated and to maintain this protest until recognition had been given to the legitimate rights of France.[28]

Hanotaux, apparently a man who had never had any desire to harangue crowds (a necessary "virtue" in French politics), prepared all his speeches with great care and never spoke without notes. "Never improvising, hardly ever replying to interruptions, keeping silence after he had once made his speech, and leaving all discussion to the Premier, he seemed to soar sublimely above the heads of the Assembly," wrote one political observer. In his first defense of the Dupuy cabinet, he made an impressive speech which was received with thunderous applause and "bravos."

The interpellators on June 7, 1894, apparently realized that the government would not accept a treaty "en contradiction si formelle avec le droit international." The purpose of the interpellation was, then, to provoke a declaration of policy on which the Chamber of Deputies could vote and, in this vote, to show the government, as well as other powers in Europe that Hanotaux had the full support of the deputies. This objective was well achieved and Hanotaux's first defense of the Dupuy cabinet yielded a 527 to 0 vote of confidence.[29] It was a good start for a minister whose appointment, only a week earlier, had surprised the public. On June 9, Delcassé, Minister for Colonies, asked for a sum of 1,800,000 francs, 1,100,000 of which was to be allotted to strengthening the approach to the Bahr-el-Ghazal, the Ubangi region. The deputies granted his request, again with an overwhelming majority and the senate endorsed the vote.[30]

On June 9, Hanotaux replied to a communication which he had received on June 6 from the British ambassador who proposed to discuss not only the French objection to the Anglo-Congolese treaty, but also all outstanding Anglo-French differences in Central and West Africa. Egypt was not mentioned, but Hanotaux agreed to proceed on the basis advanced by the British, leaving other problems to be dealt with at a later time. Both sides, though they took strong positions, seem to have been eager to arrive at a peaceful understanding. The British, though they had broken the treaties and agreements mentioned by Hanotaux in the French protest to the Anglo-Congolese treaty, were puzzled at the vehemence of the French objections. Lord Dufferin presented the British point of view when he questioned the French interest in the disputed area and pointed out that France had no more rights in the Upper Nile Valley than did anyone else. The French, of course, argued that the British had given away something that was not theirs to give. England was in actual occupation of Egypt. But it was generally felt during the 1890s that this control could become shaky for "he who holds the head waters of the Nile is potential master of Egypt." The British considered the Upper Nile and adjoining regions a British sphere of influence and wished to keep out the French.[31]

To accomplish this, the British had proposed to lease the Bahr-el-Ghazal, a large part of what the French considered as one of Great Britain's chimerical spheres because, as the French pointed out, this was Egyptian territory and British occupation of Egypt was not recognized. Also, the area had not been occupied since the British withdrawal following the defeat of Gordon at Khartoum in 1885. In leasing this vast area, Britain would gain the lessee's recognition of their own rights over the area and at the same time, the Congo State would be placed between France's Gabon and the headwaters of the Nile, blocking French advances to an area which Britain was unable to defend at that particular time. The French objections to the Anglo-Congolese treaty could not be interpreted in any other context than the Egyptian question. Even after the British had withdrawn article three, which gave them a strip of land along the Congo's frontier with German East Africa, they would not pull back from the second article which leased territories in the Upper Nile Valley to the Congo and, in effect, would block French access to the Nile.

The right of German East Africa to a common border with the Free State would have been lost if European powers recognized as valid the agreement of May 12. The German protest was therefore justified and, at first, quite moderate. But when Hatzfeldt, the German ambassador in London, suggested to Chancellor Caprivi that the Anglo-Congolese treaty be used to make "clear the disadvantage of annoying" Germany,[32] the suggestion was not only accepted but also followed up by an advance to see if the new French minister would cooperate with Germany in common action for the annulment of the treaty.

The British, in substituting themselves for the Congo Free State along the long western frontier of German East Africa, reneged on an important part of an Anglo-German agreement affecting the areas in contention. The serious diplomatic *faux pas* soon forced Foreign Secretary Lord Kimberley to annul article three of the Anglo-Congolese convention, that article having attracted the just ire of the German government. Yet, against French claims, and even before the British Foreign Office bowed to the protest of the Wilhelmstrasse, Dufferin tried to use a portion of the Anglo-German convention to counter Hanotaux's objections to the May 12 Anglo-Congolese agreement.

Britain's arrangement with Germany had implicitly recognized the Upper Nile as falling within the British sphere of influence. On June 13 Dufferin told Hanotaux he doubted that public opinion in Great Britain would allow for backtracking on concessions won through the instrument of the Anglo-German convention. But Hanotaux quickly disagreed, explaining that although England and Germany had an advantageous agreement, France was not a party to the Anglo-German convention and could not be held to its conditions. Hanotaux did not intend to recognize a British sphere of influence from "the confines of the Nile" and north to Egypt. The French had not taken any engagement not to expand into Equatorial Africa, and the British government was well aware of this fact.[33]

The German advances toward the Quai d'Orsay were reported by Jules Herbette, French ambassador in Berlin, on June 5. Anglo-French differences over Egypt had, in the past, suggested cooperation between France and Germany (as in 1882–85, for example); earlier in 1894 the two countries had amicably settled their African differences. The German advance was therefore not as brash as it might seem, in spite of the continuing conflict over the Alsace-Lorraine question. Hanotaux accepted the idea and when Baron Marshall at the Wilhelmstrasse made more specific advances to the French ambassador in Berlin, the cooperation was worked into a formula for "le maintien du *statu quo* légal africain." [34]

The Wilhelmstrasse had threatened England with a conference on the Egyptian question in a note so forceful and abrupt that even Caprivi, the German chancellor, thought it rude.[35] However, when the British relinquished article three of the Anglo-Congolese treaty, which had substituted British for Congo Free State territory next to German East Africa, Germany adhered only to the letter of her agreement with France. The Wilhelmstrasse communicated to the French the developments of its separate negotiations with England but offered France no support. As a result Hanotaux learned about the advantages and limitations of German diplomatic cooperation during his first two months of tenure at the Quai d'Orsay. Although he would again try to work with Germany on other specific questions, he never forgot the lesson of his first disappointing experiment.

After June 18 then France was left to deal with England single-handed. There were many problems involved in the continuing Hanotaux-Dufferin talks which had been suggested by Lord Dufferin on the 6th. Among the problems were the delicacy involved in referring to the Egyptian question and the infinite care which had to be taken in order not to damage the "amour-propre" of the British. The French foreign minister also had to insist on the objections he had raised in order not to ruffle the feelings of Frenchmen. He wanted a quick settlement, fearing public opinion would get out of hand and become bellicose.[36]

Hanotaux and Lord Dufferin were unable to reach agreement on the Anglo-Congolese treaty. France would not accept the treaty. Britain, after renouncing the third article of the convention which contained all the British advantages, could not give in to France and cancel the entire treaty; such action would have involved a loss of face. More was involved for both parties than appeared on the surface. Hanotaux, apparently in agreement with Lord Dufferin, therefore shifted his attention to Brussels.[37]

Reaction to the French protest had been varied in Belgium. But one thing was certain, the Belgian Chamber of Deputies would not permit its government to go to war over the Anglo-Congolese treaty. Members of the Belgian Chamber pointed out that the relationship between the Congo and Belgium was strictly a personal one, and that Belgian blood should not be shed to further the desires of King Leopold II. Moreover, the Belgian government considered France a friendly nation and did not intend to fight over the question. British rights in the contested areas dated from the 1890 agreement, the Congo government argued, but the areas had not been occupied and had therefore been considered as being, diplomatically, *terra vacua*. Thereupon, the Chamber gave the Belgian government control in the affairs of the Congo and the debate was ended.[38]

Though unwilling to relinquish the privileges that had been acquired by the Anglo-Congolese treaty, the diplomats in Brussels soon withdrew the objectionable article two which would have permitted the Congo Free State to spread into the Bahr-el-Ghazal. The pressure from Germany and France and the protest of the Ottoman Empire were too strong, especially as the opponents of the Free State apparently had right as well as might on their side.[39] The most important enemy, naturally, was Hanotaux.

Turkey had acted with characteristic sluggishness. The Turkish ambassador in Brussels apparently was the only exception. Caratheodory Effendi encouraged his Government to take a vigorous stand. His many letters to Constantinople disturbed English and Congo officials in Brussels, who dismissed the Effendi as a French stooge. But one ambassador's reaction did not make a policy. Before protesting about what should have been a vital interest, the Sultan waited to see what Europe would do. France had pushed Constantinople to this protest. Paul Cambon, the French ambassador in Constantinople, wanted to quit his job because of the Sultan's reluctance. When Turkey did take a stand, the important decisions had already been made.[40] The problems raised by the Anglo-Congolese treaty were therefore primarily European problems.

The talks between the Quai d'Orsay and the British Foreign Office had, of course, been paralleled by an active discussion between Paris and Brussels. But until June 18 when the objections of Germany were met and France was left to fend for itself, the Hanotaux-King Leopold negotiations had moved at a snail's pace. The King of the Belgians and his Congo cabinet were slow to make decisions and always hoped for strong British backing; though the government of the Congo Free State never got the support from London which they half expected, their every action was tied to Great Britain's decisions.[41]

From Brussels, Frederic-Albert Bourée, the Third Republic's ambassador to Belgium, kept Hanotaux well informed of public opinion, which enabled Hanotaux to decide how much he could demand of King Leopold's Congo government. On the 22nd, Hanotaux requested that the Belgian ambassador in Paris be given official directives and credentials to negotiate and conclude a treaty if necessary. The language used was rather strong, the note insisting that the proposed talks be held in Paris and as a *sine qua non* that the negotiations be secret.⁴² Hanotaux had apparently not forgotten the experience of the Brussels negotiations earlier in the year when Leopold, behind Hanotaux's back and while negotiating with him, had concluded an arrangement with the British.

The death of Baron Eugene de Beyens, the Belgian ambassador to France, slowed up negotiations. Leopold then appointed Baron Constant de Goffinet and M. J. Devolder who were highly placed in his government. From then on negotiations advanced rapidly though these were really one-sided with Hanotaux insisting, threatening, and getting his way. Border incidents on the Congo Free State's northern border were already exciting antagonisms.⁴³

Throughout the dispute France watched the movement of Belgian military personnel. France sent soldiers and material enough to make Leopold's agents think twice before attacking. Hanotaux had warned Dufferin of this movement early in June. The speed with which France implemented her policy was proof enough of her determination. Meanwhile a press campaign was begun in Brussels against the involvement of Belgian officers in the Congo. It was charged that a situation threatened in which Belgians would be fighting Frenchmen in an African war. This press campaign was a broadside at King Leopold's whole Congo policy. Strongly pushed at home and unable to secure British backing, Leopold could do nothing but bow to Hanotaux.⁴⁴

On August 14, 1894, the French were satisfied with the signing of a Congo-French treaty, which annulled the second article of the Anglo-Congolese treaty. The British acknowledged the decision of King Leopold's government but did not accept it. The British complained that France had done much the same in the August 14 treaty as Great Britain had done in the May 12 treaty. France had ceded to King Leopold the Lado enclave. Smaller than the area earmarked for the Congo Free State by the British, the Lado enclave was, nevertheless, Ottoman territory. Also, the question of French pre-emption over the Congo involved, in British eyes, some grotesque possibilities. Instead of large semi-arid Ottoman territories, France might inherit one of the richest parts of Africa. Grey said on August 16, 1894, that Leopold was in his right; but England was in no sense a party to the arrangement between France and King Leopold.⁴⁵ The Egyptian question, which lay behind all of the French diplomatic activity against the Anglo-Congolese treaty, remained until the French re-opened the question directly at Fashoda in 1898.

In the meantime, France was rushing along the way to Fashoda. Hanotaux attempted to solve the diplomatic problems of France, while Delcassé at the French Colonial Office ordered the Monteil expedition (September 1894). But this was not yet Fashoda, as Monteil was to be re-directed against Samory.[46] For a while at least, Hanotaux's diplomatic approach triumphed over Delcassé's weak military challenge to the British in the Upper Nile area. During the last years of the nineteenth century, France seemed to be wavering between England and Germany. The Alsace-Lorraine question was still touchy, but for the moment both France and Germany were willing to keep it down, combining in colonial affairs to the benefit of one, then of the other. Yet when Hanotaux dealt with the British, he was always very careful. While working with Berlin on the Congo business, Hanotaux cooperated with London against Berlin in Morocco. The historian Raymond Sontag has rightly labeled the years 1894–99 in French politics as years of wavering. France apparently had a choice between England or Germany. Serious objections to an alignment with either country could be raised. Germany still held Alsace-Lorraine; British and French colonial interests led to continual friction.

In the Anglo-Congolese treaty Hanotaux was faced with an inherited problem; nevertheless he attacked this treaty in an attempt to safeguard the interests of France. He centered his attack on Brussels as soon as it became clear that London would not agree to his claims. He used his training as a Chartist to prepare carefully documented diplomatic notes. Since he was academically inclined, he read scholarly and historical discourses as he lectured the deputies in defense of his own policies. For the moment, he resisted the establishment of a policy that would actually challenge the British in Egypt. He refused to allow Monteil, who was supported by Delcassé, to push into the region of the Upper Nile.

The very next problem Hanotaux chose to deal with involved the British again and the Italians. These two powers had an agreement which threatened to block another French access to the Valley of the Upper Nile. The problem created by the Anglo-Italian treaty of May 5, 1894, was deliberately put aside by Hanotaux during his first months in office. Finally he turned his attention to East African difficulties and to French differences of opinion with the Italian Government.

The Anglo-Italian Treaty
of May 5, 1894:
The Nile Once More

Chapter 4

Having won his point with regard to the Anglo-Congolese treaty Hanotaux
turned his energies to the solution of still another problem, that created
by the signing of the Anglo-Italian treaty of May 5, 1894. This treaty completed the delimitation of the spheres of influence of Great Britain and
Italy in East Africa, a delimitation which was begun by protocols signed
at Rome on March 24 and April 15, 1891.[1]

The three protocols completed the delimitation of the spheres of influence of Great Britain and of Italy in East Africa and placed all of Abyssinia, including the district of Harrar, within the Italian sphere of influence. Article II of the protocol of April 15 established Italian rights to
temporary military occupation of the district of Kassala. An ancient province of the Egyptian Sudan, Kassala, was affected by the general European
guarantee of the integrity of the Ottoman Empire agreed to at Paris in 1856
while the status quo of Harrar was provided for by an Anglo-French agreement signed in 1888.

The terms of the Anglo-French agreement of 1888 expressly stated that
the two governments, Great Britain and France, "engage not to endeavor
to annex Harrar, nor to place it under their Protectorate. In taking this
engagement the two governments do not renounce the right of opposing
attempts by any other Power to acquire or assert any rights over Harrar."[2]
There was an apparent inconsistency between the British engagements
with France and with Italy. To the French government, this inconsistency
seemed important, and it was not long before the Quai d'Orsay informed
the British and Italian governments of its opinion.

In a note dated May 28, 1894, Casimir Perier, then the Foreign Minister
of France, instructed the French ambassadors in London and in Rome to
communicate the objections of the French Republic to the Anglo-Italian
Protocol. France would protest any change in the actual political situation
of Harrar.[3] Casimir Perier could do no more, for his cabinet was overthrown

on a question of internal affairs. Hanotaux, his successor at the Quai d'Orsay and a member of the same political party, the Moderate Republicans, inherited the problem.

Though the French government officially objected to the new political order created in the hinterland of their East African colony, the considerations that motivated their protest involved Egypt. For many years France had refused to recognize British gains in the Egyptian Sudan or the British occupation of Egypt itself. Indeed official and unofficial reminders, of which M. Lavisse's was but one, of Great Britain's unfulfilled promise to evacuate Egypt were almost constantly made during the 1880s and 1890s. The promise to evacuate British military and administrative personnel from Egypt was repeatedly made by no lesser statesmen than Gladstone and Salisbury. But words had failed to bring about the actions desired by France.[4]

In 1894 France decided to change its approach to the Egyptian question from the plane of polemics and ineffective diplomatic notes to that of vigorous action. Two plans were seized upon, one involving a political penetration of the disputed areas, the other in the form of strong protests against treaties which were considered illegal as well as detrimental to French interests. The political action, considered even before Hanotaux came to power at the Quai d'Orsay, took shape in 1894, in the formation of the Monteil expedition from Gabon on the West Coast of Africa and into the Bahr-el-Ghazal. This expedition was stopped before it had gained the potential advantages envisaged, partly because the French Government would not challenge Great Britain too openly. The new Russian alliance, although enthusiastically received in France, was not sufficient to offset potential British opposition in Europe. Moreover, Russia could not be expected to offer any sustained help to the French in Africa.[5]

Hanotaux would probably have preferred only a diplomatic challenge for he realized the dangers involved in a political-military challenge on the Nile question. He ordered Monteil to abstain from penetrating the Nile basin. The question of the Egyptian Sudan was to be kept open.[6] Britain claimed the whole of the Nile Valley. Firmly entrenched in Egypt the British had once occupied the Egyptian-Sudan. But faced with the revolt of a powerful Mahdi and of his Dervishes and the massacre of General Charles Gordon and his men at Khartoum in 1885, the cabinet in London had decided to pull its effectives out of the Sudan. It was taken for granted that a campaign would eventually have to be waged to reconquer the territories lost and to avenge the death of Gordon.[7] British imperialists would not allow their government to forget injury to British honor. Great

Britain had not yet relinquished her claim over the whole of the Nile River; and to the great disappointment of French colonialists, she never withdrew from Egypt.

If British honor had been pricked at Khartoum in 1885, so also was French prestige involved in the Egyptian question. In 1882 France had lost her position as joint ruler over Egypt when she failed to act in cooperation with Great Britain in putting down a local revolt. Ousted from Egypt France never tired of demanding a re-opening of the Egyptian question while England naturally felt reticent about doing this. The French representative in London reported in June 1894 that Lord Kimberley was willing to discuss all African problems but did not consider Egypt an African problem.[8] And so the fight went on, a contest of words carried on for the French side by the "colonialists." It was a fight to correct a wrong which Hanotaux, an historian as well as a politican, judged "a painful and unexpected postscript of the Treaty of Frankfort." [9]

By 1894 the Third Republic had gotten over the defeatism which partly explains her failure to act on Egypt in 1882. It was a rejuvenated and strengthened France which called on Hanotaux to help re-establish France to her natural position as a great European power. M. Hanotaux understood his task as one of strengthening France by bolstering her colonial empire even at the cost of occasional but limited quarrels with Great Britain.

Hanotaux therefore accepted the idea of a French penetration of the Egyptian Sudan. In 1894 there seemed to be no alternative way of forcing Great Britain to agree to a discussion of the Egyptian question. But a reading of Hanotaux's dispatches during 1894 and of his own accounts reveals clearly that he would have preferred a friendlier, more diplomatic approach to the whole question. At one time he even offered England a chance to enter into a "self-denying ordinance" about the occupation of the Egyptian Sudan.[10] While this would not have solved the question of the Upper Nile, it might have made agreement elsewhere more likely.

Having accepted the idea of a French penetration of the Upper Nile Valley, a plan which was not publicly announced, M. Hanotaux prepared the diplomatic arguments necessary to secure the gains expected from the expedition and justify the planned French action. The Egyptian Sudan, abandoned since 1885 and since then occupied by no European power, should be considered *res nullius* argued Hanotaux. Or if any rights were to be recognized as legitimate, they should be those of the Ottoman Empire. This involved a volte-face on Hanotaux's part but one that did not surprise the British. In his June 1894 speech to the Chamber of Deputies,

Hanotaux had argued on the basis of Ottoman rights. In April 1895 Hanotaux would present his *res nullius* thesis and the British soon found themselves using Hanotaux's earlier argument. The Foreign Office in London had decided that Hanotaux was insincere when speaking of Ottoman rights in the Valley of the Upper Nile. France could not be brushed aside by "fictitious" arrangements. Effective occupation was in colonial matters a better right than paper claims to unoccupied territories.[11] Hanotaux summarized the whole problem when he told the Senate in April 1895,

> I am one of those who think that in assuring respect of the rights of the Sultan and of the Khedive, in reserving to each that which will belong to him according to his work, two great nations will, when the time has come to settle the destiny of those far away lands, know how to find the proper formulas to conciliate their interests and satisfy their common aspiration toward civilization and progress.[12]

French irritation at British paper claims, the feeling that Great Britain was illegally throwing stumbling blocks in the way of French colonizing activities in Central Africa, and the actual state of affairs in Abyssinia (i.e., the traditional friendship of France and Abyssinia and the unreality of Italian claims over the area) were all elements of the complex dispute of which one aspect was the French protest against the Anglo-Italian treaty of May 5, 1894. France wanted to penetrate the Valley of the Upper Nile to force a discussion of the Egyptian question. Prestige was probably the most important element behind this desire. On their side the British would not have France on the Upper Nile. French economic presence might have been acceptable, but the possibility of political occupation was rejected out of hand. This attitude was made abundantly clear in 1895, through the Grey declaration, and its acceptance by the French after the turn of the century served as a basis for the start of talks that eventually led to the Anglo-French Entente.[13]

The economic reasons which probably motivated British actions in and around the Valley of the Upper Nile involved their control of Egypt itself. And in 1894 it was argued that any civilized power in control of the headwaters of the Nile and in a position to interfere with the life-giving flow of water, would be arbiter of the fate of Egypt. French authors, including Hanotaux's colleague at the Colonial Ministry, André Lebon, supported this thesis. This kind of consideration had led Britain to claim the whole course of the Nile River, to attempt to have other African powers recognize this claim, and to try to block all French access to the regions.[14] This last aim was not openly admitted; nor did France admit, until it had been carried out, her plan to penetrate the Egyptian Sudan in a dangerous move which was sure to raise the Egyptian question because of the gravity and magnitude of the interests involved.

On May 31, 1894, Hanotaux received the Italian reply to the French protest. A note from the Italian embassy in Paris acknowledged receipt of the French protest and opened the discussion of the problem. Against the rights which France was upholding by virtue of the Anglo-French Protocol of 1888, whose terms were familiar to the Italians, Rome put forth her own case. Italian rights were based on a note communicated to the French in 1889, and giving notice "in accordance with article 34 of the general act of the Berlin Conference" of Italy's protectorate over Abyssinia. At that time the Italian note explained, Harrar was already an integral part of Abyssinia. The French Government had acknowledged the 1889 Italian claim by a note to the Italian embassy in Paris dated October 20, 1889. Certainly if objections were to be made, the French Government should have protested at that time.[15]

The British reply to the French protest was much the same as that of Italy. The argument presented by Downing Street was an illustration of the practicality of British diplomats. This practicality was a trait Hanotaux noticed when, comparing French and British diplomats, he wrote in *Fachoda:* "French negotiators want to convince, while the English negotiators are satisfied to conquer" (p. 85). The British argued that the treaty signed by Italy and the Abyssinian King Menelik in 1889 (and on which the Italian notification of October 1889 was based), had placed Harrar, an Abyssinian dependency, in the Italian sphere of influence. France had not at that time used its right of opposition as guaranteed by the 1888 Anglo-French arrangement. In signing the May 5, 1894, Anglo-Italian treaty, Great Britain had broken no previous engagements and did "no more as regards Harrar than recognize the actual state of things which has existed for several years past."[16]

There was then a complete lack of agreement as to what constituted the "actual state of things" in Harrar and as to what "rights" had or had not been observed by the treaty of May 5, 1894. On the surface the French case was apparently a weak one. Rome and London observed that France should have objected in 1889. Through their failure in 1889 to protest and reserve their rights, the French had weakened the bases of the diplomatic action of 1894. But the politicians in 1894 were members of a new generation of leaders. The Boulanger Crisis of 1889 had swept away many public figures and given a more energetic younger generation of politicians a chance to arrive in positions of leadership. Among the prestige-conscious young politicians were MM. Delcassé, Hanotaux, and Etienne, all men who were trained in the "imperialistic school" of Freycinet, Ferry, and Gambetta. These new men analyzed the "actual state of things" in East Africa and examined French interests in that area of the continent. They then decided to make known the formal objections which the French Republic found to a treaty which according to their opponents did no more than recognize "what was."

Their analysis was based on several points. First, the French Foreign Office admitted that Italy had notified the powers of her protectorate over Abyssinia in compliance with article thirty-four of the general act of the Berlin Conference on African Affairs which met in 1884–85.[17] But it also noted that Rome had failed to comply with the provisions of article thirty-five of the same agreement. This article required a power, once it had declared the establishment of a protectorate over any part of Africa, to insure the existence of sufficient authority to enforce respect of acquired rights. A minimum requirement was the insurance of freedom of commerce and transit.

Italy's failure to comply with the requirements of article thirty-five of the general act of the Berlin Conference was caused largely by the opposition of the Abyssinian Emperor, Menelik. Menelik was the king of Shoa, one of the provinces of Abyssinia which was organized as a feudal state. The lesser potentates (the king of Shoa included) owed allegiance to an Emperor. Menelik's relations with Italy had been quite good until he became, largely through Italian help, Emperor of the whole realm. The very personality of Menelik underwent a profound change with the assumption of the supreme dignity. No longer a noble owing allegiance to an Emperor, he would not acquiesce in European encroachments on Abyssinia.[18]

Menelik's prime obsession was to gather all traditionally Abyssinian territories under one crown. This brought him into immediate conflict with the Italian government which under Crispi wished to widen the territorial base of its Eritrean colony. In 1893 Menelik denounced the treaty of Ucciali following the discovery of a discrepancy between the Italian and the Amharic versions of this Protocol. Negotiations failed to lead to satisfactory settlement of the discrepancy. The Amharic version of article seventeen of the treaty of Ucciali stressed *consent:* "The Abyssinian Emperor consents to make use of the good offices of the King of Italy in his relations with foreign powers." Taken in the feudal context of Abyssinia in the late nineteenth century, consent should imply "that a feudal lord would consent to accept the services of his liege." The Italian government, however, introduced in the Italian text of the treaty of Ucciali is "obliged to" instead of "consents." Hence, Rome could claim a protectorate over Abyssinia and in October 1889 gave notice to that effect.[19]

Menelik was shocked when he discovered the humiliating wording of the Italian text. He denounced the treaty of Ucciali and since only the Amharic text had been signed, his position was strong. He also paid back a loan the Italian government had made. Yet, the French argued, Great Britain recognized the Italian protectorate over Abyssinia by becoming a party to the Anglo-Italian treaty of May 5, 1894, in spite of Menelik's denunciation of the treaty of Ucciali during the course of the previous year. By May 1894 Italo-Abyssinian relations had deteriorated as the two nations embarked on the path that was to lead them to the great Italian disaster of Adowa. France, standing aside, could easily profit from the Abyssinian objections which were brought about by Italian actions.

Indeed, while relations between Menelik and the Italian government well before the signing of the May 5, 1894, Anglo-Italian Protocol were rapidly deteriorating, the connections between Addis Ababa and Paris were noticeably improving. In 1894 Ras Maconnen, the most powerful Abyssinian king owing allegiance to Emperor Menelik, saw his pro-French attitude adopted by Menelik. Maconnen had long fought Italian influence often at great risk to his own life and property. Franco-Abyssinian relations had in any case been cordial from the start when France established herself at Obock in Somaliland. Surprisingly these relations had never been formalized and, except for a commercial treaty signed by the king of Shoa and Louis-Philippe in 1843, no diplomatic document existed to control diplomatic exchanges.[20]

Informally, however, Abyssinian-French relations were close enough. It was Paris which in 1890 pointed out the discrepancy between the Amharic and Italian text of the treaty of Ucciali. This observation had provoked a sharp diplomatic protest on the part of Menelik as early as 1891 and in 1893 the denunciation of the Italo-Abyssinian treaty. France, of course, also possessed the natural outlet for Abyssinian commerce in the Red Sea, the port of Djibouti. Most of Abyssinia's foreign trade might be channeled through the French facility. Possession of this port gave the French a potentially coercive weapon which they might have, but failed to use to force any desirable concession from Abyssinia. One French political commentator in September 1894 wrote: "We had interests and traditions in the Red Sea; yet when we saw that Italy carried on its principal colonial effort there, we discreetly stepped out of the picture, leaving her a free field of action." [21]

Given this attitude about Italian colonialism and about East African affairs during the 1880s, why then did France object to the Anglo-Italian treaty of May 5, 1894? Ernest Lavisse had given a partial answer by observing that since Harrar was the real hinterland of the French colony of Obock-Djibouti, France had been reasonable and moderate when in 1888 she was satisfied that this door should remain open and that no one would close it. With respect to Abyssinia itself, the French envisaged a pacific development of their own influence. But this did not exclude the possibility of furnishing Menelik with weapons with which to fight third powers.[22]

Undoubtedly, France was concerned about her rights and was interested in assuring respect for engagements which Downing Street apparently did not take into account when signing the two important African treaties of 1894. France could hardly be expected to stand aside while her East African Colony was reduced to a mere enclave in a sea of Italian territories, while Obock-Djibouti, a potential outlet for all Abyssinian commercial goods, became useful as a coaling station only. M. Etienne brought up the point about having French rights respected. Prestige then was involved in both the Harrar question and in the Egyptian question. In any case Italy was a bad enough neighbor in Europe.[23] Not interested in extending the territorial expanse of the Obock-Djibouti colony at the expense of Abyssinia, France wanted a free Abyssinia which would avail herself of the French commercial facilities of Djibouti. Negotiations were begun in 1894 between France and Menelik, the object of which was the securing of a railway concession from Djibouti through Harrar, to Addis Ababa (the capital of Abyssinia) and beyond. Commercial gain was the apparent reason behind the protest against the Anglo-Italian treaty of May 5, 1894. To strengthen their own local position the French extended to Menelik a gift of more than 10,000 rifles and of 2.5 million cartridges. A proposed sale had become an outright gift to Menelik at the suggestion of Hanotaux's ministry.[24] There were, however, more fundamental interests involved in the French protest. Behind many French actions about Africa during most of the 1890s was the thorny question of Egypt.

"You have sworn not to stay in Egypt," wrote Ernest Lavisse in answer to Sir Charles Dilke during the heat of the Fashoda incident of 1898–99, and "since your occupation of Egypt, we are no longer good neighbors." [25] Some years later in *Fachoda* Hanotaux, who had managed the French protest of 1894, wrote:

> ... the question of Egypt dominated all, inflamed all. Yet, the basic aim [*l'idée maitresse*] of French diplomacy in 1894, was that this Nile question, the core of all unsolved differences, could become the nucleus of a general settlement. (p. 89)

Behind Hanotaux were the colonialists, a group of French politicians and publicists motivated by considerations of prestige and united in a firm resolution and desire to "reopen the question of Egypt." [26] That the question of Egypt was really the question raised by the Anglo-Italian and Anglo-Congolese treaties of May 1894 can hardly be doubted. If there were any doubts, these were quickly dispelled by the opinions expressed by Hanotaux during his first speech as Foreign Minister of France.

From interpellators in the Chamber of Deputies on June 7, 1894, M. Hanotaux accepted the following formula: "In ceding on her own authority, Egyptian territories to Italy (and to the Congo Free State), England has usurped the rights of the Khedive and of the Sultan." Italians operating from Eritrean bases occupied Kassala in July 1894. [27] Hanotaux chose to attack the Anglo-Italian treaty on this ground as Kassala had been a khedivial province until 1885 when it had been evacuated following the defeat of Gordon. Could England now recognize Italian suzerainty over this center without breaking its pledge to work for Ottoman status quo? Ottoman and khedivial rights supposedly covered the whole of the Upper Nile Valley, the so-called Egyptian Sudan. In theory the Egyptian khedive owed allegiance to the Ottoman dynasty in Constantinople. Also in theory the territories of the Ottoman sultan were guaranteed by all European powers. Reality and theory were not the same, and while France was seeking to re-establish the theoretical order which she thought she could exploit, England was becoming firmly entrenched in Egypt and calling for Anglo-Egyptian control of all of the Nile watershed.[28]

In 1894 French colonialists felt strongly that British moves, diplomatic and military, around and about the Valley of the Upper Nile tended to upset the European powers' equilibrium in Africa. England's gifts of Egyptian territories to the Congo on the right bank of the Nile and to Italy on the other bank were understood to be illegal blocks thrown in the way of any possible French attempts at penetration in the area in question.[29]

In protesting against the Anglo-Congolese and Anglo-Italian treaties of May 1894 France was trying to preserve her two accesses to the Valley of the Upper Nile. Attempting to make these protests effective Hanotaux used what he termed "un mouvement tournant." [30] This was in diplomacy what a flanking movement is in the military. With the French protest against the Anglo-Congolese treaty this had involved working in cooperation with Germany and getting Russia and Turkey to support the French point of view. With regard to parallel action against the Anglo-Italian treaty the "mouvement tournant" involved the diplomatic help of Russia, the newly won ally of France, Turkey, the theoretical ruler of the Egyptian Sudan, and Abyssinia, a nation traditionally friendly to France whose very independence was threatened by colonialism.

The community of thought necessary for a French "mouvement tournant" was well understood by Hanotaux who on June 7, 1894, explained before the Chamber of Deputies that his position on African affairs, particularly in the Nile Valley, was based on the preservation of the rights of the sultan and of the khedive.

Earlier Hanotaux had expressed similar views in a directive to his ambassadors in St. Petersburg and Constantinople.[31] In this *communiqué* dated June 1, 1894, Hanotaux noticed the apprehension recently manifested by the Porte about a rumored Congo Free State expedition into the Valley of the Upper Nile. This rumor had followed closely behind the announced British occupation of Wadelai, the capital of the ancient Egyptian province of Equatoria. Then had come this new African arrangement. Hanotaux further stated that Russia should be approached as the ally of France, as a guarantor of the Ottoman Empire, and as a power interested in the Abyssinian Empire. Hanotaux had previously noticed the interest of the Tsarist regime. Russia and Abyssinia could not fail to notice that the objectionable Anglo-Italian treaty of May 5, 1894, "tended to consecrate the establishment of the Italians in the region between the Red Sea and the Nile." [32]

Turkish interest in supporting the French protest was assumed for self-evident reasons. The Anglo-Italian treaties affecting East Africa had violated the rights of the sultan in the Egyptian Sudan. Though the Ottoman rights over certain Italian occupied parts of the Egyptian-Sudan were ambiguously mentioned in the arrangements which London and Rome agreed upon, the British welcomed news of the Italian occupation of Kassala. And Downing Street had granted the Italians a right to "temporary" occupation of Kassala, undeniably a part of the ancient Egyptian Sudan.[33]

The territorial integrity of the Ottoman Empire placed as it was at the core of the French argument against the Anglo-Italian treaty was also the cause of M. Hanotaux's optimism about getting diplomatic support from St. Petersburg against London and Rome. The Tsar's government was one of the guarantors of the territorial integrity of the Ottoman Empire. As such and also because she was interested in Abyssinian independence from Italy, Russia objected to the 1889 Italian notification which declared Abyssinia an Italian Protectorate. When St. Petersburg was approached in 1894 about the French protest against the Anglo-Italian treaty, her foreign minister immediately expressed the opinion that Russia was probably in an even better position than France to protest against the irritating arrangement; for France had not opposed Italy in East Africa in 1889.[34]

In 1894 as in 1889 Russia had interests of her own in Abyssinia. Therefore, the Tsarist government gladly approved of its ally's protest. This approval Russia quickly followed up by demanding at London and at Rome an explanation about the meaning of the Anglo-Italian treaty.[35] A diplomatic protest was communicated to the respective parties of the objectionable African treaty. According to M. de Montebello, the French ambassador in St. Petersburg, these objections were based on Russian opposition to the effects of the May 5th treaty on the integrity of the Ottoman Empire, the independence of Abyssinia, and the neutrality of Harrar, which England had agreed to.

Of the Russian motives, that involving the independence of Abyssinia was probably the most important. Indeed, Franco-Russian cooperation in Africa and in the Balkans was an exception rather than the rule in spite of the defensive alliance which existed between the two nations. Russian interests in Abyssinia had become active when, in 1888, the Ashinov-Paissi expedition from Odessa to East Africa took place. Supposedly a pilgrimage inspired by the interest of the Russian Orthodox Church in the very similar brand of Christianity practiced in Abyssinia, the Ashinov-Paissi expedition had a definite political undertone. In the opinion of Lobanov-Rostovski, the historian of Russian colonialism, "A survey of [the] secondary theaters of Russian [colonial] activity would not be complete without the mention of a curious attempt to get a foothold also in Africa, namely in Abyssinia." [36] Whatever the real interests of Russia in Abyssinia, the first contact was succeeded by numerous exchanges of delegations. In 1894 Russian activity in East Africa was considerably intensified, much to the displeasure of the Italians who speculated that all this activity had something to do with the Franco-Russian alliance. In fact, the Franco-Russian alliance was to have practically no effects outside Europe until after the turn of the century. But the Abyssinian situation in 1894 and after did suggest the possibility of cooperation in Africa and elsewhere, which Hanotaux may well have sought to foster.

Yet Franco-Russian cooperation on the Abyssinian problem came slowly. As late as July 10, 1894, Rome could think that St. Petersburg would not object to the May 5th Anglo-Italian treaty. Russia's protest in June had apparently not been as strong as M. de Montebello had believed. On July 30 the Russian ambassador in London was still awaiting instructions from his government. Decrais, the French charge d'affaires, regretted his ally's sluggishness thinking a firm word from the Russians "would not have been useless." [37] The early enthusiasm of Frenchmen about possible Franco-Russian cooperation in Africa—a feeling which enabled someone at the Quai d'Orsay to suggest the possible cession of the port of Obock to the Tsar—soon waned. Obock was never offered to the Russians though French authorities in Obock-Djibouti were carefully instructed to cooperate with Russian missions to Abyssinia and to facilitate Russian shipments to Menelik in every possible way. [38]

In Europe Franco-Italian relations had deteriorated during the period of growing Franco-Russian rapprochement and negotiations about an alliance. By 1894 France and Italy were conducting vigorous tariff wars against each other to the detriment of both. The Abyssinian matter only added to the fuel of the press war in which both sides indulged and when Sadi Carnot, the French President, was assassinated in 1894 by an Italian anarchist, Franco-Italian relations were strained almost to a breaking point. Yet, during the time he was at the Quai d'Orsay Hanotaux worked almost constantly to reestablish friendly relations between Paris and Rome and to woo the latter away from the Triple Alliance. [39]

Franco-Italian relations did not improve until after the Crispi ministry at Rome was thrown out of office following the great Italian disaster at Adowa. Italy had thought imperialistically, but she had not the strength to be a great power. Menelik, with considerable French and Russian help, defeated the Italians decisively at Adowa, where 14,000 to 17,000 well armed but poorly organized Italians were beaten by some 80,000 Abyssinians. In Menelik's army there were about as many rifles as men, many of the weapons being quite modern. Menelik's guns, furnished by Frenchmen and Russians in the years which preceded the Abyssinian-Italian conflict, were superior in accuracy and range to those of the enemy. [40] The Italians were not blind to Franco-Russian aid, as is revealed in the polemic attacks in the Roman press. But the culpability of European enemies in East Africa was not proved, and much of Italy's case was destroyed because she herself had furnished Abyssinians with the machine guns which were turned against Italian soldiers. [41]

Events and accidents, then, played a more important role than diplomatic maneuvers in the success of the French protest against the Anglo-Italian treaty. Indeed, neither Rome nor London had withdrawn their agreement after the Adowa disaster of 1896. Great Britain could no longer count on Italian protection after the defeat of the Italians by the Abyssinians at Adowa. This influenced Britain to carry out the Dongola expedition into the Egyptian Sudan. The Quai d'Orsay was well aware of the relation between the Italian disaster and the British decision to send a military expedition into the region of the Upper Nile. France had gained the support of Russia and Turkey on East African affairs. The Quai d'Orsay had, undoubtedly, also gained Menelik's support. Yet, perhaps because France was helping Menelik against Italy but was not admitting it, a letter from Menelik asking for a formalization of Franco-Abyssinian relations was not answered for over a year. Also, railway concessions involving the building of a Djibouti-Harrar-Addis Ababa line which were granted in 1894 were not exploited until after the Fashoda incident in 1898.[42]

Abyssinia was only a secondary theater of French colonial interests while the Upper Nile was the center of attention. The attitude is clearly expressed by M. Delconcl, a colonialist who in February 1895 said:

> We gave ourselves an access toward the Upper Nile, not to establish ourselves there, since these regions belonged to the Ottoman Empire . . . , but we are in a good position to take by surprise [*prendre à revers*] certain positions from our rivals and [thereby] furnish new elements to our diplomacy for negotiations that will be indispensable.[43]

The French protest against the Anglo-Italian treaty of May 5, 1894, was not carried out to weaken Italy. Nor was there much truth in the Italian claim that Menelik had been provoked by France and assisted by Russia, "to engage Italy in a fight to wear her out in Africa and weaken her in Europe." [44] France and Russia were active in East Africa and probably against Italy. But the motivation was not that which the Italian press saw. Russia had her own reasons for wanting to maintain Abyssinia free and it was the question of the Nile and Egypt which made for French action and seemed to force French action. French colonialists wanted to reopen the Egyptian question. Great Britain wanted it to be a closed affair and tried to block French accesses to the Upper Nile. One facet of the British effort to block any possible French attempt toward the Nile was the Anglo-Italian treaty of May 5, 1894. For the French, and particularly for Hanotaux, the problem was quite clear:

> If one lets things alone, the question of Egypt, one might add the question of Africa, was regulated in one stroke. The colonial policy followed in France for fifteen years would have been but a vain parade. No means to negotiate once more, no elements of exchange or compensation would have remained at the moment when the great African negotiations were about to begin. (*Fachoda*, p. 74)

So Gabriel Hanotaux fought diplomatically by attempting to abrogate the Anglo-Italian treaty of May 5, 1894, by reluctantly accepting the idea of a French penetration of the Nile Valley, and, later by protesting against the Grey declaration.

The plan for penetrating the Egyptian Sudan, known as the Marchand expedition, was taken up during 1895–96. Starting from a base in Gabon Jean Baptiste Marchand with a few French officers and some Senegalese contigents numbering less than two hundred soldiers in all, reached the Nile at Fashoda in 1898. On their way from the Congo to the Nile, this handful of French officers and their hundred Senegalese soldiers had crossed through the Upper Ubangi and Bahr-el-Ghazal districts of Central Africa.[45] They were to have been met by another French expedition from Djibouti through Abyssinia, and diplomatic negotiations to secure the necessary transit right through Menelik's empire had actually been engaged in as early as 1894. But the planned junction of the Congo-Nile and Djibouti-Nile expeditions was not realized. As a result, Marchand did not get expected supplies and men at Fashoda while his presence there precipitated a crisis between France and Great Britain—the Fashoda incident. In an uneven conflict of will, Marchand's small band weakened by months of marching through tropical Africa—often in swampy districts—and lacking fresh supplies faced the full force of the well supplied and relatively fresh Anglo-Egyptian expedition of more than 20,000 men. The military fait accompli expected to leave France in a strong political position from which a diplomatic attack on the English occupation of Egypt might be launched simply did not occur, partly because the French expedition to the right and left banks of the Nile never met.[46]

In all of the planning involving Marchand's expedition to Fashoda, France never considered taking Abyssinia. Instead, the French dealt with an independent Emperor Menelik whom they tried to strengthen. Gabriel Hanotaux and the cabinet in which he served during 1894–95 refused to accept the proposed "partition" of an independent empire, Abyssinia. This refusal was based on commercial considerations—French plans to develop Djibouti into the main outlet for Abyssinian commerce but also on questions of prestige, French desires in the Upper Nile region and Egypt itself. The protest which Hanotaux directed against the Anglo-Italian treaty of May 5, 1894, was as strong and as effective as it could be made. In the end, however, and as Hanotaux himself recognized, it was the Italian defeat in 1896 at the hands of the Abyssinians which "left the field open" to the political and commercial activity of France.[47]

Victorious against the Italians, Menelik was faced with the necessity of keeping together a large portion of the huge army he had gathered together. He decided to continue his conquests: the area of Abyssinia nearly doubled during Menelik's reign. In this campaign approved by the French whose enemies the Emperor was fighting, Menelik assumed the role of Christian ruler set against infidels, mostly Muslims. While Africans occupied Menelik's attention, European powers competed for the right to furnish the military needs of the foremost independent ruler in Africa. Italians complained bitterly about French shipments of weapons.[48] For a while Menelik seemed to threaten the Nile Valley. The British reactions, as well as the reactions of France and Italy, were a far cry from what either "the white man's burden" or the *"mission civilisatrice"* were supposed to be. The Europeans involved struggled diplomatically—often involving the King of Abyssinia as a third party. In the pursuit of their own interests they fought for prestige, and for commercial and strategic considerations. They rarely demonstrated much concern for the East Africans' well-being or civilization.

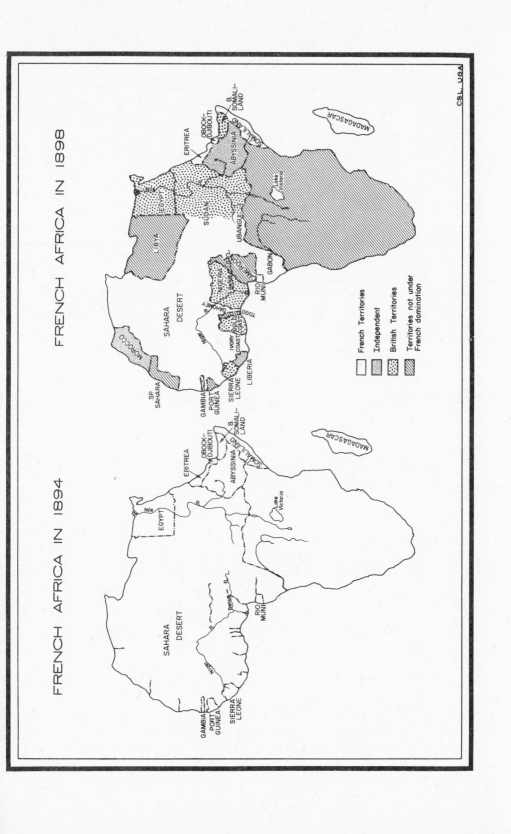

FRENCH AFRICA IN 1898

FRENCH AFRICA IN 1894

French Territories

Independent

British Territories

Territories not under
French domination

CSL. UGA

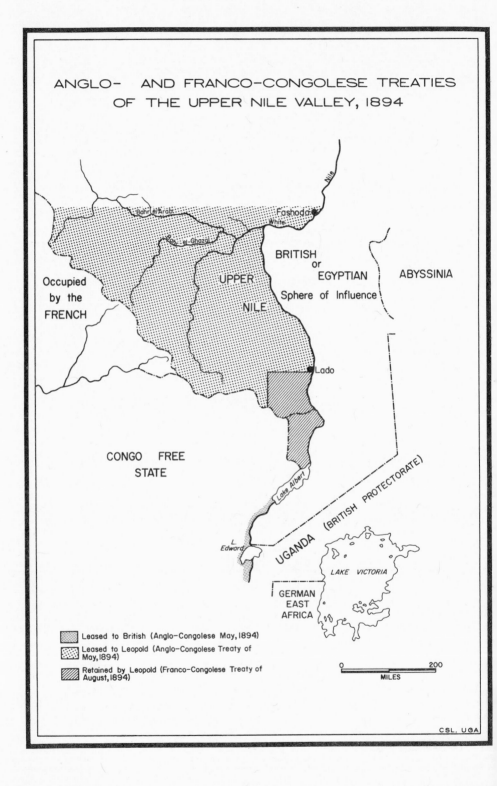

ANGLO- AND FRANCO-CONGOLESE TREATIES
OF THE UPPER NILE VALLEY, 1894

Nile

Bahr el Arab

Bahr el-Ghazal

Fashoda
White

Occupied
by the
FRENCH

UPPER

NILE

BRITISH
or
EGYPTIAN
Sphere of Influence

ABYSSINIA

Lado

CONGO   FREE
STATE

Lake Albert

UGANDA (BRITISH PROTECTORATE)

L.
Edward

LAKE VICTORIA

GERMAN
EAST
AFRICA

Leased to British (Anglo-Congolese May, 1894)

Leased to Leopold (Anglo-Congolese Treaty of
May, 1894)

Retained by Leopold (Franco-Congolese Treaty of
August, 1894)

0   200

MILES

CSL, UGA

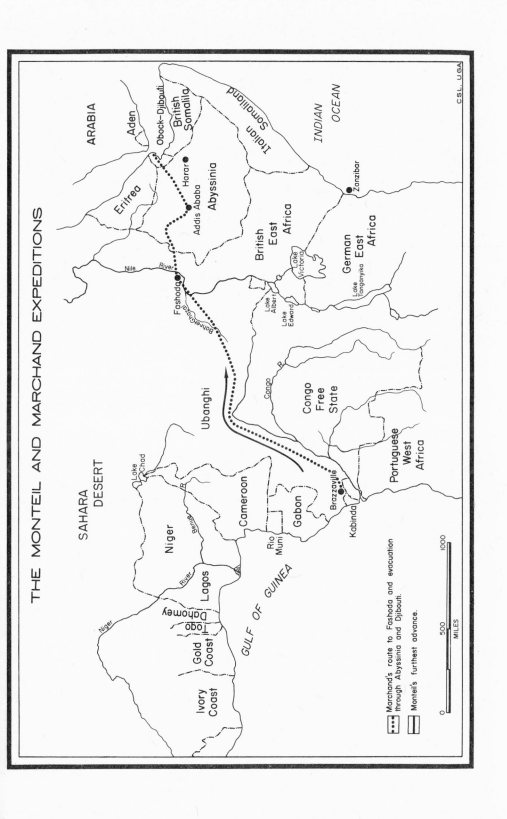

THE MONTEIL AND MARCHAND EXPEDITIONS

ARABIA

Aden

Eritrea

Obock–Djibouti
British Somalila

Italian Somaliland

INDIAN OCEAN

Harar

Addis Ababa   Abyssinia

Nile   River

Fashoda

Bahr-el-Ghazal

British East Africa

Lake Victoria

German East Africa

Zanzibar

Lake Albert

Lake Edward

Lake Tanganyika

Ubanghi

Congo R.

Congo Free State

Portuguese West Africa

SAHARA DESERT

Lake Chad

R.

Niger

Benue R.

Cameroon

Rio Muni

Gabon

Brazzaville

Kabinda

Niger River

Lagos

Dahomey

Togo

Gold Coast

Ivory Coast

GULF OF GUINEA

:::: Marchand's route to Fashoda and evacuation
     through Abyssinia and Djibouti.

▯▯ Monteil's furthest advance.

0   500   1000
            MILES

CSL, UGA

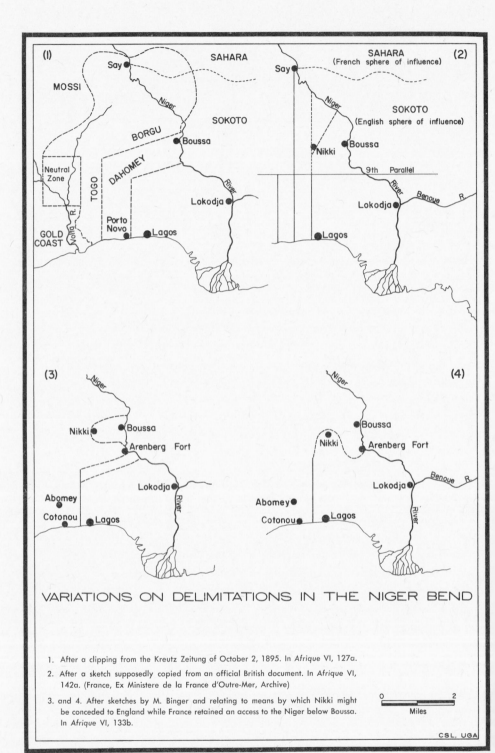

VARIATIONS ON DELIMITATIONS IN THE NIGER BEND

1. After a clipping from the Kreutz Zeitung of October 2, 1895. In *Afrique VI*, 127a.

2. After a sketch supposedly copied from an official British document. In *Afrique VI*, 142a. (France, Ex Ministere de la France d'Outre-Mer, Archive)

3. and 4. After sketches by M. Binger and relating to means by which Nikki might be conceded to England while France retained an access to the Niger below Boussa. In *Afrique VI*, 133b.

0 — 2 Miles

CSL, UGA

The Anglo-French
Colonial Talks
of 1894–95

Chapter 5

Discussions between London and Paris, begun when the French objected
to the Anglo-Congolese and Anglo-Italian treaties of 1894, made possible
further talks about outstanding Anglo-French differences throughout Africa. The limited cooperation achieved on Moroccan issues during the first
several weeks of Hanotaux's tenure at the Quai d'Orsay indicated the possibility of agreement between France and England, although Downing
Street gave Hanotaux little satisfaction with respect to his Central and
East African protest. Only after the French foreign minister had achieved
his ends by pressuring the British allies in Brussels and Rome did London suggest further African negotiations. Hanotaux, who had consciously
fought his own growing reputation for Anglophobia, accepted the British
offer. Selecting Hausseman to assist him, he engaged in a long and drawn-
out series of talks with two British representatives, Dufferin and Phipps.
That he himself chose to negotiate rather than to appoint a representative
was a clear indication of the importance Hanotaux attached to these talks.
They would touch on most African problems, but particularly on questions about West Africa and the Upper Nile Valley. The unspoken corol-
lary of the Upper Nile question and the most important element in the
disputes which these four men attempted to solve was the Egyptian question. The Anglo-French colonial talks of 1894–95 revealed a great deal
about the positions and attitudes of the British and the French, and particularly about Hanotaux.

French pride had been pricked when in the 1880s she lost her predominant position in Egypt to Great Britain. The debate about Egypt was
temporarily closed but far from forgotten, for an able and vigorous group
of French colonialists urged their government to reopen the Egyptian question. France had lost when she failed to support British efforts to resist the
Mahdist revolt of 1882. Having acted alone in the face of this native rebellion Great Britain began to engage in an even more active occupation of
Egypt. France remained on the side lines, bitter, but unable to act. The

Quai d'Orsay dared not challenge Great Britain directly. Continental considerations after the war of 1870 made such policies inadvisable at best. The British Foreign Office for its part did not wish to discuss the Egyptian question. Great Britain had the upper hand and talks could only weaken her position, an important one involving India.[1]

Both parties realized that the Upper Nile question was linked to the Egyptian question. During the spring of 1894, both France and Great Britain opened negotiations with Leopold II. Hanotaux attempted to keep the Belgians from blocking French access to the Nile. Great Britain naturally wanted to keep France out of the Upper Nile Valley for the same reason that France wanted to get into that area. There was an element of dishonesty in Leopold's double negotiations and the agreement with Great Britain was reached secretly while separate talks were under way with Hanotaux. But Hanotaux discovered the subterfuge by which the date of the agreement was changed so the Anglo-Congolese treaty appeared to have been signed after the Franco-Congolese talks had broken down.[2] The insult, added to the bitterness of failure, may explain Hanotaux's harshness towards Leopold in the later negotiations which led to the Franco-Congolese treaty of August 14, 1894, and in the talks about French pre-emption rights in the Congo. Then the tone changed and the Quai d'Orsay became more friendly to Leopold II. The real conflict was between Paris and London; and, in the pursuit of political goals which involved the Upper Nile, Hanotaux needed transit rights for men and material on the Belgians' Congo railway.[3]

The Anglo-French dispute was bitter because control of the headwaters of the Nile would put a power with sufficiently advanced technology in a position to squeeze almost unlimited concessions from any power in actual political control of Egypt. Such concessions would be obtained by threatening to hold back or to divert the water supply that has always been the life line of Egyptian agriculture.[4]

It was probably speculation on the possibility of controlling the water supply of Egypt and on the political consequences of such tampering which drove French colonialists to advocate the military occupation of the Upper Nile Valley. There were of course legalistic undertones involved in the plan. The French considered the British presence in Egypt illegal. France in occupation of the Upper Nile Valley would ask Great Britain to withdraw from Egypt. If this were accepted, France would agree to withdraw from the Upper Nile. Another alternative to the occupations and withdrawals outlined would have been for Britain to find adequate compensation for France somewhere else. In 1894 no compensation was suggested.

Britain was not yet ready to offer Morocco to France in exchange for a free hand in Egypt. Nor was France, which used every possible means for making nuisances for the British in Egypt, ready to change its policies on the question.

The Fashoda incident in 1898 put an end to Anglo-French rivalry about the Upper Nile. This rivalry had broken out in earnest as a result of the French protest against the Anglo-Congolese and Anglo-Italian treaties of 1894. The former treaty was nullified when Hanotaux, through diplomacy backed by the Monteil expedition, forced Leopold II of the Belgians, the owner of the Congo Free State, to sign a treaty with France. The Franco-Congolese treaty which was signed on August 14, 1894, secured for France "son chemin libre" to the Upper Nile Valley. Great Britain neither acknowledged nor protested the arrangement between Paris and Brussels.[5]

Even earlier, probably to force the British to discuss the Egyptian question, Carnot, the president of the Third Republic, Delcassé, the undersecretary for colonies, and Monteil, a colonial officer, had drawn up in 1893 a plan for the occupation of the "Soudan nilotique." [6] The former Anglo-Egyptian Sudan or the Upper Nile Valley was the objective of a Gabon-based French expedition in 1894. The Monteil expedition, however, was called back when France gained satisfaction with respect to the Anglo-Congolese treaty. But the plan to penetrate and occupy the Upper Nile Regions and to force a reopening of the Egyptian question remained; throughout 1894 and 1895 the colonial office over which Delcassé now presided as minister put pressure on the Quai d'Orsay to allow the proposed plan to go into effect.[7] First Liotard, then Marchand were ordered to carry out a plan which in 1898 led to the Fashoda incident. Since that time many French historians have complained not about the plan but about the procrastination which they detected in the implementation of the Upper Nile occupation.[8] In the mid–1890s Hanotaux promptly tried to keep French options open while at the same time attempting to reduce some colonial problems and particularly to eliminate all possible Franco-British African differences.

Hanotaux's achievements in the Anglo-Congolese treaty kept the French approach to the Upper Nile from West Africa open. But he was unable to duplicate this success with the Anglo-Italian treaty. The Italians proved to be as stubborn as the British, who never gave in to France on these disputed African arrangements. In early 1896, however, Hanotaux gained all that he wanted for France when the Francophobe Crispi cabinet fell as a consequence of the Italian colonial disaster of Adowa. Now the East African route to the Valley of the Upper Nile was open to potential French expeditions. Hanotaux, however, remembered Italy's reticence and probably sought revenge against Rome in the settlement he forced on Europe in 1896 when he suspended the capitulations treaties and the extra-territorial rights enjoyed in Tunisia by several European powers.

In East Africa Italy was left to her own devices, as the Congo had been two years earlier, by an ally who had signed treaties for her own interests alone. Great Britain never gave up the advantages she had gained through the Anglo-Congolese and Anglo-Italian treaties. The French foreign minister might well criticize the British treaties as meaningless but irritating "paper arrangements." Still, the Foreign Office had won recognition of its claimed sphere of influence from all but one of the powers which could possibly be interested in the Upper Nile. The British imperialists meant to ignore the French protest. Evidence of his negative attitude can be seen in the British ambassador's actions and words during the weeks which followed the conclusion of the Anglo-Congolese treaty.

Though the British government received the French protest about the Congo treaty on May 28, 1894, the British representative in Paris, Lord Dufferin, claimed complete ignorance on the subject on June 6. Having made repeated requests for instructions Dufferin was finally told what the British position was. He immediately sent a letter to Hanotaux, stating he was authorized to discuss without prejudicing British freedom of action "the grounds upon which the Government of the Republic" objected to the treaty of May 12th. The British note also proposed "a general review of all . . . pending African questions." ⁹

The proposed review of Anglo-French differences in Africa was first made on June 5. The proposal was made to M. Decrais, the French ambassador in London, by Lord Kimberley, foreign secretary in Lord Rosebery's cabinet. According to the report sent to the Quai d'Orsay on the same day, the British were willing to discuss all Central and West African questions. But the offer was limited for it did not include the Egyptian question, which was of prime importance to France. Indeed, Kimberley judged the Egyptian question "un trop gros morceau qui mérite d'être traité à part." In any case, Hanotaux wished to have the dispute raised by the Anglo-Congolese treaty settled before a wider discussion began.¹⁰

If Dufferin's attitude is to be trusted, the British understood even the Upper Nile question as being excluded. The expression *Central Africa*, according to this report, was to be applied to the regions of Lake Chad, and not as the French had understood it, to the Sudan and Equatorial Africa. Hanotaux concluded that the Anglo-German arrangement, completed when the article of the Anglo-Congolese treaty to which the Germans objected was withdrawn, had led to a determined effort on the part of the Foreign Office "to resist French demands vigorously." [11] The British offer was, in any case, an offer to discuss, not an offer to negotiate.

Perhaps the withdrawal of the *article* of the Anglo-Congolese treaty to which the Germans had objected was followed by a stiffening of the British attitude toward the French protest. This article, the third, would have granted Great Britain a 25 mile strip between lakes Albert Edward and Tanganyika. This was the article which, because it separated German territories from those of the Congo Free State, had drawn the ire of Germany. But even before June 18 when the partial cancellation of the Anglo-Congolese treaty occurred, there seems to have been little sincerity in the British advances toward France. In the Dufferin-Hanotaux meeting on June 11 all words approaching negotiation and compromise were said "à titre privé," without instructions from the British government. On the 20th Dufferin was still powerless to negotiate, nor did the British ambassador receive positive instructions during the following week.[12]

While the British would not commit themselves, France insisted on the cancellation of the Anglo-Congolese treaty. The Foreign Office, whose case was weakened by the abrogation of half its treaty with the Congo on June 18, could not see how it could retract an engagement so recently signed without putting the British Government in a bad light. Hanotaux argued that the British were already in a poor position, for their agreement with Leopold II had broken previous engagements with other powers. For some time this impasse seemed insurmountable, and until the difference about the Anglo-Congolese treaty could be settled, no progress could be expected in the Anglo-French colonial talks.[13] Until Hanotaux negotiated with Leopold II nothing was accomplished.

In Brussels Leopold II, unable to gain British backing and faced with opposition within his own government, quickly came to terms with France by signing a Franco-Congolese treaty that conceded all of Hanotaux's demands. The way was then cleared for the first real negotiations between Paris and London. Three days after the conclusion of the Franco-Congolese treaty, Dufferin received some definite instructions and went to Hanotaux with specific proposals on the basis of which negotiations could begin.[14]

Hanotaux, as the exponent of an arrangement with Great Britain in colonial matters, was opposed by the colonial minister, Théophile Delcassé, who wanted to occupy the Upper Nile Valley. Delcassé wished to accomplish militarily what he felt Downing Street would never concede diplomatically.[15] Hanotaux was also a colonialist and thought the greatness of France would be enhanced by a vast empire. But he was unwilling to approve actions which might arouse Great Britain. There was really not so much difference between the policies of Hanotaux in the period 1894–98 and of Delcassé from 1898 on. Delcassé when he was colonial minister in 1894–95 was a strong colonialist; this tendency he apparently suppressed after he became foreign minister. Hanotaux became a much stronger colonialist once he was out of office. But as long as there was a chance of accomplishing peaceably by diplomatic means rather than by military expedition a settlement of the Upper Nile question, Hanotaux refused to sanction the planned Nile penetration. During 1894 and 1895 he sparred almost continually with his colleagues at the Colonial Office.[16]

Hanotaux forced a radical change in the character of the Monteil expedition. Originally, the plan devised by Delcassé and Monteil would have had the latter penetrate the Nile Valley and set up a French post at Fashoda. As finally ordered on July 18, 1894, however, the Monteil expedition was strictly forbidden to enter the Nile Valley. This represented a concession to the British with whom Hanotaux was apparently conducting successful negotiations.[17] Delcassé and the colonialists, however, did not give up their projected Nile expedition lightly. Pressure was soon put on the Quai d'Orsay to allow another expedition into the Valley of the Upper Nile. In late 1894 Delcassé maintained that Liotard could be on the Nile within one year. Hanotaux had to yield to pressure from colonial activists as the negotiations with the British were not progressing satisfactorily and as he was unable to get the British concessions he needed in his dispute with his own Ministry for Colonies.[18] Hanotaux later blamed Delcassé among others for the failure of the 1894 West Africa talks.[19]

When the Marchand expedition had been proposed, Hanotaux had taken a lead in helping to determine its eventual character. Two notes, one prepared by Captain Marchand and the other by some unnamed official at the Foreign Ministry, reviewed the negotiations which went on between the Quai d'Orsay and the Colonial Office.[20] Reading these, one gets a clear idea of the moderation exercised by Hanotaux. His idea was that the expedition should be a diplomatic tool to be used with care. In the end, Hanotaux was forced to accept the concept of a penetration of the Nile Valley by French military contingents when the Anglo-French colonial talks failed to yield appreciable results.

Hanotaux was temporarily out of office when the Marchand expedition was actually ordered to proceed. He had refused to join the Radical cabinet led by Léon Bourgeois because he disagreed with the new government leader on two counts: (1) on the Radical policy towards taxation and (2) with that party's policy on Madagascar. According to Félix Faure, who was president of the Republic at the time, Hanotaux thought that his refusal to join the cabinet would force the defeat of the Bourgeois cabinet in short order. Faure, though he would have liked to see Hanotaux remain at the Quai d'Orsay, was very critical of Hanotaux's Upper Nile policy. Though he would have preferred more diplomatic means to settle the Upper Nile question, Hanotaux, nonetheless, approved of the Marchand expedition.[21] He saw it as a diplomatic tool to be used to reopen the discussion about Egypt.[22] In 1898 when Marchand's presence on the Nile triggered the Fashoda crisis and France and England were perilously close to war, Hanotaux claimed he had not expected war over Fashoda.[23] Perhaps he had overestimated his own powers as a diplomat; he never had a chance to prove his views. Shortly before the Fashoda incident reached its climax, Hanotaux fell from power with the Méline cabinet, and Delcassé assumed control of the Quai d'Orsay. But it might rightly be said that Hanotaux's colonial policies were far too ambitious, considering the state of the French navy during the years he held power. Had an open conflict about African matters occurred between France and England, the French would have found communications with their colonies closed. Even Algeria might have been isolated.

Consideration of Hanotaux's attitude toward the Anglo-French negotiations in 1894–95 has carried the story far afield. However, it is necessary to make another aside and consider the attitudes of some of the leading persons in the British cabinet. Hanotaux's British counterpart, the Earl of Kimberley, was willing to come to terms with France. Unfortunately, he was usually influenced or overruled by Rosebery, whose attitude toward France was quite different. Other parliamentary figures who were partisans of the entente with France included Sir Henry Labouchere, Charles Dilke, and Sir William Harcourt. Harcourt, one of the few members of the Rosebery cabinet who trusted the pacific attitude of Hanotaux, believed Great Britain should evacuate Egypt.[24] Opinions such as Harcourt's were not the most influential during the Rosebery administration. Imperialists who believed France should be kept out of the whole course of the Upper Nile were dominant. Indeed, Sir Percy Anderson, a Foreign Office African specialist, was much closer to Prime Minister Rosebery than was Harcourt or Kimberley. Anderson and Rosebery were the key persons on African affairs in the British government, and they made many important decisions affecting African affairs without consulting the cabinet members.[25]

In spite of the dominant attitude vis-a-vis France which existed in Rosebery's cabinet, the British offered to discuss the Anglo-Congolese treaty and to review outstanding differences in Central and West Africa. Hanotaux accepted the offer with "alacrity" and clearly expressed his attitude in his first defense of the second Dupuy cabinet. Speaking before an aroused Chamber of Deputies on June 7, 1894, the day after he received the British offer to discuss outstanding problems, Hanotaux reserved his harshest comments for Leopold II with whom he had been negotiating a few days before the news of the Anglo-Congolese treaty was made public. Great Britain, a partner in this "illegal" territorial arrangement, escaped all but moderate criticism. Two days later Hanotaux officially accepted the British offer and expressed his readiness to begin negotiating by making himself available to Dufferin, the British ambassador.[26]

The concession made to France by the British foreign office was granted in the face of the obvious Franco-German cooperation on the Congo Treaty question and of the known existence of a Franco-Russian alliance. Lacking in the British offer was the willingness really to resolve Anglo-French differences in Africa. The first obstacle to agreement on any specific issue was centered around the unwillingness of Downing Street to retract the Anglo-Congolese treaty although Hanotaux insisted that the treaty should be abrogated. Faced with an impossible task in London the French foreign ministry turned to Brussels.

By turning on Leopold II Hanotaux reached his own ends without ruffling British feelings. With Downing Street he tried to retain as flexible a position as possible. Early in August, for example, he gave in to British demands to have his objections to the Anglo-Congolese treaty put in writing.[27] At first he had resisted the request for a written statement arguing with good foresight that to put in writing the objections to the Congo Treaty would force him into a rigid position which he thought incompatible with the general good will necessary in the search for a solution of Anglo-French problems. But since the British insisted, on August 6, 1894, Hanotaux wrote his objections to the Anglo-Congolese treaty. Basically he simply restated his speech of June 7 and reviewed the Anglo-French talks down to August 6. The British reaction to the written objections was uneventful except on one point. Hanotaux claimed Dufferin had accepted his own observations on the Congo treaty as being reasonable. Dufferin, however, claimed to have accepted Hanotaux's proposal as debatable.[28] Hanotaux accepted Dufferin's objections without comment and waited for new developments. The next move was made by the British government three days after the conclusion of the Franco-Congolese treaty on August 14, 1894.

Meeting Hanotaux on August 17 Dufferin, acting for the British government, proposed that "France recognize the 1890 Anglo-German agree-

ment in as far as it affected the Upper Nile; in return, England would take
an engagement to occupy these regions only under the same conditions as
Italy might, according to the 1891 arrangement, occupy Kassala." [29] The
British overture further proposed to regulate in a spirit of conciliation the
delimitations in the Niger basin and in the hinterland of Dahomey. The
June 6 proposal to discuss and to pass in review all Central and West African questions had by August 17 become a proposal to negotiate about specific problems in the same areas.

Hanotaux was quite willing to begin the limited negotiations suggested
by Dufferin. In the offer insofar as it affected the Upper Nile question,
Hanotaux saw two things. First, the British were asking France to recognize
the Anglo-German treaty of 1890. Second, the British believed that their
offer to occupy the Upper Nile Valley only until the khedive could reas-
sert his authority in the region represented a concession to France. But to a
France with plans of her own about the Upper Nile Regions, it made little
difference whether the area was in British hands temporarily or permanently. The British offer included no concession to France except perhaps
in the proposed settlement by delimitation of outstanding questions in the
Niger basin and in the hinterland of Dahomey. The decision to accept or
reject the British proposal of August 17, 1894, was too important a decision for Hanotaux to take on his own authority. He wished to consult with
other ministers who were on vacation. With some difficulty, Hanotaux convinced Dufferin to accept a suspension of the debate until after the French
cabinet met on August 30. [30]

One of the principal difficulties involved in the British proposals of
May 17 was that it referred to the 1890 Anglo-German and 1891 Anglo-
Italian treaties both of which partly defined the British sphere of influence
in the Upper Nile in terms of "the confines of Egypt." [31] The two questions, that of the Upper Nile and that of Egypt (*actually, the question of
the British evacuation of Egypt*), were so closely linked as to make separate
treatment of either practically impossible; also closely connected to the
Upper Nile question was the still unsettled dispute between France and
Britain in Uganda.[32] It is important to stress that mention of the Egyptian
question, however indirectly, made a solution of the Upper Nile dispute
more difficult.

The problems involved in the two questions can be defined in British
as well as in French terms. In the realization that the question of Egypt
could be raised again should an unfriendly power get control of the Upper
Nile, the British government attempted to create a sealed preserve for itself in that region. Downing Street, led by imperialists who had no in-

tention of fulfilling the promised evacuation of Egypt, considered the Egyptian question closed. France, for its part, had never become reconciled to the British occupation of Egypt. The Quai d'Orsay continued to make vigorous attempts to reopen a question which, in accepting the June 6 British proposal, France had agreed to reserve for future settlements.[33]

The Egyptian dispute was an ever-present shadow. It loomed threateningly over the whole of the Anglo-French colonial talks of 1894–95. Hanotaux and the members of the third Dupuy cabinet (Dupuy's second cabinet resigned following the death of President Carnot and was reconstituted after Casimir Perier was elected President), would not compromise on the Upper Nile question and hence on the Egyptian question without first securing some adequate compensation. That there was a price for French recognition of the permanence of British occupation in Egypt was mentioned by responsible persons in France and in Great Britain. No one could suggest exactly what should be given in compensation. In any case, Hanotaux could make no commitments on so important an affair without consulting the cabinet. Having received the British proposals on August 17 Hanotaux followed the lead of his cabinet colleagues and went to Vichy for his summer vacation.[34]

On August 30 Hanotaux was back in Paris for a cabinet meeting. At this meeting he was apparently given the authority necessary to proceed with the Anglo-French colonial talks on the grounds presented by Dufferin on August 17. Accordingly the Anglo-French colonial talks were renewed on September 5.[35]

Dufferin was still away on vacation so the talks were resumed with Sir Constantine Phipps, a secretary at the British embassy. Phipps, a Foreign Office specialist on Africa, was much more competent to negotiate Central and West African Anglo-French differences than Dufferin. Indeed, Dufferin knew very little if anything about the details of the African disputes. To have him replaced with a more qualified negotiator made the promise of progress in the colonial talks brighter although Phipps, being lower than Dufferin in the official hierarchy, could easily be repudiated should the results of his work prove unsatisfactory to the British government.

The conversation on September 5 was introduced with a recapitulation of the Dufferin proposal of August 11. In addition, Phipps, who had seen Rosebery a few days before, was able to bring some new elements into the discussion. Revealing an appreciation of Hanotaux's "on nous demandait" of August 17 the British offered a number of concessions to France. For example, the indemnity asked by Casimir Perier in connection with the British occupation of Uganda would be paid. In addition, the Sierra

Leone border would be drawn in accordance with French desires, the hinterland of Dahomey would be assured as far back as Say, and Britain would accept the August 14 Franco-Congolese treaty. The Waima Affair would be dropped as would the Mizon Affair with no reparations from either side. Finally, the Say-Barrowa line would be rectified so as to leave the whole of the kingdom of Sokoto in the British sphere.[36]

Though the new overture included several concessions to France, Hanotaux could not help noticing how unimportant these concessions were. The rectification of the Say-Barrowa line was to British advantage. In return for what small concessions she got, France was expected to recognize the Anglo-German treaty of 1890, i.e., the Third Republic would accept the British sphere of influence in the Upper Nile Valley. Something more would have to be found before such French consent could be willingly granted.[37] Indeed, Germany, Italy, and the Congo Free State had received considerable adjustments in exchange for their recognition of the British sphere of influence in the Upper Nile Valley. Hanotaux pointedly asked what Great Britain was prepared to offer France.

The British proposals of September 5 as well as that of August 17 included the same difficulty, namely, they mentioned Egypt. Hanotaux mentioned the 1890 Anglo-German treaty and asked: "Must one then conclude that it is the whole Nile basin, that is all of Egypt, which England claims? Certainly not since during the present negotiations it has been repeated that the questions of Egypt should be left aside." Hanotaux also asked: "What new demarcations would one introduce into the 1890 treaty to put it in accord with recognized rights, with the unchanging facts, and with the character which the British government itself wished to give to the negotiations in process?" [38]

Asked to define the Upper Nile, the British could not. Between British and Egyptian claims the whole of the Nile Valley was covered, but exactly where the one ended and the other began remained a mystery. On June 17 Rosebery wrote a memorandum declaring that "the Nile is Egypt and Egypt is the Nile." This was not communicated to Hanotaux who, nevertheless, rephrased his question from the taboo "Qu'est ce que l'Egypte?" to "Qu'est ce que le Haut-Nil?" [39]

While settlements were reached regarding West Africa, where France was getting some of the token concessions she had been promised, discussion about the Upper Nile became even more difficult. Hanotaux suggested a self-denying ordinance. If the area could be defined in terms that would not require France to recognize the British occupation of Egypt, Hanotaux could recognize the British sphere of influence on the Upper Nile. But both the limits of the Upper Nile and the concession to be made to France remained mysteries. The self-denying clause proposed by Hanotaux represented the high water mark of the Anglo-French colonial talks. Phipps, who thought the offer would satisfy British designs in the area, i.e., keeping France out of the Upper Nile Valley, was overridden in London. And after the proposed self-denying clause was rejected, no solution for the Upper Nile question could be found.[40]

The negotiators themselves made one more attempt and in January 1895 proposed a formula by which "France obtained a definition and a limitation of the claims England had asserted over the equatorial regions: the disputed provinces were, in a way, neutralized under the surveillance of the two powers." This formula was rejected as was the October 1894 self-denying ordinance which Hanotaux had proposed. After the breakdown of talks in October 1894 Hanotaux was still willing to negotiate but he was getting impatient. If the negotiations were to be bogged down anew in minute details, and the failure of the talks about the Upper Nile seemed to forecast such a development, he would have to delegate the discussion to one of his officials. There was another worry for Hanotaux. If the negotiations broke down, he would have no arguments with which to fight off the Colonial Ministry's demands for an expedition to the Upper Nile and similar movements in various parts of West Africa.[41]

Before Dufferin and Hanotaux met again, Lord Rosebery and Paul d'Estournelle de Constant, the French Chargé d'affaires in London, had a stormy session. Speaking at Sheffield on October 25 Rosebery had expressed some sentiments that were taken as being against France and against the resumption of the suspended colonial talks. D'Estournelle saw Rosebery on the 31st and complained that the resumption of the suspended negotiations depended only on the British government. Send Dufferin, d'Estournelle told Rosebery, adequate authority and you will find Hanotaux more than willing to pick up where things had been on the 20th of October. Rosebery himself had a complaint: why would Hanotaux not recognize the British sphere of influence in Central Africa? D'Estournelle could give no answer.[42]

If d'Estournelle had not answered, Hanotaux had at least hinted at possible answers. On several occasions he had complained about the unimportance of British concessions to France. Apparent concessions such as the supposed willingness to guarantee the Dahomey hinterland as far back as Say proved unsatisfactory. And throughout the course of the colonial talks of 1894–95 only once was a concession mentioned which might have proved suitable in exchange for French recognition of the British occupation of Egypt and eventual occupation of the Upper Nile. The price was Morocco and the unofficial suggestion was made in the fall of 1894 by Cecil Rhodes, the British imperialist.[43] Rhodes's concept, however, never entered the official debate. Meanwhile other imperial questions made negotiations about Central and West African problems more difficult than ever.

Madagascar was quickly becoming another crisis center of Anglo-French rivalry as an old dispute began to erupt again. On November 13, 1894, Hanotaux went before the Chamber of Deputies to ask for credits for a military expedition to enforce the 1885 protectorate. The British felt that they lost some vested interest when the expedition proposed by Hanotaux led to the establishment of a French colony during 1895. The Madagascar problem was, however, not the only Anglo-French difference which weighed unfavorably on the Anglo-French colonial talks.

Another Anglo-French difference arose in 1894 because of the Japanese seizure of Korea and Port Arthur. The Chinese Government appealed to the Western powers for their support in an effort to regain these lost territories. France, eager to please her new Russian ally, found herself in the middle of a dispute over how to regulate the Asian problem. Hanotaux, who at first was disposed to follow a British suggestion for collective action by all Western powers, was unwilling to displease Russia, which refused to follow the British plans.[44] The Sino-Japanese dispute was not likely to smooth Anglo-French relations. In April 1895 France, following her Russian ally, found herself in the same camp as Germany while Britain refused to join the concerted action to force Japan to evacuate Port Arthur. For a while England was apparently isolated.[45] These differences between London and Paris had advanced far enough by November 1894 to leave a dampening effect on the Anglo-French colonial talks.

The Anglo-French colonial talks about Central and West Africa continued during November 1894. On November 1, 1894, Hanotaux and Dufferin reviewed the general character of their discussions which had been conducted with a view toward a possible general African settlement. Hanotaux insisted that a failure to arrive at a general settlement should not preclude the settling of specific points of contention. But Dufferin, who had received no new instructions, could not commit his government.

On November 7 the British ambassador returned to the Quai d'Orsay with the first official British definition of her sphere of influence in the Upper Nile Valley. According to Dufferin, the British thought the Fashoda parallel to be the northern limit of their Central African sphere of influence. This definition, derived from the May Anglo-Congolese treaty, was rejected by Hanotaux. Citing the August 14 treaty the French foreign minister stated that, though Downing Street had not formally recognized the Franco-Congolese treaty, the British had been consulted about it by Leopold II and had not opposed its ratification. Hanotaux could not relinquish France's rights in the Congo Basin without receiving in exchange adequate compensation. As no offer of compensation was forthcoming, negotiations on the Upper Nile question were suspended.

On November 17 Hanotaux noted that the French Cabinet had ordered Delcassé and his ministry to proceed with the Liotard Congo-Nile expedition. Another method would be used to preserve French rights and advantages since diplomacy had failed to solve the problem. On other points in dispute, however, settlements seemed possible. Accordingly, Hanotaux ordered the dormant commission, set up in 1890 for the delimitation of French and English possessions in the Niger basin, to resume its task. He also proposed that the Sierra Leone arrangement, until then the only problem on which London and Paris had reached an agreement, be signed as soon as possible.[47]

The Sierra Leone treaty signed in January of 1895 was the only arrangement salvaged from the general treaty proposed by the Anglo-French negotiators at the end of 1894. Rejected was a general settlement of West and Central African differences, including proposed clauses to end Anglo-French disputes in the Niger basin and in the Upper Nile Valley. The Upper Nile question and the differences centered around the Niger basin, though almost solved in 1894, continued to embitter Anglo-French relations until 1898. Only then, with Hanotaux still directing French foreign affairs, was a treaty signed regarding the Niger basin. Also, in 1898 the Fashoda incident would end French activity in the Upper Nile, but it would not resolve the Upper Nile and Egyptian questions. These were not solved until Great Britain supported France in her Moroccan ambitions.[48]

In 1894 however, Great Britain was not ready to offer Morocco nor was France ready to take it in exchange for her recognition of the British occupation of Egypt. France, with her Algerian colony's long border with Morocco, thought that land an area in which she had special rights. But, in 1894 Paris did not judge the Moroccan situation ripe for the establishment of a French protectorate: the Quai d'Orsay was simply interested in preserving the Moroccan question for future settlement to French advantage. Britain was still not sure of the permanence of her domination of Egypt. Should Egypt be evacuated, the British thought they would need a coaling station in Morocco, and they were consequently not ready to offer France a concession there.[49]

South of Morocco Anglo-French disputes were much more lively. Indeed, West Africa was the location of numerous small scale expeditions similar to Marchand's to the Nile. British and French representatives were racing each other to strategic points here and there in an attempt to acquire prior treaty rights. In this game, France apparently had an advantage. By 1894 the Republic had acquired a sufficient expanse of territories to reduce Portuguese Guinea, Sierra Leone, Liberia, Gambia, the Gold Coast and Togoland to enclaves in a sea of French colonial holdings. The French were in 1894 apparently also attempting to reduce Lagos and Nigeria to mere enclaves.[50]

The French plan to unite all French possessions in Africa at Lake Chad was grandiose. The fate of Gambia, Sierra Leone, and the Gold Coast, and the threatened fate of Lagos and of Nigeria aroused British imperialists. Even if unsuccessful, France could give the appearance of making concessions when she pulled out of territories which she had no right to occupy in the first place. F. A. Edwards, an official at the British Foreign Office, wrote, "We have failed to follow up our treaties (in West Africa) with 'effective occupation.' " Edwards's term was often used to describe Hanotaux's policies: French colonialists based their claim squarely on "effective occupation" during the 1890s.[51] Hanotaux denied the validity of this judgment of his policies. The French thesis, he told the Senate, was not based on "effective occupation" but on open discussion.

Hanotaux attempted to insure the success of the Anglo-French colonial talks of 1894. He was not only willing to negotiate, but he himself negotiated on questions which he might well have delegated to one of his subordinates. If he received worthwhile concessions, he was willing to sacrifice French rights in return. Late in 1894 he appointed his best ambassador, Baron de Courcel, to London. And when it became apparent that the proposed treaty which he had helped formulate would be rejected, he agreed to salvage the Sierra Leone clause. This would at least secure a large portion of the Niger basin for France. But his efforts to secure a general settlement were to no avail, for both Paris and London rejected a treaty which might have become the basis of an Anglo-French entente. The end of the 1894 colonial talks represented an "entente manquée," and the difficult work had to be started again from the beginning.[52]

When the fruits of months of work were rejected by the French cabinet, Hanotaux's whole policy of seeking an entente with Great Britain was also rejected. Hanotaux stayed at the Quai d'Orsay only because of the grave situation in which France found herself in January 1895 as a result of the beginning of the Dreyfus case. In February France and England were again discussing colonial disputes. Hanotaux, more insistent on French rights then he had been in 1894, would lead the French side of the new negotiations.

"L'Affaire Madagascar"

Chapter 6

Hanotaux's action in connection with the Anglo-Congolese treaty of May 12, 1894, revealed a statesman bent on securing all possible gains for France while respecting the national pride of Great Britain. He did not, like Lord Dufferin, try to force concessions by theatening an ultimatum.[1] When the Anglo-French colonial talks, begun in the wake of the French protest, theatened to break down, Hanotaux turned to Leopold II to force the issue. The French foreign minister had apparently analyzed the situation correctly: Britain had leased the Bahr-el-Ghazal and part of the Upper Nile area to the Congo in exchange for recognition that this area was, in fact, a British sphere of interest. The British were safeguarding something they were not in a position to defend, for the moment at least, and they would probably not fight to support Leopold when it was not to their advantage to do so. Leopold was left to fend for himself in the face of French and Belgian opposition, and though Britain never adhered to the ensuing Franco-Congolese treaty, the French foreign minister received what he wanted. Though he later earned his reputation as a colonial zealot, Hanotaux would never humiliate the British or let it appear that Downing Street had been badly defeated. When the effects of the Anglo-Congolese treaty were nullified by a new arrangement between France and Leopold II, Britain took no action. Their treaty had been in contradiction with earlier agreements, a blunder had been committed at Downing Street; nothing could be done but to accept the nullification.

Throughout his ministry, Hanotaux always insisted on French rights or on reserving French rights for the future. If a power acted on some African question without the consent of France, Hanotaux protested. He presented the opponents with logical arguments which left them disarmed. When his opponents realized what had happened, the crisis was usually over and France had emerged victorious. So it happened that France, during the years of Hanotaux's service at the Quai d'Orsay, advanced everywhere in Africa: in area after area, piece by piece, an empire was being built which, in the end, was second only to that of Britain. Hanotaux's first problem was the Anglo-Congolese treaty. Simultaneously, he directed the French protest against the Anglo-Italian treaty of 1894, and he worked to keep the Moroccan situation such that it might be settled to French advantage at some future date.

Another crisis, "l'affaire Madagascar," came to a head less than three months after Hanotaux took charge of the Quai d'Orsay. Again Britain was to be the most important opponent. The Madagascar problem had been in the making for many years. As usual, French rights had been tampered with. These rights or claims—for they were not uncontested, in some instances not even recognized, by other powers interested in "la grande ile" —dated back to the time of Richelieu. As the French historian Jacques Stern wrote in *French Colonies Past and Present:*

> In 1642, the *Compagnie des Indes Orientales* was granted the monopoly of trade in Madagascar. Naval Captain Ricaut, according to his letter patent, obtained from Monseigneur L'Eminentissime Cardinal de Richelieu, the concession and privilege "to bring spices and export, along with the word of God, civilization and charity." According to the French historian, Gabriel Hanotaux, such was the Cardinal's main idea [about colonialism].[2]

Hanotaux, who, before taking office in the Dupuy ministry, had published a first volume of what became a massive multi-volume study of the Cardinal, must have felt his historical heritage as he approached the question of Madagascar.

There were other connections with earlier imperialists. It was on the basis of an agreement reached in 1885 that France founded her most recent claims. This had been a treaty negotiated between France, with Freycinet at the Quai d'Orsay, and the Queen of Madagascar, which had created a protectorate over the isle. Still another historical treaty which Hanotaux enforced was a concession secured by Waddington in 1890. One of Hanotaux's predecessors at the Quai d'Orsay and an imperialist, Waddington had relinquished French claims to Zanzibar, claims that were as old and just as valid as those of Britain, in exchange for British recognition of the French protectorate over Madagascar. France had demanded a similar arrangement for Tunisia. But she had been unsuccessful in Tunisia when Salisbury had proposed French recognition of exclusively British rights in Egypt as an equivalent concession. This had been too high a price for France who, throughout the nineties, continually tried to reopen the Egyptian question, to force Britain out, or secure elsewhere some sizable concession acceptable to French public opinion. The Germans had followed suit recognizing the French protectorate over Madagascar in return for concessions in other areas.[3] France did not, however, follow up these concessions by strengthening her hold on the island. Nothing more was done until 1894 when Hanotaux took it upon himself to establish effective control.[4]

An excuse was not hard to find. The protectorate arrangement of 1885 had never worked well, and the history of "la grande ile" in the period 1885–95 can be told in a simple listing of incidents of vandalism against French settlers and other foreigners. Moreover, Rainilaiarivony, Prime Minister of Madagascar, did not seem disposed to rectify the situation.[5] By January 1894 dissatisfaction with the situation was so general that the Casimir-Perier ministry received a unanimous vote of confidence in the Chamber of Deputies on the simple and old formula: "The Chamber resolves to sustain the government in whatever it undertakes to maintain our situation and our rights in Madagascar, to restore order, to protect our nationals, and to make our flag respected there, and passes to the order of the day." By the time Hanotaux was named foreign minister in Dupuy's "ministère des jeunes" (May 30, 1894 to January 20, 1895) which succeeded the Casimir Perier cabinet, nothing effective had been done. There had been some talk of reinforcing French garrisons on Madagascar, but no real use of the Parliamentary "carte blanche" voted on January 22 had been made.[6] Strangely enough, Hanotaux, to whom Dupuy had granted a free hand in the conduct of foreign affairs, made no use of this vote of confidence. The question of Madagascar was debated in the cabinet and Hanotaux's disposition to push through a vigorous policy was generally accepted. All told, it was decided not to use the "carte blanche" but to play for time to avoid "any precipitate action in Madagascar which could not be plausibly rationalized." Time was needed to play a diplomatic game in Europe and to offer the Hovas, the ruling caste of the island, a chance to agree to a peaceful solution.[7]

Just as important in the foreign minister's view was the necessity to allow French public opinion time to ripen. In 1894 the French as a whole were still not very keen imperialists But most could be expected to demand a harsh reaction against rebellion and to protect French nationals from the terrorism of Malagasy "rebels." Hanotaux was also aware of a developing issue involving English missionaries who were apparently encouraging the Hova authorities and their people to resist the French attempts to affirm their own control over the great African island.[8] Newspaper accounts and an effective propaganda campaign launched by the colonial lobby led by Eugène Etienne quickly did this work for Hanotaux. An article published in 1896 but illustrative of reactions that were typical by the end of 1894, proves that Hanotaux correctly evaluated the situation. The most characteristic sentence, which approaches xenophobia in tone was "qui dit catholique dit français, qui dit protestant dit anglais." [9] Hanotaux also prepared a European base for his action. Therefore, when he asked the Chamber for credits for a military expedition to Madagascar, he had ready support at home as well as abroad.

Before the military expedition was accepted as policy, however, the French attempted to find a peaceful solution to the Malagasy problem. During the summer of 1894 Hanotaux decided to send Le Myre de Vilers to negotiate with the Hova government. De Vilers had been governor of Madagascar shortly after the 1885 protectorate agreement had been arranged, and was familiar with Malagasy affairs. Now he was called to carry on negotiations with Rainilaiarivony. De Vilers was in France and it would take him well over a month to reach Madagascar. In the meantime P. Larrouy, French resident general at Tananarive, the capital of Madagascar situated in the center of the island, was called back. The evacuation of French nationals, strongly urged by Larrouy preceding his recall, and at first thought unwise by the government, was ordered by a telegram dated September 9, 1894. Only the Resident's military escort would remain at Tananarive. It would stay, under the orders of M. d'Anthouard, who would be accredited and would continue to represent France until such time as a complete break would become policy. A diplomatic rupture had become inevitable but one last effort would be made. De Vilers was sent to examine the situation "sur place." [10]

Hanotaux's instructions to de Vilers[11] make up an interesting document. First he presented a short historical *résumé* of Franco-Hovas relations from 1885 to 1894 with a review of the many incidents against French nationals. This was followed by a short retelling of the French Parliament's activities in connection with the problem of its repeated manifestations of its will to maintain French rights in "la grande ile." De Vilers' letter of instructions included the right to conclude, if possible, a treaty, the bases of which were annexed to the letter. Finally there was a whole program, a sort of anticipation of events: if the Malagasy government refused or procrastinated in answering and signing the proposed treaty, de Vilers was to set a date on which, if the Queen's government had not moved in the desired direction, relations would be broken off.

The "projet de traité" was little more than a clarification of the 1885 protocol. It envisaged a French protectorate over Madagascar, as Hanotaux wrote: "un protectorat avec toutes ses conséquences." This sentence was very significant as Hanotaux was to prove later with respect to Tunisia. It might embody a situation hardly to be differentiated from that of an outright colony. What was meant by a protectorate? With the control of all the foreign relations of the "protected" nation, the dominant country could create for itself a closed market. In the case of Madagascar, these included the French right to build telegraphs, railroads, canals, roads, and other projects helpful to the economic development of the island, should the Hova government fail to do so itself.[12]

In the early months of 1896 when he was temporarily out of office Hanotaux defended his policy which his successor was in the process of altering, "We had no other intention but to assure in uncontested manner, the position of a protector state which belongs to France." His formula, "Le protectorat avec toutes ses conséquences" had one great advantage: other European powers had accepted the French protectorate. This acceptance included that of England which had extended it in return for French concessions regarding Zanzibar. Hanotaux's policy, well expressed in the documents and explained in this *exposé* just two years later, was well thought out; indeed he appears to have foreseen everything that actually happened in Madagascar.

The Franco-Hovas negotiations begun soon after de Vilers arrived in Madagascar on October 8, 1894, quickly deteriorated, and the diplomatic break occurred, followed closely by a French military expedition. Rainilaiarivony, the Malagasy prime minister, was strongly anti-French and, according to Larrouy, he had decided to disregard French rights on the strength of information furnished him by European informants who had told him that France would not cause an armed conflict. Even if they should, Rainilaiarivony appears to have been determined to restore more independence to his government and therefore was willing to risk a show of arms. While Rainilaiarivony's attitude was more extreme than that of Grand Vizier Ba Ahmed in Morocco, both sought to keep their own countries out of the grasp of European imperialists. Both men failed and western technology, as represented by France, imposed its control for its own purposes on Madagascar then, somewhat later on Morocco. But there was an epic quality to the resistance which in Rainilaiarivony's case was termed banditry by French authorities. In any case, the Hova Minister's diplomacy reflected his outspoken opposition to French penetration and his willingness to risk an armed conflict. In answer to the projected treaty prepared by Hanotaux and presented by de Vilers, Rainilaiarivony offered a greatly watered down counter-project. While expressing warm friendship and a desire for peaceful relations with France, Rainilaiarivony denied all the advantages sought by the French and attempted to assert himself as an independent leader of an independent Madagascar.[13]

To France, of course, this was completely inadmissible. She prepared for a conquest of the island by breaking her relations with the native government and evacuating all her nationals to a few defensible ports.[14] By November 2 the evacuation of all Frenchmen had been completed. The time for which Hanotaux had bargained had been gained and opinion in the Chamber of Deputies had been allowed to ripen. Ostensibly France had made all possible efforts to settle its differences with the Hovas by peaceable means. This having proved impossible, two alternatives existed: France could evacuate *completely* and relinquish her rights or she could attempt to enforce her claims by an armed demonstration against the recalcitrant Queen of Madagascar's government. Thinking the first alternative impossible, Hanotaux went before the Chamber of Deputies on November 13, 1894, and reviewed the whole situation: the history of French rights on the island, their violation, the last efforts at peaceful assertion of these rights—sixty-five million francs would be needed for an effective military invasion which, in view of the Malagasy record, would be the only way to maintain French rights over "la grande ile." [15] There was some opposition and a demand for a special commission of twenty-two. This motion defeated, a commission of eleven members was organized. When, on November 23, 1894, this commission reported, Hanotaux had another chance to present his case with respect to Madagascar.

It appears from Hanotaux's discourse on November 23 that economic considerations were not the primary reasons for insisting that French rights be respected in Madagascar. Certainly France's trade with "la grande ile" was minimal in comparison with the proposed sixty-five million francs requested to assert French supremacy. Hanotaux himself said there was no more than about 100,000 francs profit on about 10,000,000 francs invested. But the possibilities were much greater as Hanotaux did not fail to point out. The sense or essential meaning of what Hanotaux said may be summarized in one word, prestige. Prestige, indeed, seems to have been a large part of Hanotaux's imperialism. Certainly he believed, as had Gambetta and Ferry before him, that France would be strengthened by the acquisition of colonies, but a large part of his—and the colonialists'—desire for an empire was the question of prestige for the French nation. France was vigorously reasserting herself in Europe after the "débacle" of 1870, and one of the avenues to her rightful position was thought to be imperialism. In the conclusion of his November 23 speech Hanotaux dramatized the choice which events had left open to the Chamber: 1) to evacuate, renouncing all claims and forgetting all injuries inflicted upon French nationals, and forgetting, as well, the engagements taken by France to Europe and the oft-repeated engagements of the Chamber to control Madagascar, or 2) to accept the sacrifices entailed by an appropriation of sixty-five million francs for the definitive invasion of the island, assertion of France's protectorate "with all its consequences," and possibilities of economic development for the future. The plan for evacuation was unacceptable to Hanotaux because of the damage to French prestige. Clearly the second alternative—invasion of Madagascar—was the one which would most benefit France.[16]

Economic considerations were not of great significance in Hanotaux's colonial system. Of course, he did use the promise of good economic returns to convince the deputies to approve the credits necessary to finance the military expedition to Madagascar. Some months later, however, Hanotaux offered the following definition of his own attitude towards imperial expansion in a revealing defense of his own Hova policy when he published "Le traité de Tananarive" in *La revue de Paris:*

> Whatever might have been said about it, a colony is not a farm given to the mother-country for exploitation, [and] which has no value unless it earns a rent by the end of each year. The expansion of a great power throughout the world has a quite different character. Carrying and perpetuating its name, language, [and] thought to new countries, a civilized nation already accomplishes a good deal if it thereby prolongs its own existence in space and time. (Jan. 1896, p. 14)

As his policies in West Africa and Madagascar show, Hanotaux was an advocate of the use of military might for colonial expansion when it could enhance the prestige and power of France. Just as obvious was the foreign minister's acceptance of Jules Ferry's arguments for colonial expansion and at least an implied approval of various racial judgments used to justify proposed French conquests of non-European areas. In the mid–1880s Georges Clemenceau had thrown telling barbs at Ferry by pointing out that some Germans had proved scientifically that French civilization was inferior and should therefore be defeated by the superior Germans in 1870. The colonialists' arguments based on the opinion that European scientific civilization was superior to more traditionally oriented societies in Africa and Asia, Clemenceau had concluded, made no more sense.[17] Hanotaux, and Ferry before him, ignored the arguments of anti-imperialists. But Hanotaux was forced to fight fellow colonialists on the issue of Malagasy administration.

Before the end of 1894 the French government's resolve to send a military expedition to reconquer Madagascar was clear. Even before this resolve became a policy, however, a debate began between Hanotaux and his supporters, who advocated continued use of the protectorate system and their opponents, who worked to annex the great African island and turn it into a colony directly administered by French officials. Delcassé was the chief supporter of the annexationist or "Tonkinois" solution. He was joined by leading military men such as Gallieni and by quite a few administrators who were afraid that if the protectorate system were allowed to continue, the same abuses and misunderstandings that had led to the impasse of 1894 would occur. To avoid this they argued for annexation and for military control of the colonial administration.[18] The "Tunisians" who advocated a modified protectorate argued that direct rule would be cumbersome and expensive and that Hanotaux's proposal could lead to effective French control of Madagascar without running the risks of annoying other European powers who were involved in the area.[19] The debate was resolved in favor of his opponents in 1895 while Hanotaux was temporarily out of office. Hanotaux's opposition to the annexationist thesis may have been personal, a matter of power. Under the protectorate system Madagascar was administered by the Quai d'Orsay. The "Tonkinois" solution transferred authority over the island to Hanotaux's colleagues in the Colonial Ministry, Delcassé if the change had occurred before January 1895, then Pierre Guieysse in the Bourgeois ministry in 1896.

In November 1894 the military expedition was not yet policy. First of all, the French negotiator in Madagascar had set December 26 for accepting an answer from the Queen's government. It was just a matter of time, for this answer was not expected to come, and in fact the ultimatum was not heeded. Indeed, all the legal preparations were effected. On November 26, 1894, the Chamber approved the credits requested by a vote of 372 to 135. The Senate followed suit on December 8 by a strong majority of 267 to 3, following a discourse by Hanotaux which he concluded by noting that persuasion had failed in Madagascar and that if war came, France should be ready. By the end of 1894 it was obvious that an invasion would occur.[20]

While the Ministry for the Marine worked out the technical aspects of the proposed military expedition, Hanotaux prepared European diplomats and the French public for the events to come. As intended, de Vilers' mission attracted the attention of the press. In France newspapers launched a vigorous campaign which helped swing public opinion behind the government's Madagascar policy.[21] Foreign newspapermen were also interested in the de Vilers mission. Abroad, however, there were numerous speculations about possible French double-dealing. Hanotaux's insistence on French legal rights and his attempts to prove the peaceful designs of the Third Republic by pointing to the "peace mission" which was sent to the Hova Queen did not quell British suspicions. Press campaigns on either side of the English Channel were well-advanced before Madagascar was first mentioned in official Anglo-French diplomatic talks.

The French had felt and even feared that the British would try to use the troubled Franco-Hova situation to secure advantages for themselves. There were already several outstanding problems disturbing Anglo-French relations in Madagascar. The English press campaign begun in reaction to the first French reports on de Vilers' mission tended to confirm suspicions about British motives. Britishers, in any case, never fully accepted French domination over Madagascar. France was a protectionist nation and wherever she ruled, high tariff walls were inevitably put in the way of British goods. Hanotaux himself was not a protectionist, but he could naturally be overruled by his colleagues. It was felt that Salisbury's recognition of the supremacy of France in Madagascar had been a blunder. While most newspapers in Great Britain recognized that the French control could not be changed, some took violently Francophobe attitudes which led to unfortunate articles and press reports. One account (Reuter's) was strong enough to motivate the Foreign Office to disassociate Her Majesty's government entirely.[22]

On September 26, 1894, Phipps brought up the subject of Madagascar. Hanotaux took advantage of the occasion to communicate a few thoughts of his own. He was not one to be upset by press reports but he could not understand why the British press was in such an uproar. "The campaign in which the English press has engaged on the subject of Madagascar appears to me to have no sense," Hanotaux said, "since in recognizing our protectorate with all its consequences England gave us a carte blanche in the area." In sending de Vilers France had chosen to stand on clearly established rights and had acted with great moderation. The Republic could accept no unwarranted intervention on the part of a foreign government.

Several questions other than the press campaign strained Anglo-French relations in Madagascar. For example, the activities of British nationals in any way connected with Madagascar were carefully watched. Sir Abraham Kingdom was reported to have placed an order in England for the minting of silver coins destined for Madagascar. The activities of Mr. Kingdom were reported and a query was addressed to the Foreign Office. London replied with assurances that the matter would be investigated and Sir Abraham was soon thereafter pulled into court.[23]

Somewhat later, an officer formerly connected with the British military, Colonel Shervington, was reported to have made attempts to draft British officers for service in the Hova army and to have ordered weapons of various descriptions in the United Kingdom and in South Africa. Another suspect was General Willoughby, formerly a military advisor in the service of the Hova government. French complaints about these matters led to renewed British assurances. Actively engaged British officers could not hire themselves out to foreign governments, and the activities of British nationals, though embarrassing to Her Majesty's government, could not be stopped. This did not imply official approval of the activities of such nationals. As the second French military expedition to Madagascar began, two important questions remained unresolved. First was the old thorny question of consular *exequatur*. Second was the problem involved in the possible British declaration of neutrality in the Franco-Hova conflict and the consequent application of the Foreign Enlistment Act.[24]

If France was in fact the protecting nation, her representatives should introduce foreign diplomatic personalities to the native government. Should foreign consuls and other diplomatic officials receive *exequatur* from the Malagasy Queen or prime minister directly, the French protectorate would be but a fiction. Seen in this light, a procedural question took on enormous importance to the French who had fought diplomatic battles from 1885 when they instituted their protectorate until 1890 when they received recognition of their *fait accompli* in exchange for their own withdrawal from the affairs of Zanzibar. By 1894 the problem of *exequatur* had been complicated by the policy of the Hova prime minister, Rainilaiarivony, who urged foreign representatives to seek *exequatur* directly, even refusing to recognize those who came to his government through the French resident.[25]

The beginning of war—for though the French treated the Madagascar question as an internal question, and the expedition as a police action, it was war—added another complication to the *exequatur* problem. The French, of course, had broken diplomatic relations with the active authority in Tananarive. As the French in Madagascar withdrew to ports along the coast, with whom were those Europeans who remained behind, to deal? Negotiations between Paris and London soon led to an agreement. The British consul, during the crisis, would be permitted to deal with the Hova government directly though unofficially.[26] The amicable spirit which made possible such an agreement was carried over to the discussion of the problems involved in a possible British declaration of neutrality.

For the French a British declaration of neutrality would have seemed an inimical act. Great Britain, in declaring itself neutral, hence recognizing a state of war, would have given the Hova Government an independent existence which the French were not ready to admit. In his attempt to avert the British neutrality declaration, Hanotaux warned that if a state of war were recognized, French ships would stop and search ships for contraband all around the area of Madagascar. Kimberley simply turned the matter over to Her Majesty's *juris consultes* and announced that the government's decision would be based on their report. Within a few days the desired report was at the Foreign Office at Downing Street. "There exists," the report stated, "a state of hostilities between France and Madagascar which may involve the exercise of belligerent rights towards British trade, and, therefore, if Her Majesty's government thinks fit, they would be at liberty to issue a Proclamation of Neutrality." Such action would recognize Madgascar as a belligerent and

> recognition by a neutral of belligerency between a protected State and a protecting State, especially where the former is semi-civilized, might be interpreted as an unfriendly act towards the latter, unless clearly required by the legitimate interests of neutral commerce.

Should France use a belligerent's rights, she would not be in a position to object to a British declaration of neutrality. Kimberley could choose his own course and not wishing to alienate the French, he decided not to recognize a state of war in Madagascar.[27]

As soon as Hanotaux knew that Kimberley would not intervene, he probably sighed in relief. The French expeditionary forces had engaged several British ships to transport men, animals, and materiel to Madagascar. Had Her Majesty's Government decided to declare the existence of a state of war in the African island, British nationals whose ships had been hired to the French government would have been censured. The expeditionary forces would have been deprived of necessary means of transportation and have been put in a precarious situation indeed.

During his four-year tenure at the Quai d'Orsay Hanotaux's gravest mistake was to advocate an active colonial policy though France did not have the naval strength necessary to support and protect the gains sought. The error seems amazing when cast against a background of British naval supremacy on all seas including the Mediterranean. Had an Anglo-French colonial war occurred in Africa, and the possibility of such a conflict in the period 1894–98 was indeed great, the British could easily have intercepted most supplies sent by the French Republic long before such could reach the hypothetical theater of war. Early in 1894 the French discovered that six of their best naval ships were top heavy. Yet Hanotaux continued his active policies of colonial expansion without, on the home front, making any intervention for naval improvements. The President of the Republic, Felix Faure, though in another context than that of Madagascar, quite just-

ly brought Hanotaux to task for the failure to have sufficient might to
back up his diplomacy. It is indeed surprising that the anxiety created by
the threatened British intervention, at a time when a French military expedition depended on British shipping, did not lead Hanotaux to push for
more and better ships for France.[28]

In the gathering of supplies for the expedition to Madagascar, the
French were again at odds with the British. The French, for example,
bought mules from Menelik. But to feed these in Djibouti and during transshipment to Madagascar, they had depended on hay from Aden, a territory on the Arabian peninsula controlled by the British. This source of hay
failed, the British delegate claiming a local shortage had prevented the
usual export.[29] When the Franco-Hova war began, there were still numerous Anglo-French differences to be solved, but most of these were put off
until 1896.

In 1895 a successful French expedition arrived at Madagascar under the
leadership of General Duchesne. For a short time Hanotaux's "protectorate
with all its consequences" was established apparently with considerable
success. As Hanotaux explained, the protectorate represented a restraint
of French rights "in form" but not necessarily in actuality. This policy
envisaged the pacification of "la grande isle" by the recognized native
government.

In France the Dupuy cabinet gave way to the Ribot ministry (January
26, 1895–November 1, 1895) but Hanotaux, because of France's difficult
position (in Madagascar as well as in Europe the Dreyfus case had led to
complications with Germany) remained at the Quai d'Orsay. The Alexandre Ribot government in turn was succeeded by that of Léon Bourgeois,
Pierre Berthelot taking over the Foreign Ministry. Public opinion was not
satisfied by the results of the Madagascar expedition since the sixty-five
million francs budget had been overdrawn and the cost in men had risen
above the numbers anticipated. Of a total of 15,000 soldiers and 6,000
porters, nearly 6,000 men died, four-fifths of them young Frenchmen. The
loss in life was not from combat but from diseases induced by the climate
and from woeful military planning. Fewer than twenty of the dead were
killed by the enemy. Whatever the reason a closer union was demanded
between France and Madagascar, and Berthelot and Bourgeois began to
work for outright annexation. Native rebellion rose at once.

Léon Bourgeois, Felix Faure has recalled, wanted Hanotaux to retain
his portfolio at the Foreign Ministry. A Moderate Republican, Hanotaux
refused to join in a government dominated by the Radicals. Even before
Bourgeois constituted his cabinet, members of his party had advocated a

policy of outright annexation of Madagascar. Such a policy negating Hanotaux's own protectorate thesis was in fact implemented while the Radicals
were in power. Hanotaux's first refusal to join in Bourgeois' cabinet seems,
then, to have been amply justified.[30]

Bourgeois himself finally had to take charge of foreign relations. His
government was nearing its end. With Hanotaux the Bourgeois ministry
might have survived a few months longer. President Faure, himself a member of the Moderate Republican group, helped the Radical Premier, and
strongly criticized Hanotaux's African policies. Yet Faure admitted that
Hanotaux had grown while in power, and that he had succeeded completely with respect to public opinion. And the President seemed to have
been disappointed, if not upset, at Hanotaux's opposition to Bourgeois'
cabinet. Whatever the reasons, whether through political calculations or
simply because of his opposition to the Radicals, Hanotaux refused a second time to join the Bourgeois government. One month later the Moderate
Republicans were to return to power with Jules Meline assuming the Pre-
miership.[31] Once again Hanotaux took on the duties of foreign policy making, this time as a member of a governmental combination which was to
rule France for the next twenty-four and one-half months.

While out of office Hanotaux had turned to the press to defend his
Malagasy policy, a policy the Radicals, momentarily in control of the
French government, were in process of cancelling. In one article the politician-historian compared the economic and social progress of Algeria and
of Tunisia while under French domination. Sixty years of French civilizing
missions in the Algerian colony, Hanotaux claimed, had been less fruitful
than ten years of protectorate rule in Tunisia. Mentioning Tunisia enabled
Hanotaux to capitalize on the great successes of Paul Cambon who as resident general in Tunisia had evolved and felicitously applied a protectorate
system just a few years earlier.[32] Under a political arrangement similar to
that in existence in Tunisia, Hanotaux continued, France could have done
for Madagascar all that needed to be done and still have reaped rich profits
for itself. Colonizing could have been left to individual initiative. Instead,
the Radical Government had saddled Madagascar with an administration
that was too elaborate for local conditions and which was centralized in
Paris and therefore quite inefficient and expensive. The Bourgeois government, though it attached Madagascar to the Colonial Ministry, had mud-
dled the situation since the debate in the Chamber of Deputies had led to
no clear solution. Hanotaux pointed out that when the Radicals forced
the Queen of Madagascar to sign a second treaty which recognized the
French *prise de possession* and greatly diminished her own power, they had

diminished a flexible tool with which to govern. Though he did not say so, Hanotaux implied that the Radical policy led directly to the revolts which spread throughout the island soon after the second treaty was imposed on the Malagasy native government. While foreign powers protested against the new French order in Madagascar, the deputies handed Bourgeois a vote of no confidence which led to the return to power of the Moderate Republicans.[33]

Hanotaux, when he returned to office in 1896, rallied to the "annexation outright" point of view and it was he who actually had Madagascar declared a French colony. The protectorate policy might have worked—as it had and continued to work in Tunisia—but when Hanotaux returned to office in 1896, he decided not to further confuse the situation by applying a policy which had already been discarded. The Radicals had failed in their attempt to close Madagascar to British traders without formally annexing the great African island. Hanotaux began to work for a clearer political status for the territories so recently reconquered. First, on May 3, 1896, he announced that Madagascar had been annexed to France. Two months later on Hanotaux's request the Deputies voted in a law which declared Madagascar a French colony. The next problem to be solved was that involved in convincing the other powers to accept the new French order in Madagascar.[34]

Advocates of the annexation of Madagascar had argued that the protectorate arrangement left important disadvantages in permitting the continued existence of engagements previously agreed to by the Queen of Madagascar with powers other than France. These were, Hanotaux argued, but juridical arguments brought forward by the foreign powers, which France would have been in a position to combat successfully. In power, however, the proponents of annexation had pushed their policy forward. Months later though Madagascar had been attached to the Colonial Ministry, foreigners other than Frenchmen were still not under the jurisdiction of French courts in the island, and France did not enjoy the closed shop which the change from protectorate to colonial status was supposed to have brought about. "Enfin, ce qui est fait est fait," Hanotaux concluded, and since the Queen had signed a second treaty, there could be no question of having her sign a third. The protectorate system having been pushed aside, the annexation policy had triumphed. The future would judge according to results.[35] In the meantime, Hanotaux set himself to the task of having the new order recognized by other powers.

The British found it difficult to accept the change from protectorate to colonial status for Madagascar, although in strict international law, France, having conquered and militarily occupied the territories, had a "right to extinguish the independent existence of the State of Madagascar." By extension all treaties contracted between the Hova government and foreign powers would also cease to exist, should "the French Republic think fit to exercise this right." The British legal expert at Downing Street recognized as much.[36] Yet herein lay the real British objection to the political change the French had wrought. British trade treaties could be cancelled and this eventuality the British Foreign Office dared not ignore. Bourgeois, during his last month as premier and foreign minister of France, had apparently implied that the cancellation of treaties would have to be negotiated. Hanotaux, however, as soon as he was back as director of the affairs of the Quai d'Orsay, let it be known that "treaties between Madagascar and foreign powers are extinguished by reason of the island having passed under the absolute sovereignty of France, and having become a French territory by conquest." The American Secretary of State, Richard Olney, did not feel he would challenge the French thesis. And Great Britain, which had thought of allying itself with the United States in a diplomatic accord to counter French designs in Madagascar, was left to fend for itself. Salisbury who was again Prime Minister in London was inclined to seek better relations with Paris.[37]

The French government was busily reorganizing the whole administrative structure of Madagascar, particularly the judiciary, and attempting to create a closed market for itself by abolishing tariffs on French goods, while maintaining the ten percent tax on foreign goods, and on some items, even raising the duties. The tariffs ostensibly helped pay for the new administration. But Great Britain and other powers that had had most favored nation treaties with the Hova found little to rejoice about. In Madagascar itself, the new policies apparently led to a severe drop in the total volume of trade, though the continuing rebellion and consequent unsettled political situation within the island undoubtedly contributed to this drop.[38] Madagascar was not pacified until the first years of the twentieth century.

The British government protested against the tariffs, but to no avail. In another dispute Downing Street was more fortunate in that a *quid pro quo* was found. This second disagreement involved the judicial jurisdiction of consular tribunals over their own nationals. When the French substituted their own judicial system for that of the native government which they had destroyed, they also declared consular tribunals abolished. Great Britain was not ready to abandon the right to try its own subjects in Madagascar, a right that had been sanctioned in a treaty with the Hovas before the island became a French protectorate. In the argument that ensued,

Salisbury eventually offered to accept the cancellation of British consular courts in Madagascar in exchange for a similar cancellation of French extraterritorial jurisdiction in Zanzibar. Hanotaux protested that European courts had not yet been established in Zanzibar and threatened to involve Germany since the East African Sultanate had been under a tripartite rule until 1890 when Great Britain had gained sole control.[39] The British insisted until Hanotaux accepted. On April 22, 1897, he could write his colleague at the *Ministère des Colonies* that "the exercise of the jurisdiction of our tribunals over British subjects residing in Madagascar is assured"; the foreign secretary of Great Britain sent instructions to that effect to his agents in the African island.[40]

The Madagascar question was solved though it left a trace of bitterness in Anglo-French relations. By the spring of 1897 the attention of European chancelleries had shifted away from Madagascar. Not unwilling to ease Anglo-French tension, Salisbury had authorized a resumption of negotiations on West Africa, and Hanotaux had begun his work to free Tunisia from all its treaties with powers other than France. Having accepted the annexation and the transfer of administrative authority for Madagascar from the Foreign to the Colonial Ministry, Hanotaux still had in Tunisia, a chance to prove the merit of a colonial system he preferred.

The Tunisian
"Mouvement Tournant":
The Making
of a French Tunisia

Chapter 7

During the last decade of the nineteenth century while Gabriel Hanotaux presided over the Quai d'Orsay, Tunisia became in fact a French colony. In name the patrimony of the Bey of Tunisia remained what it had been since 1882, a protectorate. But after 1897 the government in Paris dominated the protectorate completely and without foreign encumbrances. The new political order was introduced by Hanotaux, who negotiated the cancellation of Tunisian capitulations treaties during the years 1895–97.

An interesting chapter in the diplomatic history of Europe, the negotiations for the revision of Tunisian treaties with powers other than France provide a clear illustration of the colonial policies of Hanotaux and of France at the end of the last century. In Tunisia as in Madagascar and in West Africa, Hanotaux finished the work of earlier colonialists by completing situations already created and, where necessary, correcting the errors of his predecessors—Ferry, Gambetta, and Waddington.

When faced with the Anglo-Congolese and Anglo-Italian treaties of 1894 Hanotaux was forced to react to the activities of foreign chancelleries. In the middle of June 1895 he provoked the Tunisian debate himself when he queried his representatives in Rome and in London. He took this initiative because several facets of the Tunisian situation bothered him. Although France was the protecting power and paid the whole defense budget of Tunisia, Frenchmen had to pay the same custom duties and tariffs as did the nationals of most other European nations. Since 1882 France itself had guaranteed all treaties that were in force at the time of the French invasion of Tunisia, and since most European nations had previously secured most-favored-nation clauses in their treaties with the Bey, to grant Frenchmen preferential treatment proved impossible. Any advantage afforded Frenchmen by the Tunisian administration had to be extended to the nationals of all the powers that held valid capitulations treaties. Added to this apparent injustice was the fact that one treaty at least, the Anglo-Tunisian treaty of 1875, had no terminal date. Such a treaty might be demanded of a "barbaric" country but not of a civilized power such as France. In any case, the possibility of changing the Tunisian order appeared promising in mid-1895. During the next year the Italian treaty with the Bey of Tunisia signed in 1868 would expire. By simply denouncing this treaty one year before its expiration, the privileges secured for Italy would be cancelled. If no action were taken, the treaty would be automatically renewed for a period of twenty-eight years.[1]

On receiving Hanotaux's dispatch about the Italian treaty of 1868, Baron de Courcel brought up the subject with Sir Percy Anderson at the Foreign Office. In the middle of August Courcel reported that not much more could be done until the new British cabinet had established itself. He had, however, indicated to Sir Thomas Sanderson, another African specialist at Downing Street, that France wished to reopen negotiations about Tunisia so that benefits secured in an Anglo-French agreement might be extended to Italy. In the margin of this report, Hanotaux wrote "M. Courcel va bien vite!" A few days later the French ambassador was reminded that he had been asked for a personal opinion only.[2]

To broach the Tunisian problem with Great Britain involved the possibility of starting negotiations which, as was the case in the Anglo-French West African talks, might have no satisfactory end. The consequence would be to heighten Anglo-French irritations, something Hanotaux wanted to avoid at all cost. The conclusion of detailed instructions to Courcel were words through which Hanotaux set the tone for the whole negotiation which was about to begin: "But above all, whatever happens, avoid the great evil of negotiations that advance too far (before) breaking down in failure. Anything is preferable." [3]

Hanotaux's instructions to Courcel clearly illustrate his policies vis-a-vis Great Britain on the Tunisian question as well as on colonial questions in general. He would have liked to see Anglo-French relations established on a friendlier basis than they were. But though he would not risk a negotiation that would break down, he intended to insist on French rights and achieve his objective, a French Tunisia unencumbered by foreign rights based on capitulations treaties. If negotiations could not lead to a satisfactory solution, there was the possibility of annexing Tunisia, thus automatically cancelling all previous treaties. This had just been done in Madagascar, a fact the British were well aware of, and would be quite legal in terms of international law. Legal or not, London could be expected to disapprove strongly.

Long before such arguments were aired in Anglo-French talks the
Italian treaty of 1868 was denounced.[4] The Italian government was not
surprised by the French decision to denounce the Italo-Tunisian treaty of
1868. As early as October 1894 Count Tornielli had approached the Foreign Office in London to discuss the Tunisian question. He had then asked
the British to refuse to give up their own most-favored-nation clause. Such
refusal "would be considered by Italy as a new proof of friendship." When
their treaty with Tunisia lapsed, the Italians planned to fall back on their
capitulations treaties which gave them most-favored-nation treatment; this
right had apparently not been abolished or supplanted by the Treaty of
1868. But for their most-favored-nation clause to be worthwhile, Italians
needed some power other than themselves with privileges which they might
claim because of the Italian most-favored-nation clause. The future commercial and financial relations of Italy and Tunisia apparently hinged on
the British treaty, which explained the great interest of Italians in the
progress of possible Anglo-French talks about Tunisian treaty revisions.[5]

Officially Italy and Great Britain were on the best of terms about Tunisian affairs, Downing Street invariably replying to Italian queries with
promises to keep Rome informed of any French advances on the subject.
In the press, however, Anglo-Italian relations were at times heated. In
March 1895 *La Tribuna* had published several articles which were critical
of the British Consul in Tunisia. Sir W. H. D. Haggard's offense was to
have given a speech in which he had favorable things to say about the
French protectorate in Tunis. What was taken to be the British Consul's
pro-French attitude inevitably led to the conclusion that steps had been
taken toward a revision of the Anglo-Tunisian Treaty of 1875, which would
be to the "detriment of Italian interests." But in spite of occasional un-
favorable press articles Anglo-Italian relations continued to be quite warm
in Tunisia as in Morocco and East Africa.[6]

Early in 1895 there was a change in the attitude of Italy toward France,
but this change did not really affect relations between Rome and London.
Billot, the French ambassador in Rome, thought he observed a slacken-
ing of the anti-French campaign in the Italian press. Also Count Tornielli
was transferred from his ambassadorial post in London to Paris. His instructions at the time of the change, it was believed, included orders to help
prepare better Franco-Italian relations. These had been poor throughout
the Crispi era, conflict having been engendered by the French occupation
of Tunisia in 1881–82. Before the French annexation Italian nationals had
migrated to Tunisia by the thousands and the government in Rome had
assumed that the Bey's territories would fall under their domination.[7]

The Italian arguments that supported this assumption about Tunisia were much the same as those used by Spaniards about Morocco. Of course, Rome and Paris were also in contention about East Africa where the latter supported Abyssinian independence in spite of an Italian claim that they had a protectorate over the area. Even as Italy was preparing to improve its relations with France, events in Tunisia threatened to deepen old wounds.

On August 17, 1895, the French denounced the treaty which guaranteed the relations between Tunisia and Italy. This treaty had been signed in 1868 and, because of the denunciation, would expire in September 1896. In effect, the Italian government was given one year in which to find alternative guarantees for their important trade and other relations with Tunisia. When he brought up the Tunisian question in a conversation with Ambassador Tornielli, Hanotaux was apologetic. The French foreign minister also offered to initiate negotiations for a new settlement, but Tornielli had no instructions and the matter was left dormant. In their search for alternatives to the cancelled 1868 arrangement, the Italian government had turned to London.[8] Detecting a certain reluctance in Rome, Hanotaux also turned his attention toward Downing Street.

Acting on Hanotaux's instructions Ambassador de Courcel asked the British Foreign Office how negotiations about a new Anglo-Tunisian treaty could be initiated. This treaty would replace the 1875 agreement, made to last in perpetuity. In complementary instructions to his ambassador in London Hanotaux warned that it would be to British advantage to come to terms with him. His own ministry might be replaced by one of protectionist leanings which might well apply the French minimum tariff to Tunisia.[9]

Asked what the effect of the denunciation of the Italian treaty of 1868 might have on Anglo-Tunisian affairs, Sir Percy Anderson said that Great Britain would continue to pay the same tariff as France. This was exactly what Hanotaux wanted to avoid for he thought France should be entitled to a privileged position in Tunisia. In exchange for the cancellation of the British Treaty of 1875 Hanotaux offered certain specific concessions. A new Anglo-Tunisian treaty would set eight percent *ad valorem* as a ceiling of tariffs to be charged on British goods entering Tunisia. In addition, a special concession would be extended to British cotton goods, perhaps even a tariff as low as five percent *ad valorem*.[10]

Though unwilling to give up their treaty of 1875 the British could not refuse to consider the French advance. A clause in the 1875 treaty had stipulated that either party could initiate talks about a new arrangement with a view toward an amelioration of existing relations at any time. In

1895 the protecting power, France, spoke for Tunisia. Great Britain, however, quickly pointed out that Hanotaux's proposals would improve French relations with Tunisia but did not offer Britishers a better position than they already enjoyed.[11]

When Salisbury asked the Board of Trade to comment, the answer was that any change in the Tunisian treaty along the lines indicated by Hanotaux would be commercially undesirable, though political considerations might lead to a different conclusion. After further consultation between Downing Street and the Board of Trade and a representative of the Manchester Chamber of Commerce, proposals emerged for conditions that should be carefully guaranteed if the government should decide to sign a new Tunisian arrangement with France. One suggestion involved a British surrender of "the Tunis Treaty *en bloc*" in exchange for a French acceptance of "concurrent instead of preferential fishing (rights) in Newfoundland." Manchester would not be satisfied with such an arrangement, and the Tunisia-Newfoundland deal was never officially proposed.[12] Not until 1897 was a basis found on which France and England could willingly negotiate on the Tunisian question.

Meanwhile, Marcellin Berthelot and Léon Bourgeois replaced Hanotaux at the Quai d'Orsay from November 1, 1895 until April 29, 1896. Though the Anglo-French dialogue about Tunisia continued during this interim in Hanotaux's tenure at the French Foreign Ministry, the negotiations made no progress. Back in office as a member of the Méline government of April 29, 1896, Hanotaux at once set himself to the task of building up diplomatic pressure that might force the British to come to terms with him. To do this, he made treaties about Tunisia with all the European powers, leaving Great Britain isolated in her opposition to Hanotaux's program for the French protectorate in the eastern Maghrib.

This "mouvement tournant," as Hanotaux called it, began when France came to terms with Austria-Hungary on July 20, 1896. Through the instrument of a joint declaration, Austria-Hungary promised not to invoke the capitulations regime which it renounced. As important from Hanotaux's point of view, was the second paragraph of the declaration which guaranteed Austria-Hungary the most-favored-nation treatment in Tunisia with respect to all nations save France. In exchange for the two concessions he received, Hanotaux agreed that the special terms offered Italian wines entering the dual monarchy would not, until January 1, 1904, be claimed by the government of the French Republic. In effect, France agreed to an exception to its own most-favored-nation clause in Austria-Hungary.[13]

Even before Paris and Vienna settled their relations about Tunisia,

Franco-Italian negotiations about the same question had been initiated by
Rome. The Italian government was in the hands of Marquis di Rudini who,
in an answer to an interpellation on May 25, 1896, had announced that
he wished for a reconciliation between France and Italy. In Europe itself,
these two nations had waged a tariff war which had lasted for over a decade.
Italian intransigence on colonial matters had kept the conflict open, though
Frenchmen were by no means innocent. On March 1, 1896, however, Italian
armies were defeated by Menelik at Adowa. A time had come for Rome to
adopt pacific programs in Africa.[14]

Desiring a rapprochement with France the Italian government
watched with interest the political developments of the Third French
Republic throughout the spring of 1896. At the end of April Méline replaced Bourgeois as Prime Minister. This served as a signal for a long com-
parative report about the policies of the two French leaders by the Italian
ambassador in Paris. An agreement, Tornielli wrote, might have been
reached more quickly with the Bourgeois ministry. But at the moment of
ratifying such a possible convention on Tunisia and on the commercial
relations of France and Italy, there would almost certainly have been an
insurmountable parliamentary obstacle. With Méline in power success
would be assured if agreement could be reached on an executive level. But
the new government would be reluctant to enter the negotiations desired
in Rome.[15]

In the opinion of the Italian ambassador in Paris the best chance of
bringing the French to negotiate about the Tunisian question as well as
about Franco-Italian commercial relations would be to win Hanotaux
over to the cause of better Franco-Italian relations. Tornielli thought
Hanotaux would be willing enough to help improve the poor relations
existing between Rome and Paris. But he also warned that the French
foreign minister would insist on a Tunisian settlement before he would
consider commercial qeustions in Europe itself. Tornielli was also convinced that Hanotaux carried considerable weight in the government, and
he based this judgment on information he had gathered in a private conversation with Méline. The new French prime minister, Tornielli reported,
had told him that he would have refused the task of organizing a government if Hanotaux had not agreed to accept responsibility for the Quai
d'Orsay. Tornielli therefore concluded that Hanotaux could probably convince Méline of the beneficent effect of better Franco-Italian relations. On
May 19, 1896, Tornielli received a telegram from his foreign minister asking if he thought it possible to negotiate a one-year prolongation of the
Italo-Tunisian treaty.[16] Thereupon, Tornielli sought an interview with

Hanotaux, and the two quickly laid down the basis for much wider negotiations about Tunisia that were to begin in early June.

Hanotaux's willingness to come to an agreement with the Italian government was confirmed in a conversation with Tornielli later in May. The new French foreign minister went to great lengths in defending the peaceful intentions and attitudes of the French ambassador in Rome: Billot had been misunderstood in Rome. The rumor that he would be moved to Berlin was false as such a move had become unnecessary because of the change that had occurred in the Italian government. The advent of the new ministry in Rome would mean that Billot could work more effectively for peaceful commercial relations between France and Italy. He had always been a partisan of better Franco-Italian relations, and his reported anti-monarchial opinions were destitute of any foundation in facts. The French government, whether Hanotaux himself was in it or not, could not and did not wish to interfere with the royal regimes of either Italy or Spain.[17]

With Billot still in Rome and Hanotaux back at the Quai d'Orsay, Tornielli concluded, the time to propose the talks envisioned in Rome seemed opportune. The Italian foreign minister, Duke Caetani de Sermoneta, was aware that Hanotaux had worked under the orders of Albert Billot in the mid-1880s, and concluded as had Tornielli that the influence of Billot on Hanotaux was apparently quite strong and that it might be profitably used in pursuance of Italian objectives. Billot himself was approaching retirement and could be counted upon to work for a substantial improvement in Franco-Italian relations that would permit him to leave the service on a diplomatic success.[18]

From the French point of view the return of M. di Rudini as head of the Italian government had seemed propitious. With Crispi out of office the Italians could be expected to be less demanding in colonial matters. And it was probably with an idea about a bettering of relations between Paris and Rome that Hanotaux presented Billot to Tornielli as an ambassador in sympathy with Italy and as a man who wished to see tensions diminished. Fortunately, press polemical writing about Abyssinia and about Tunisia subsided in France and Italy as responsible leaders in both countries began to reexamine the economic differences which could only hurt all involved.[19]

In the face of the French denunciation of the Italo-Tunisian treaty of 1868, the Italian government had kept an official silence until late May 1896, that is for about nine months. During this time lapse Rome tried to find some way out of the impasse created for Italian trade in Tunisia which would not force them to seek a new treaty on French terms.[20] But with the expiration date of September 28, 1896, only a few months away the di Rudini government initiated talks in order to settle the Tunisian question with the real masters of the Bey's territories.

In the first days of June 1896 Tornielli approached Hanotaux with a proposal which foresaw not only negotiations about Tunis but a broadening of a possible agreement on that question into a series of agreements about Franco-Italian commercial relations as well. Unfortunately, public opinion in France was not ready for such wide sweeping settlements. Or at least Hanotaux thought Frenchmen were not ready to become more friendly with Italians overnight. While insisting that any settlement favorable to Italy should be considered a mark of good will on the part of France, Hanotaux was willing to explore possible solutions to the Tunisian question. In August 1895 he had himself suggested such talks, but the Italian government had not followed up his opening.[21]

Negotiations about Tunisia began in June 1896 though Tornielli and his government continued in their efforts to broaden the scope of the talks so as to include Franco-Italian commercial relations. The two parties held basically opposed theses. The Italian government considered that a recognition of the privileged position of France in Tunisia would represent a double concession, one political, and the other economic, on their part. In return Rome hoped Hanotaux would agree to offer a guarantee that Italian goods not be taxed by more than the minimum tariff of France; French goods should be assured the conventional tariff of Italy. Hanotaux, however, thought any Tunisian settlement would represent a concession to Italy. He firmly maintained his refusal to broaden the discussion, though he later agreed to ask the French cabinet for an opinion on a more moderate Italian proposal presented by Tornielli on July 1, 1896.[22]

On July 2, 1896, Tornielli presented a new proposal which involved a three-point program. France and Italy should come to some settlement about Tunisia. Navigation would be regulated in a second agreement. And the French government would promise to open, at some later date, negotiations about Franco-Italian commercial relations. In effect, the Italian government agreed to drop its insistence on immediate commercial talks. The weaker stand was made in the face of Hanotaux's assertion that after September 28, 1896, Italy would have no treaty rights in Tunisia unless a new settlement had been signed with France. Only an assurance that the French government did not wish to apply the rigors of the *strictum jus* that would be created by the expiration of the 1868 Italo-Tunisian treaty mollified Hanotaux's strong stand.[23]

During the negotiations, several incidents threatened to make agreement impossible, though both sides protested their good will. On June 29, 1896, for example, the di Rudini government had to fight off a francophobe attack by Crispi elements in the Italian Chamber of Deputies. During the debate that ensued, members of the opposition asserted that as France had done in Egypt, Italy should not renounce any of her rights in Tunisia. In answer to criticism about the governmental policy about Tunisia, the Duke de Sermoneta, who was foreign minister, assured the deputies that Italian rights would be protected by a reversion to the capitulations which had not been cancelled. Hanotaux, of course, found this thesis unacceptable. Capitulations could be applied to barbarian countries only, but France, the master in Tunisia, was civilized. Billot pointed to the precedent set by the Habsburgs when they had cancelled capitulations on taking Bosnia-Herzegovina.[24]

As late as September 22, 1896, Haggard, the British consul in Tunisia, reported that Franco-Italian negotiations were apparently not advancing satisfactorily. There had been concern expressed throughout the Italian press that if no new treaty were signed by the deadline of September 28, the maximum French tariff would be applied to Italian goods entering Tunisia. In Paris Tornielli and Hanotaux were feverishly hammering out three conventions and two protocols to regulate Italian commerce, navigation, consular establishments, and extradition in Tunisia. These diplomatic agreements were signed on the very day the 1868 Italo-Tunisian treaty expired, September 28, 1896. Though Hanotaux's conditions had been met, the Franco-Italian Tunisian agreements were judged much more favorable toward Italy than expected. The Italian demands about a commercial settlement had been dropped when Visconti Venosta took control of the Italian Foreign Ministry, and Italy had thereafter yielded to all French demands. Haggard wondered why the Italian government had not sought German support in the negotiations.[25]

Having settled their Tunisian differences with France, the Italian government would have liked to go on to settle their European differences with their northwestern neighbor. The situation which developed as a result of the cross currents of differing wills has been interestingly described by the British chargé d'affaires during the crucial month in Franco-Italian relations, that of October 1896. According to F. A. Edwardes, di Rudini was trying hard to achieve a reconciliation with France. A first step had been taken with the Tunisian agreement; French moderation at a time when they could have ruined Italian trade in Tunisia should be credited with that initial success. In retrospect, Edwardes continued, even the fact that the French had supplied weapons to the enemies of Italy in East Africa seemed to be an act of hatred directed more against the Francophobe Crispi than against his nation. With Crispi out of office France had shown herself willing to make real concessions. As a result, Rome was beginning to lean towards France and away from the Triple Alliance, and it was Hanotaux's actions about Tunisia that had helped the development of this new tendency. The Franco-Italian Tunisian agreement was a beginning, though it was easy to exaggerate its importance. Hanotaux had consistently put off talks about the commercial difficulties which Rome wished to end, at one time simply informing Billot that agreement would cost French producers too much. Hanotaux was a member of a protectionist cabinet, and though he might himself have been willing to make concessions to Italy, he would have had a difficult time securing Méline's approval.[26]

Towards the British the Italians were apologetic about their new Tunisian treaty. The diplomatic agreements of September 28, 1896, had been signed behind Great Britain's back, just over one month after the last Italian request that the British stand firm on their Tunisian treaty had been delivered. On August 14 the Duke of Sermoneta had accompanied the Italian ambassador in London to the Foreign Office for an interview. During the course of the discussion Salisbury was asked about the progress of British negotiations with France about Tunisia and especially about capitulations. When Salisbury had answered that the British were about to make counter proposals, but that not much was expected from these, his interlocutors seemed relieved. The Duke of Sermoneta noted that since Austria had abandoned its capitulations, and Italy had had its Tunisian treaty denounced, both had no one to turn to but Her Majesty's government. If the British were to abandon their treaty, Italy's position would become untenable. Also, Hanotaux felt that British opposition to a new Anglo-Tunisian treaty was supported by the opposition of Italy to his policy. In this respect, Hanotaux had gained an important diplomatic victory in securing the Franco-Italian agreement on the Tunisian question.[27]

In a conversation with Lord Dufferin in Paris a few weeks later Count Tornielli explained that Italy had not found itself in as strong a "fortress" as Great Britain on the Tunisian question. Left without a treaty Rome had had to negotiate to avoid a serious crisis. The Italian government had also wished to work for the resumption of normal Franco-Italian commercial relations and had seized on the Tunisian question as a possible starting point.[28]

While Franco-Italian negotiations about Tunisia were advancing satisfactorily, Franco-British talks were deadlocked. Great Britain and Italy had been the strongest opponent of Hanotaux's proposed new order in Tunisia. Having secured Italian approval to a privileged position for Frenchmen in Tunisia, Hanotaux was still faced with unbending British opposition. Great Britain's insistence that her subjects should receive the same treatment as the nationals of France in Tunisia was based on a treaty that the Quai d'Orsay itself had guaranteed. Salisbury had not failed to point this fact out when de Courcel, at Hanotaux's suggestion, had complained that France might be forced to annex Tunisia, thereby eliminating all previous treaty rights.[29] But Hanotaux did not like this solution. He wished somehow to bring Salisbury to negotiate and to agree to his terms. With Austrian and Italian approval of his Tunisian program Hanotaux continued to build diplomatic pressure against London on the Tunisian question by coming to terms with one European nation after another.

On October 2 and 14, 1896, a Franco-Russian Tunisian agreement was signed in St. Petersburg. In a joint declaration the two powers agreed that all treaties and conventions in effect betwen them should be extended to Tunisia. Russia agreed to abstain from demanding any rights and privileges for its consuls or dependents in Tunisia that were not established in France. Finally, it was clearly stated that the most-favored-nation treatment for Russians in Tunisia did not include a right to equality of treatment with Frenchmen. On October 14 Hanotaux himself signed a similar declaration with the Swiss representative in Paris. The wording of the Franco-Swiss declaration was the same as that of the Franco-Russian one with the exception of an additional clause about the exchange of ratification.[30]

Germany also joined the ranks of governments that recognized a special status for France in Tunisia and abandoned the capitulations system. In a declaration signed in Berlin on November 18, 1896, Germany specifically renounced its right to invoke the capitulations regime in Tunisia in exchange for the extension of all rights acquired through treaties with France to Tunisia. Germany recognized a special position for France provided Germans be guaranteed the most-favored-nation treatment with respect to all other powers in matters of customs and navigation. The French government also agreed to extend to Germany any new benefits that might be granted any power save France. Tunisians were to enjoy the same rights in Germany as Germans enjoyed in Tunisia. Finally, the joint Franco-German declaration stipulated that the agreement should become effective as soon as ratifications had been exchanged, which date was not specified, and until December 31, 1903. The fact that a terminal date was set was important. It was a precedent to serve in Franco-British negotiations. Great Britain had a perpetual treaty with the Bey of Tunisia. To introduce a terminal date to this Anglo-Tunisian treaty was one of Hanotaux's primary objectives.[31] The Franco-Italian arrangement about Tunisia, of course, had also provided for a terminal date.

In terms of the powers' trade in Tunisia France led and was followed by Great Britain, Italy, and Germany in that order. With the Franco-German declaration Hanotaux secured the approval of the second of the four most important powers interested in Tunisia to his policy of "Frenchi-fying" the Maghribi protectorate. Three powers not so vitally interested in the area had already agreed to accept a special position for Frenchmen in Tunisia, these being Austria-Hungary, Russia, and Switzerland. Belgium, Denmark, Holland, Spain, and the United Kingdoms of Sweden and Norway followed suit, agreeing to declarations that were worded in much the same terms as those concluded between France, and Russia and Switzerland. There were no special bargains such as those reached between France and Austria, Italy, and Germany. Finally, all the Hanotaux-sponsored diplomatic agreements granted most-favored-nation treatment for the nationals of all European powers in Tunisia save Frenchmen, who were to be allowed an even more advantageous position, and Englishmen, who still claimed the right to be treated on parity with Frenchmen. After May 5, 1897, with the signing of the declaration by the Scandinavian dual kingdom, all European powers, save Great Britain, had agreed to Hanotaux's Tunisian program.[32]

Great Britain remained unreconciled throughout the period of the ten Tunisian settlements that left Her Majesty's Government alone in opposition. The British attitude had been clearly exemplified in a report sent to Hanotaux by de Courcel after a conversation with Salisbury on October 3, 1896. Great Britain would probably remain stubborn about its Tunisian rights, de Courcel had written, and would not be budged by eloquence about the superior rights of France as the protecting power. Perhaps the British would make concessions to France about Tunisia in exchange for French concessions in the Egyptian question. The French ambassador in London had concluded by suggesting that French goods be allowed free entry into Tunisia while other goods be forced to pay tariff duties in spite of treaties.[33]

De Courcel's suggestion was pragmatic but not good diplomacy. Although probably tempted to follow his representative's advice, Hanotaux used other means to achieve his own ends in Tunisia. In February 1897 at France's bidding, the Bey of Tunisia published decrees that abrogated all treaties with Germany, Austria-Hungary, Denmark, Spain, Italy, Russia, and Switzerland that had been in effect before Hanotaux's series of declarations of 1896–97. Another decree by the Tunisian Regency brought Belgium into the fold of the powers whose relations with Tunisia were redefined in accordance with Hanotaux's policies.[34] Though Great Britain's relations with Tunisia were not directly affected by these decrees any more than they were by the ten Hanotaux-inspired declarations, the fact that London was out of step was clearly brought out. There is no way of determining whether the psychological pressure on the British had any effect on policy making. Indeed, the new agreements all involved most-favored-nation clauses and the powers thereby gained an interest in the preservation of the British Treaty of 1875 which would guarantee all a treatment equal to that of France itself in Tunisia.[35]

On February 15, 1897, Sir Thomas Sanderson, permanent under-secretary at the London Foreign Office, wrote the Board of Trade that on general political grounds, agreement or conciliation should be found. This attitude more than anything else probably made possible an eventual Anglo-French agreement. Hanotaux strongly opposed barters involving the Egyptian and the Tunisian questions. To regulate the Tunisian difficulty on its own merits was the French Foreign Minister's aim. This, of course, made for a certain stiffness on the part of the French negotiations in the Franco-British Tunisian talks. Other trades of concessions involving Algeria and Madagascar were suggested by the British. If France would agree to a lowering of its Algerian tariffs on cotton goods to the Tunisian levels, the British were willing to give up their perpetual clause in the Anglo-Tunisian 1875 treaty. Still another British proposal would have involved the lowering of the tariffs charged in Madagascar on Manchester goods in exchange for British concessions on the Tunisian question. If, for example, British cottons were placed at a disadvantage with respect to French cotton goods in Tunisia, the ten percent *ad valorem* tariff on those charged in Madagascar should be lowered for a period of twelve to fifteen years. These possible solutions were all rejected by Hanotaux who insisted no outside elements should be brought into the Tunisian negotiations.[36]

Negotiations about the revision of the Anglo-Tunisian treaty dragged on. When Salisbury was in Paris in late March 1897, he told both Hanotaux and de Courcel that agreement would be reached as soon as the French made concessions to the cotton-goods manufacturers of Manchester. Hanotaux promised to bring up the matter with Méline and to insist that such concessions be made.[37] Still, another five and one-half months would be required to determine exactly what these concessions should be.

Earlier in March Salisbury had informed de Courcel that the ultimate concession the British might make involved the application of not more than a five percent tariff on British cotton goods and of not less than three percent on similar French products. Madagascar and Tunisia would be involved in such an agreement. The proposed treaty would last not less than fifteen years and Great Britain should be granted the most-favored-nation treatment in all other respects. A memorandum containing the proposal Salisbury had made orally was sent to the French ambassador in London on April 22 though a few changes had been introduced. As expressed in the memorandum French "cotonnades" should pay no less than two-fifths of the duty applied to Manchester goods. The most-favored-nation clause in respect to all other relations should be granted in perpetuity, though Great Britain would no longer claim equality of treatment with France. Finally, the tariff agreement should last until December 31, 1912.[38]

A week later de Courcel answered the British memorandum of April 22, 1897. He rejected the perpetuity clause asked by Her Majesty's Government with respect to the most-favored-nation treatment. For the French government de Courcel also rejected the obligation to impose a tariff on French goods entering Tunisia. This rejection was not based on considerations of the commercial consequences of such a clause but on principle. Should Great Britain insist on these two conditions, agreement would be impossible.[39]

In a British Foreign Office minute, apparently written in reaction to de Courcel's rejection of the proposal that represented the ultimate British concessions, there is the complaint that the French persisted in acting as if they were making concessions and in ignoring the guarantees they themselves had given to the 1875 Anglo-Tunisian treaty. If agreement were still deemed necessary protection against all sorts of hidden taxes should be specifically stipulated. The tariff to be charged on British cotton goods entering Tunisia might be dropped from five percent to four percent in an arrangement that would replace the suggested two-fifths clause presented by the Foreign Office. Finally, a perpetuity clause might be waived in exchange for a twelve-year duration for a new treaty and a six-months notice thereafter for cancellation. In the minute it was noted that the French claimed perpetuity for their fishing rights off Newfoundland while refusing to recognize perpetuity for British rights in Tunisia.[40]

In a new counter proposal communicated to Downing Street on May 19 the French offered to recognize a most-favored-nation clause for British goods in Tunisia for a period of twenty years. The treatment of Frenchmen, of course, would be exceptional. The tariff provisions would last until

January 1, 1910, and thereafter until six months after denunciation. The British noticed that their perpetuity clause had been dropped, that the French had omitted a six months' notice before the proposed new treaty should become effective, and that the wording of the May 19 proposal excluded British colonies from the most-favored-nation clause. Salisbury wrote the following note: "I am very sorry that the law officers held that we could not enjoy most-favored-nation treatment under the existing convention without specially mentioning it in the new one. It was certain to wreck the negotiations." [41]

In a dispatch to his representative in Paris, Salisbury added that British colonies should be included in the most-favored-nation clause because of an important indirect trade via Malta and that he had suggested fifty years instead of perpetuity for the duration of such a clause in the face of strong French opposition. Nevertheless, Salisbury wrote Chamberlain, the colonial minister, that agreement with France was desirable if at all possible. Indeed, Great Britain had no real defense against a possible full annexation by France that would *ipso facto* abrogate all treaties. The possible protection of a French guarantee of the Anglo-Tunisian treaty of 1875 seemed almost useless. Also, the Madagascar precedent made it especially desirable to come to terms with France directly. Annexed to this letter was a resumé of the terms that would be acceptable to France.[42]

The disagreement over the inclusion of British colonies as most-favored-nations in a new Anglo-Tunisian treaty continued throughout the summer. In late July Salisbury judged a suspension of negotiations probable. But Hanotaux secured the approval of the cabinet of which he was a member for a concession which would permit direct shipment from and transshipment at Malta.[43]

Though the British Colonial Office accepted a possible treaty on the basis of agreements reached by September 10, 1897, Salisbury asked Sir Edmund Monson to try to secure the same conditions for Gibraltar as had been granted for Malta. Hanotaux brought up the question for the consideration of his colleagues in the French cabinet. Méline and his government refused to extend the most-favored-nation treatment to Gibraltar. On September 17, 1897, nevertheless, Monson received authorization to sign a new Tunisian treaty, and on the next day a Franco-British Tunisian treaty was duly signed.[44]

As in other treaties Hanotaux had concluded with European powers about Tunisia, all treaties and conventions in effect between France and Great Britain were by extension applied to Tunisia. Her Majesty's Government agreed to abstain from demanding any rights for its consuls or dependents in Tunisia that were not secured for them in France. Most-favored-nation treatment was reciprocally guaranteed for forty years, and all British goods, whether sent directly to Tunisia or whether transshipment occurred at Malta, benefitted from this clause. Exception was made in favor of Frenchmen who might be treated as deemed desirable by the French government without bringing about the necessity of treating Britishers on a parity. A second article dealt specifically with cotton goods, though the French term "cotonnades" was used in the official text of the treaty. These goods were to be subjected to no duties whatever save a five percent *ad valorm* tariff. This clause was to be effective until December 31, 1912, and thereafter until the expiration of the sixth month after a possible denunciation by either party. Finally, tariffs actually enforced should be effective until ratifications of the new treaty had been exchanged, at which time the new condition would become operative. The exchange of ratifications should occur as soon as possible.[45]

In the last mentioned article Hanotaux had clearly won, since the British request that a six month notification period should elapse before a new treaty would become effective was ignored. In the second article the Salisbury government did not secure the four percent tariff it had deemed necessary if French goods were to be allowed in duty-free. But Great Britain did secure a fifteen year duration for the special terms on cotton goods, which term was longer than Hanotaux had proposed. With respect to the most-favored-nation clause, a compromise had been reached between Salisbury's insistence on an "in perpetuity" clause and Hanotaux's absolute refusal to recognize the possibility of such a thing, between the British substitute suggestion of a fifty years' duration and the French proposed twenty years' limitation. But much more important than any of these considerations was the fact that Hanotaux had finally managed to eliminate the last serious opponent to his policy of making Tunisia a true French dependency. Because of his diplomatic success, reached without any concessions having been made in other colonial fields, Frenchmen could henceforth be treated more advantageously than other non-Tunisians in Tunisia.

When the Franco-British agreement was finally signed, *Le Temps* could write with satisfaction that all the powers, England included, save Greece, had signed Tunisian agreements. Hanotaux was already completing his "mouvement tournant" by negotiating a Franco-Greek Tunisian treaty.[46] Anglo-French differences of opinion about Tunisia were by no means over. By the end of 1897 Salisbury and Hanotaux were engaged in disputes again, this time about the meaning of the term "cotonnades" used in the Franco-British Tunisian treaty.[47] But the French position in Tunisia was definitely secured; thereafter, the main Anglo-French contest in colonial affairs involved West Africa. The debate about Tunisia had revealed two different British attitudes toward France; Salisbury had obviously been willing to compromise and even to make concessions but Chamberlain wished to resist French advances everywhere. In West Africa Hanotaux was to meet the British on Chamberlain's terms.

West African Disputes and Negotiations: 1895–1897

Chapter 8

During 1894 Gabriel Hanotaux and Sir Constantine Phipps drew up a convention which would have put an end to Anglo-French differences in West and Central Africa. The failure of existing British treaties with Germany and with the Congo Free State to block French western access to the Sudanese Nile had apparently led the Rosebery-Kimberley cabinet to seek an understanding with Hanotaux. With agreement in sight in 1894, the Hanotaux-Phipps talks were, however, doomed to failure. Paris refused to grant the strict guarantees designed to safeguard the Upper Nile valley as a British sphere of influence, on which London insisted. Since London would not sign a treaty which would leave France free to embarrass Great Britain in the Sudan, the possible beneficent result salvaged from the proposed general settlement was an agreement on the delimitation of Sierra Leone and surrounding French Guinea. Months of hard negotiations on the entire African continent, save Egypt, yielded only the recognition of a *fait accompli* in the hinterland of a small West African British colony. This petty accomplishment was formalized in a treaty signed January 21, 1895.[1]

In principle, Sierra Leone had been delimited by the convention of August 10, 1889. This convention was, however, never fully put into effect. The treaty of January 21, 1895, took up the discarded diplomatic instrument and completed it. Between December 1895 and May 1896 a delimitation survey was carried out, the frontier was marked on the ground, and a protocol regarding the results was signed. The British and French commissioners who carried out the delimitation worked throughout in a spirit of friendliness and cooperation. They referred back to their respective governments only on one problem, that involving the ownership of the village of Simitia in the northeastern corner of Sierra Leone. The diplomats, after a period of hard and difficult bargaining, awarded Simitia to Great Britain. Although French colonialists complained, British newspaper opinions were correct in judging the delimitations as a striking French success.[2]

Sierra Leone was now definitely hemmed in on all sides. Gambia, another British territory entirely surrounded by French possessions, was also delimited in 1895–96, in accordance with a treaty signed August 10, 1889; Gambia seemed dead. The same fate was expected to befall Sierra Leone, which had been as unable as Gambia to challenge a vigorous French advance. The French appeared ready to treat the Gold Coast and Lagos in much the same manner. Cambon's plan to unite French possessions in North Africa to those of the West seemed closer to reality than ever. Lake Chad and most of the Niger were in the center of the vast area controlled by France.

With tongue in cheek politicians on both sides of the channel expressed satisfaction about the Gambia and the Sierra Leone frontier settlements. Throughout the first half of the decade, border incidents in the hinterlands of these British colonies had embittered Anglo-French relations. It was hoped that the marking of the borders would permanently avert incidents which had occurred because military and civilian officials had often not known whether they were in their own, or foreign, territory.[3] Unfortunately, the spirit of cooperation and friendliness which had animated the commissioners of the Sierra Leone delimitation did not have much effect on the imperial calculations of diplomats and colonialists in Paris and in London. Competition for the remaining unsettled portions of West Africa became fierce.

The Gold Coast and Lagos, and the neighboring French territories had been delimited from the coast to 9° north latitude. Beyond this geographical line the outcome of Anglo-French territorial competition had been left to be settled by effective occupation, and this principle was one which Frenchmen understood well. Throughout the 1894 talks Hanotaux had warned the British that if diplomacy failed, the West African differences would be solved in this far more dangerous manner. In April 1895 he explained to the French Senate that the government had had no recourse but to safeguard the rights of the Republic through effective occupation. This represented Hanotaux's apologia for the undiplomatic events which were brewing in West Africa. Until the Hanotaux-Phipps talks failed to bring about a settlement of Anglo-French differences in West Africa, Hanotaux had been able to force a postponement of military expeditions into contested areas. Diplomacy failing, he had no choice but to approve the plans of colonialists who were more eager than himself to carve out large African districts for France.[4] The Third Republic started pouring money and soldiers into West Africa, while British initiative was taken by merchants and not by the government. British West African policy did not begin to change until well after Chamberlain became Colonial Secretary in the Salisbury cabinet of June 25, 1895. When he assumed office, Chamberlain knew very little about West Africa, an area in which he became quite interested in 1897.[5]

Salisbury, of course, was much more interested in strategically important East Africa and in the Mediterranean than in commercially remunerative West Africa. He followed the favorite expedient of British imperial policy—to give way in West Africa in exchange for concessions elsewhere. The French were already threatening the Upper Nile, Hanotaux having managed to keep open the road which the Anglo-Congolese treaty of May 12, 1894, was supposed to close. Salisbury would not compromise on an area, which, if controlled by the wrong power, might threaten Egypt and the road to India. In the Mediterranean Italy was proving itself an unreliable British ally. Then, in April 1895 Germans, Frenchmen, and Russians combined to force Japan to disgorge part of the bounty she had so recently gained in her war with China. Great Britain was left diplomatically isolated and the time had come for London to seek a better understanding with Paris. Salisbury offered to negotiate on the Siam question. With the one exception of the Upper Nile question, which was important in his strategic system, Salisbury always tried to settle in a friendly manner the differences that kept antagonism alive between France and Great Britain.[6] Negotiations quickly led to a settlement. On January 15, 1896, a treaty on Siam was signed that included an agreement to have the Anglo-French Niger Commission resume its sessions.[7]

At the Berlin Conference it had been stipulated that trade and navigation on the Niger should be free. In reality though, only Europeans enjoyed the free trade "which was writ large over the Berlin Act"; native middlemen were forced out of business soon after the white man established himself. Naturally African leaders and merchants opposed European domination as long as they could.[8] After 1890 Europeans who did not happen to be members of the British Royal Niger Company, also found it difficult to navigate or trade on the Niger.

In the fall of 1890, for example, Lieutenant Louis Alexandre Antoine Mizon of the French Marines was sent to sail up the Niger to the Benue from which he was to explore in the direction of Lake Chad. He was stopped at the beginning of his river trip by officials of the Niger Company who announced that he would be unable to secure wood and provisions on company territory without a permit from company headquarters in

London. After long delays, Mizon was finally able to proceed. He then
found himself in territories over which there existed not the slightest evidence of European authority although the company claimed possession
of all lands south of the Say-Baruwa line and east of a line drawn from
Say to the point on 9° north latitude. This was the terminal point of the
Anglo-French delimitations of Lagos and Dahomey.[9]

Mizon's discovery was of great consequence to the French. Colonialists
in France felt that Salisbury had somehow tricked the representatives of
the Republic when he had secured their agreement to the 1890 treaty that
established the Say-Baruwa line as the limit of French and British spheres
of influence in the backlands of Nigeria. The Ministère des Colonies sent
Mizon back to the Niger in 1892. He was to continue his exploration and
to conclude treaties with independent native rulers in the Niger bend.
Again Mizon had to face the opposition and delaying tactics of the Niger
Company which was making a farce of the freedom of trade and of navigation on the Niger. A succession of events led to the confiscation of the
Sergent-Malamine, one of two boats placed under Mizon's command in
1892, and the Malamine incident became another diplomatic question
which was to parallel differences about the ownership of the Borgu and
Nikki kingdoms in the Niger bend.[10]

Anglo-French disputes in the Niger bend originated in differing interpretations of the 1890 Say-Baruwa treaty. The British would have extended the agreement to include French recognition as being within the
sphere of the Niger Company's large territories west of the Niger and east
of a line drawn from Say to the terminal point of the Dahomey-Lagos delimitation. Paris never accepted this contention and argued that the 1890
arrangement had concerned territories on the left bank of the Niger.
Though the text of the treaty proved the French to have been correct, the
argument was left for settlement by means other than those of diplomacy.
By the end of 1894 the scramble for West Africa had begun in earnest.
Britishers, Frenchmen, and Germans tried to outsprint each other to be
the first to secure treaties with uncommitted native rulers, particularly in
the Niger bend. The representatives of each nation attempted to secure
pawns and to create *faits accomplis* which would give their respective governments an advantage as occupants of the territories in question. Effective
possession, it was calculated, would also help to establish titles to the contested areas when ownership would be decided around the diplomatic negotiating tables of Europe. Between the French and the British, two questions—the domination of the Nikki and Borgu kingdoms—quickly over-
shadowed all others about West Africa.[11]

In August 1895 Salisbury and Hanotaux were rejecting each other's treaties with the rulers of Nikki and Borgu. Control of these two kingdoms was vital to the French, who could thereby gain access to the lower portion of the Niger River, which was navigable to the sea. The British, in order to preserve a hinterland for Lagos as well as to safeguard the monopoly of the Royal Niger Company, wished to keep the French from acquiring a foothold on the lower Niger. The intensity of the diplomatic bickering brought about by the creating of the d'Arenberg fort in Boussa during 1895 is a clear index to the importance which both parties of the dispute attached to the question of the control of the lower Niger. The creation of the Fort d'Arenberg revealed, as well, the adaptability of the men who led the Third Republic.[12]

Faced with difficulties which the Niger Company created to discourage navigation on the Niger, Hanotaux and Delcassé, without abandoning the diplomatic and legal fight to have free navigation enforced, found another way to reach the disputed territories on the right bank of the river. The new route, a back door to the Borgu and Boussa, started at the coast, went north through the Dahomean "corridor" to the ninth parallel, then turned sharply east toward the Niger. This was the approach used by Major Georges Joseph Toutée on his way to the point facing Badjibo where he created Fort d'Arenberg. This was the very expedition which Hanotaux, who was still willing to work for diplomatic solutions, had opposed until overruled by his own government in November 1894.[13]

Toutée was stranded at his new station for several weeks while a diplomatic uproar about his presence in territories claimed by the British raged between Paris and London. Although Toutée was recalled, France did not admit that this was done in recognition of British sovereignty. That Fort d'Arenberg had been abandoned, Lebon argued in 1897, had nothing to do with respective rights over the region. Hanotaux transmitted this interpretation of the facts to the British, adding that Fort d'Arenberg had been evacuated because it was in disputed territory about which negotiations were taking place. When the British occupied Fort d'Arenberg, the French protested, insisting on their own rights, and blamed the British for acting in a manner that might have an adverse effect on West African talks then under way.[14] The French particularly denied an assertion advanced by the president of the Niger Company who claimed that Fort d'Arenberg had been evacuated because ordered by a foreign minister who recognized British rights over Boussa.[15] Not even this could be admitted.

Back in Europe and long before the Anglo-French argument about Fort d'Arenberg was settled, Toutée was preparing a brief on the freedom of navigation on the Niger. After a careful study, which included British documents, Toutée concluded: even French warships were allowed to sail on the Niger, and Great Britain could not contest their right seriously since she herself sent gunboats on the exclusively Portuguese waters of the lower Zambezi River. In question was a new regulation of Niger navigation which the Niger Company was attempting to impose on all. The proposal, Toutée concluded, had only one article which was in accord with "l'acte général de Berlin." [16] Meanwhile the dispute about the territories on the left bank of the Niger raged on, the British having replaced the French expeditionary corps led by Toutée at d'Arenberg with troops of their own.

Though the British occupied Fort d'Arenberg and Boussa, they did not immediately secure their claim to the whole of the Borgu by effective occupation. Since Borgu was north of the ninth parallel where Anglo-French territorial delimitations in the area had stopped, the French considered it land to be claimed by effective possession. France certainly meant to be in contest for these areas, and quickly recovered from the withdrawal of Toutée by sending Lt. Henri-Etienne Bretonnet. Bretonnet's orders involved sailing down the Niger from Ilo to Roufia, a city some eighty kilometers above Boussa, which he was to occupy. But he was absolutely not to enter Boussa. Finding no sign of British authority, Bretonnet occupied Boussa. The British protested to the ill-informed Hanotaux, who questioned his colleague at the Colonial Ministry. Lebon who had received reports from Bretonnet and from the active governor of Dahomey, Marie-Paul-Victor Ballot, who was Bretonnet's immediate chief, met Hanotaux's request for information with a battery of arguments in favor of the existing French occupation of Boussa. Though somewhat befuddled, Hanotaux was left with no choice but to defend the new *fait accompli*. An earlier request for information about the Bretonnet mission had resulted in a communication informing Hanotaux that the colonial ministry knew nothing about the whereabouts of the mission, the roads back to Dahomey having been cut off by Baribas who were up in arms.[17]

Faced with what they considered a violation of their own territory, the British arrested Bretonnet's messengers who, unable to stay north of the ninth parallel because of the Baribas, cut through Lagos on their way to Dahomey. Justifying the arrests and the confiscation of mail, the British claimed Bretonnet was not only operating on their land but had attacked natives under British protection. The French countered with arguments based on the thesis that territories which lay north of the ninth parallel and on the right bank of the Niger had never been recognized as a British sphere of influence. British authority was not effective in the sense required by the Berlin Act.[18] Until negotiations settled the problems, competition led to numerous incidents and near armed clashes between opposing European missions.

Negotiations between France and Great Britain began in February 1896 in accordance with article five of the Siam treaty of January 15 of the same year.[19] But the beginning of negotiations did not lead to an end of competition between expeditions representing France, Germany, and Great Britain in West Africa. The French had Toutée, Bretonnet, Ballot, and half a dozen other colonial officers and officials heading expeditions in the Niger bend, along the Say-Baruwa line, and in other parts of Africa. The Niger Company had its own expedition against the protected Ilorin people; Chamberlain was beginning to think about the creation of the West African Frontier Force. The Germans also had explorers active in West Africa during the 1890s. All were making treaties with local chiefs and kinglets, and the treaties they made complicated a confused political geography. The treaties represented as well an accumulation of arguments and guarantees to serve in a great diplomatic negotiation which was to put a finishing touch to the partition of Africa among European powers. When the Anglo-French Niger Commission resumed its sessions in February 1896 the great final partition began.

Hanotaux was out of office so Marcellin Berthelot presided over French policy. Though he was willing enough to come to terms with the British, Berthelot was ill-informed about diplomacy particularly about African affairs. Moreover, personal problems kept him away from the Quai d'Orsay. When in March 1896 London announced its decision to send an expedition to Dongola, Berthelot's blustering opposition created a crisis which nearly ended in a diplomatic break. The Niger Commission, which had convened in February 1896, quit its deliberations indefinitely. Shortly after, Bourgeois assumed the responsibilities of the Foreign Ministry. He attempted to handle the problem in a more tactful manner than had his predecessor. But the Premier was unsuccessful, the Chamber of Deputies voting the Radical Government out of power on April 23, 1896.[20]

Hanotaux returned to the Quai d'Orsay, this time in the Méline government. He inherited a new phase in the Egyptian question which had recently been aggravated by an Anglo-French dispute about the financing of the Dongola venture. The British wanted to pay for it with Egyptian funds, and for this purpose, they obtained a majority vote in the Egyptian Debt Commission. The French, supported by their Russian allies, maintained that a unanimous vote would have been required to legalize the transfer of funds from the Caisse which the British made, and brought their case before an international tribunal. The court sustaining the French thesis, the British loaned the Egyptian government the money required to repay the illegally borrowed sum and cut discussion short. For a time it was impossible to reopen the deliberations of the Niger Commission, the affairs of eastern Europe, as well as the Dongola expedition, commanding the attention of European diplomats throughout 1896.[21]

For a time the British attempted to tie up the Tunisian and Egyptian questions in the way the Madagascar and Zanzibar questions had been equated. The British would allow France a completely free hand in Tunisia if Paris would renounce all French claims in Egypt. Hanotaux vehemently refused discussion on such grounds. Tunisia was already in French hands, legally and effectively. The French claimed that although British control of Egypt was also effective, it was illegal. Tunisia could not be considered as a compensation for the position France had lost in Egypt. Yet Hanotaux wanted to raise the Egyptian question and he apparently tried to do so in connection with the Anglo-French diplomatic discussions on West Africa.[22] A more dangerous reopening of the Egyptian question was already under way in June 1896, with Marchand about to undertake his expedition to the Nile.

Hanotaux did not order the Marchand expedition. He had expended much energy throughout his earlier tenure of office at the Quai d'Orsay to hold back the expedition while he attempted to solve the question diplomatically. But while Hanotaux was out of office, Berthelot, who was not a professional diplomat, nor as careful a man as his predecessor, ordered Marchand to proceed. Back in office, Hanotaux did not insist on a cancellation of the Congo-Nile mission or the recall of Marchand. But he did modify the character of the mission which henceforth was absolutely not to consider military conquest. What the political character of the mission might be, remained undecided. In any case, the British could not be told about a policy which was clearly intended to counter a British advance into the same area. The Marchand expedition contributed to the foreign minister's growing reputation as an Anglophobe.[23]

Hanotaux denied the anglophobia ascribed to him. He protested that he tried to calm colonial enthusiasts and limit the objectives of his government's missions throughout Africa. In his apologia, a book written soon after he was ousted from the Quai d'Orsay in 1898, Hanotaux claimed that the Méline cabinet always tried to take up again the threads of talks that were always broken, the threads of the "African negotiations." [24] With so many points of disagreement existing between France and Great Brit-

ain, it was simply too difficult to negotiate all at once. As a member of
the Méline government, he resolved the Madagascar question first; then he
negotiated about Tunisia, and only when a Tunisian settlement was in
sight, did he agree to take up West African affairs. He would have liked
talks about the upper Nile and Egypt, and he thought West Africa could
furnish him concessions to offer Great Britain in exchange for a recognition
of the territorial status he wanted in the Sudan. But since this was impossible, he resolved to strengthen his diplomatic hand by agreeing to have
Marchand plant a French flag at Fashoda. The expedition was a trump
card Hanotaux had to be used after the failure of talks. The Marchand
mission was an accepted instrument of Hanotaux's African policy.[25] Yet
that potentially provocative instrument did not necessarily reflect anglophobia on Hanotaux's part.

After Hanotaux's masterful diplomatic work in the fall of 1894 failed,
however, he seems to have been somewhat embittered against the British.
More than the British, however, he blamed his own president, Casimir-
Périer, and his colleague at the Colonial Ministry, Delcassé, "who re-
proached me for having not obtained all of Egypt." [26] Also, he never quite
accepted German diplomatic help in the way he had during his first weeks
in office. The Germans had dropped his case about the Anglo-Congolese
treaty of May 12, 1894, as soon as they had achieved their own ends, and
Hanotaux remembered. Added to his own failure vis-à-vis the British on
West African questions was that of Berthelot who agreed to a resumption
of the Niger Commission sessions in February 1896. These deliberations
had quickly bogged down in a morass of technical discussions about the
relative merits of French and English treaties with native rulers in the
Niger bend. After two weeks the talks had broken down, thus creating
more Anglo-French ill-feeling instead of leading to a settlement. Hanotaux refused to have talks break down again, which would perhaps have
a disastrous effect on Anglo-French relations; he therefore hesitated to
begin negotiating anew, at least until the spring of 1897. [27]

In April 1896 the British offered concessions in West Africa. Salisbury
faced embarrassing situations in the Sudan as well as in South Africa where
the Jameson raid had led to an Anglo-German diplomatic incident and
much ill-feeling. Hanotaux, momentarily in a strong bargaining position,
asked for more. The German government had approached Hanotaux's
predecessor to ask if he would join in a guarantee of the *status quo* with
respect to the Boer Republic. Not vitally interested in this area the French
had answered by asking if the Germans were ready to give a *quid pro quo*.
Would they support France in Egypt? Before taking office in 1894 Hano-

taux had negotiated a delimitation of Cameroun with German representatives, and cooperation seemed possible. The Wilhelmstrasse wouldn't support France in Egypt, and the proposed Franco-German colonial alliance was dropped. But the British who might still be embarrassed in South Africa made their own bid to avoid French interference. With the knowledge that both Germany and Great Britain were bidding for the support of France, to ask for more than was offered seemed safe enough; Hanotaux was not in a hurry to plunge into West African negotiations anyway. When Berlin made its offer once more, one year after the Jameson raid, Hanotaux's reaction was the same as to the first Wilhelmstrasse proposal on South Africa.[28]

By spring of 1897 there was a somewhat greater willingness to resume negotiation. Salisbury had maintained his conciliatory attitude toward France with respect to West African affairs. On the French side Hanotaux was becoming aware of Chamberlain's growing influence and knew that the British colonial secretary was unwilling to make concessions to France. But the French foreign minister still had to cope with pressure from his colonialist colleagues. Lebon, for example, urged him to repeat protests about the British occupation of Fort d'Arenberg lest silence be interpreted as approval. Hanotaux agreed. When Geoffray reported that both Salisbury and Sanderson had told him that Badjibo and Fort d'Arenberg were occupied by British contingents, Hanotaux had reacted with "one must protest, negotiations are under way!" Then, Salisbury's assurances that a Niger Company expedition being prepared would not go into the disputed areas proved unsatisfactory. Indeed, the British foreign secretary also insisted that Great Britain had a right to go north of the ninth parallel of north latitude. Hanotaux continued to protest and raise demands, leading Chamberlain to conclude that the French were advancing preposterous claims only to back down later on, and thereby to get a much larger slice than was legitimate.[29]

Chamberlain was just beginning to make his influence felt in West African affairs.[30] Ready to fight the French in this area, particularly over Boussa, which he despaired of securing through negotiations, he was opposed by other members of Salisbury's cabinet. Men such as Lord Goschen and Sir Michael Edward Hicks Beach, for example, were ready to make considerable sacrifices in order to reach an Anglo-French settlement in Africa. But the moderates were forced to make concessions to Chamberlain, agreeing first to send Sir Frederick Lugard into contested areas, and, eventually, to permit the creation of the West African Frontier Force. The activities of Lugard, who was to direct the W.A.F.F., and of Sir George

Taubman Goldie, both in the hinterland of Lagos, disturbed the French. Lugard was hated in French colonial circles because of his part in the expulsion of French Roman Catholic missionaries from Uganda in 1894. The same Frenchmen disliked Goldie because of his systematic opposition to the French in West Africa throughout the 1890s. The Quai d'Orsay questioned the sincerity of the British offers to negotiate since London was simultaneously sending antagonists of France into the territories in question.[31]

The Quai d'Orsay was undoubtedly aware of the creation of the W.A.F.F. well before it was actually put on foot in West Africa. Its very appearance must have seemed a belligerent political move.[32] The French understood that the time in which to reach a settlement with the British was quickly running out. Goldie and Lugard were in West Africa, where they were backed by a military body such as the W.A.F.F. which would, in terms of power, soon put Great Britain on as strong a footing as the French in the area. The preponderance of force which France had enjoyed through 1895 was passing as the British abandoned their policy of trusting merchants to forward and protect imperial claims in the Niger regions. There was even talk of withdrawing the charter of the Niger Company and of making her territories a colony.[33] Hanotaux wished to begin negotiations before it was too late. There was a note of urgency in the French foreign minister's instructions to his ambassador in London whenever the subject of negotiations about the Niger came up. In October 1897 the Niger Commission resumed once more its periodic sessions.[34]

Toward
The Anglo-French Convention
of June 14, 1898

Chapter 9

In the spring of 1897 Salisbury and Hanotaux met in Paris. Though the
principles which were to serve as the basis for talks about the Niger were
agreed upon in this meeting, seven months would pass before the actual
negotiations on the technical bases of a possible convention were under-
taken, and it would take a total of fifteen months to reach an agreement.
The delay was not due to ill will; both men emerged from their high level
discussion with mutual admiration for the other's abilities and duly impressed with each other's will to find a solution to Anglo-French differences.[1] The delay was caused by the very complex situation which had
developed in West Africa, and by the difficulty of compromising on seem-
ingly irreducible and contradictory claims. Also the partition of West
Africa was not solely an Anglo-French problem. The Germans also wanted
access to the navigable lower Niger River, and though their claims in the
Niger bend were not as strong as those of Great Britain or France, they
did have claims which the others could not ignore.

The Wilhelmstrasse approached Hanotaux about free navigation and
trade on the Niger early in his first tenure at the Quai d'Orsay. Thereafter, Franco-German negotiations about West African problems usually
paralleled Anglo-French talks about the same area. Well disposed toward
Berlin at first, Hanotaux had been inclined to combine French diplomacy
with that of Germany to oppose new rules about Niger navigation which
the Niger Company was attempting to introduce and enforce. But pressure from his colleague at the Ministry of Colonies, Delcassé, who did not
like the source of information through which the Niger Company's plans
had reached France, and the failure of Germany to support France in the
Congo cooled what might have been cordial relations. Wild demands put
forward by German colonialists began to antagonize Hanotaux. If the
proposals and claims of the *Kölnische Zeitung* had been accepted, Togo
would have dominated all of the Dahomean hinterland and given the
German colony an access to the Niger. Such a settlement would have re-

duced the French colony to an awkward and isolated strip of territory running south to north then west to east and never more than one hundred kilometers wide. To the French such a solution was clearly unacceptable, even though the Germans agreed to draw frontiers which would give Dahomey access to the lower Niger. It would have left Dahomey in a poor strategic position and isolated from the rest of the French empire. The proposal was never brought forward in serious diplomatic talks, though a Niger access for Togo was discussed.[2]

Hanotaux was at times willing to explore the possibility of giving Togo a Niger access. But he always considered that such an eventuality would represent a French concession, for which the Germans would have to make a high bid. In considering such rather improbable possibilities, the French foreign minister was apparently thinking in terms of using German claims against the British. Hanotaux was never impressed by the German claims on the Niger; he never considered them a threat to French plans in the area. The French occupied Nikki before the Germans could do so.[3] French policy was aimed at uniting all African colonies, except Madagascar, around Lake Chad. The policy would have been spoiled if the Germans had been permitted to gain a Niger access. During the summer of 1897 Lebon suggested delaying talks with Great Britain until Franco-German negotiators completed the Dahomey-Togo delimitation. Hanotaux had objected that such a move might seriously threaten Anglo-French talks about the Niger, and Lebon dropped his plan.[4] Now Hanotaux seemed eager to get Anglo-French Niger negotiations under way. He realized, no doubt, that only the British could concede an access to the Niger that would be safe and that, in any case, only the British could keep France from reaching the navigable Niger. The importance of a Niger access involved the possibility of draining trade through some easy water communication from the vast central African domain expected to fall to France.

The claim advanced by the *Kölnische Zeitung* for Togo—a claim which would have cut off the hinterlands of Dahomey and of Lagos—seemed incongruous since it was not based on acquired rights or local might. But in the scramble for West Africa the German colonialists' dream was no worse than those of their rivals. A second and almost comic proposal was advanced before the Anglo-French Niger Commission in February 1896 by Gustave Binger, a leading French colonialist who was governor of the Ivory Coast. Willing to concede Nikki to the British but not Boussa and the area around Fort d'Arenberg, Binger sketched two maps which embodied his views. Dahomey took on a strange shape and Nikki appeared as if it were a cancerous growth from Lagos or from Nigeria. A third proposal said to have been made by the British during the same period conceded Nikki to France but denied Dahomey an access on the Niger below the Boussa cataracts. Strangely enough, the British proposal (supposedly copied from an original document) represented a settlement which would have been acceptable to France in 1894. But by 1897 to secure an access to the lower Niger had become a cardinal point of French colonial plans.[5]

The access to the Niger above the Boussa cataracts was useless to the French. But no country based her claims on considerations for the objectives of other nations. Claims were advanced which were usually much greater than could legitimately be achieved. Chamberlain complained that French claims were preposterous, and was only half convinced when Salisbury retorted that with the exception of the Boussa claim, British claims were quite shaky. Completely forgotten in Franco-German and Anglo-French negotiations were the rights of West African tribes to stay united. What the claims failed to do, the final delimitations did not correct. Between Europeans strategic considerations were more important than concessions to existing social and political units.[6]

Franco-German delimitations between Dahomey and Togo were agreed upon in July 1897 and marked on the ground soon thereafter. Between Paris and Berlin discussion about the navigation of the Niger and about a possible Niger access for Togo was passed over and forgotten. Understandably, Germany lost interest in these questions. Togoland had become completely enclosed while Dahomey had maintained unlimited access to the Niger. An Anglo-French dispute began over this access.[7]

By now Hanotaux was in a hurry to reach a West African settlement with the British. He was, however, hard pressed by Colonial Minister André Lebon who wanted to wait on the results of French expeditions that were still in the field. Although he followed Lebon's wishes, Hanotaux indicated that he feared the consequences of delay. Downing Street also hesitated, refusing to engage in the final round of talks until Lugard could report the results of his latest mission and before the French had answered a new protest about Boussa. Bretonnet reoccupied Boussa for France in 1897. Since the British asked for a delay in order to ascertain the results of Lugard's mission, Hanotaux was able to blame the British for procrastinating, and thereby threatening the negotiations.[8] Meanwhile, he waited for his own reports from Bretonnet and Baud, leaders of two French missions in the Niger bend during late 1897 and early 1898. In October 1897 Lugard was back in Europe and the French had received reports from their representatives. It was therefore agreed that the negotiations should resume, and the first renewed session of the Niger Commission was held before the end of the month. The business of the commissioners included technical discussions of treaties, local customs, geography, and principles put down by Hanotaux and Salisbury during their March meeting and elaborated upon in the intervening months.

The negotiations advanced at a snail's pace. Not only were French and British claims contradictory, the problem was further complicated by ignorance of the geography of West Africa. This lack of knowledge was reflected in disputes such as that involving the 1896 edition of Sir Edward Herstlet's *The Map of Africa According to Treaties*. Ambassador de Courcel complained that the British map showed all of the Bahr-el-Ghazal as being under the control of Great Britain. French holdings in the Ubangi and Chari basins were shown as no more than small strips of territory while French advances toward Lake Chad were shown as stopping some one hundred kilometers from the actual advances.[9]

On the first day the Niger Commission met, Hanotaux wrote Lebon that Salisbury was eager to settle the whole Niger business, but that he was being pushed by Chamberlain. Chamberlain, Hanotaux thought, demanded much more than he expected and was unwilling to pay a high price for a settlement. With Chamberlain thinking much the same about Hanotaux's aims, it was a difficult business for the commissioners to find solutions that would please both. Herstlet's maps showed British demands in West Africa; a map by the French marine infantry lieutenant, Lt. Spick, "corrected" accomplished delimitations to suit French designs in the same area. This had drawn a complaint from Salisbury, who wrote that the Dahomey-Lagos frontier, though settled to the ninth parallel of north latitude, stopped at latitude 8°. Also, various important centers appeared on Spick's map as being independent, though under British control, or at wrong latitudes.[10]

Asked to comment on the British complaint about the map drawn by Spick, Lebon simply noted that left with the choice between Lugard's and Toutée's astronomical readings for certain centers, he had seen no reason to accept Lugard's. The centers Spick had pictured as independent, though claimed by the British, were found to be abolutely independent by all French visitors. One point of contention involved the African village of Bouna; this settlement was effectively occupied by the British, but claimed by the French. Hanotaux himself stoutly defended this French claim. Though Bouna was incorrectly placed in Spick's map, it was recognized as falling under French domination in a map which, though incorrect, was an integral part of the Anglo-French frontier arrangement of July 12, 1893.[11]

The spirit which led to arguments such as those involving the Herstlet and Spick maps, and which had led to the drawing of such maps, inevitably left a mark on the Niger Commission's debates. Arguments in Europe were paralleled and supported by the activities of expeditions throughout West Africa. British military strength was quickly being brought up to par with the dominant French. There were, inevitably, numerous incidents which also influenced negotiations. But at last, there were negotiations.

On October 29, 1897, the first session of the Niger Commission was held. A procedural discussion led to decisions to have the talks kept secret and to consider as binding nothing that was not written. Then a review of work previously done by the commission, whose sessions had so often been suspended, led to further decisions to skip examinations of respective titles and to proceed with a search for a compromise delimitation on which it would be possible to agree.[12]

The decision to skip the examination of titles proved to be futile optimism. The second session, held on November 2, 1897, was entirely devoted to technical examinations of treaties. The third meeting, held a week later, yielded no more than renewed enunciations of differing interpretations of frontiers as these might be drawn according to previous Anglo-French treaties. The fourth session was an interesting review of the Boussa question, largely about recent events but devoid of new elements. Officers who had been on missions in West Africa were called in to answer questions about their experiences and about African customs. Voulet was a Frenchman called in, while Henderson was to represent British activists. By the end of December 1897 the geographical positions of disputed centers were discussed though agreement was still not to be found.[13]

During the twelfth session the eventuality of a French evacuation of Boussa, which they had reoccupied early in 1897, was discussed. Though Hanotaux reacted with a "haut le corps" on hearing about this, he did not forbid the continuation of the discussion begun by the French delegates. Indeed, in the backstage negotiations with his own colleague at the Colonial Office in Paris, Hanotaux had insisted that the delegates should be granted as much power as possible. Now he instructed the delegates to insist on the conciliatory nature of such a potential concession. The least that could be accepted in return would be some secure point on the navigable Niger around the ninth parallel of latitude north.[14]

Throughout the spring of 1898 delegates to the Anglo-French Niger Commission were again involved in technical discussions about the relative merits of their respective treaties. Was the African signer or marker of a given treaty really a king? Was a treaty a protectorate treaty through which both sides gained or a scrap of paper signed by an African who had not understood the meaning of the contract? These were some of the questions discussed by the commissioners. For a time, agreement was an illusory objective as Hanotaux demanded much more than Salisbury, who had to cooperate with Chamberlain, could concede. Hanotaux also wanted to negotiate about the Sudan; to convince him that there would be no such negotiation was a difficult task.[15] During the spring of 1898 however, Hanotaux became worried. The press on both sides of the channel threatened to burst into polemics over West Africa which might have undesirable effects on the negotiations. Another danger sign was the launching of the West African Frontier Force in February 1898. Concessions would become harder to make or receive. Faced with these dangers and well aware that Marchand's presence at Fashoda would create a critical diplomatic crisis, Hanotaux eased French demands in the west and a settlement about this area was quickly completed.[16]

When the Anglo-French West African convention of June 14, 1898, was signed in Paris, French and British troops were facing each other in many parts of the Niger bend. Officers on both sides had, of course, received strict orders not to fight and always to address opponents in diplomatic terms. But the danger of conflict had been imminent and the territorial situation had become very complex. The practice of creating numerous small posts around important centers which one's opponent had managed to occupy first only enhanced the confusion. The French had practiced this policy all along. In the spring of 1898 the British did the same, creating concern in Paris, and perhaps helping to force Hanotaux to back down.[17] The June convention limited the probability of clashes, though these were not eliminated from the realm of the possible until actual delimitations took place somewhat later. Unfortunately, no concession was found for the Sudan where Anglo-French rivalry remained intense and where the Fashoda crisis was about to erupt.

An important part of the June 14, 1898, settlement dealt with the territorial possessions of France and Great Britain around Lake Chad; it also touched on the question of the Say-Baruwa line agreed upon in principle in the 1890 agreement about the Nigerian hinterland. The French claimed the northern and eastern shores of Lake Chad, a claim the British were willing to concede. Raising no objection, however, the British Foreign Office realized that possession of these areas around the lake would give France an easy access to the Nile. As the British ambassador in Paris put it, the acceptance of French claims on the Chad should not "be understood to admit that any other European Power than Great Britain has any claim to occupy any part of the valley of the Nile." To substantiate the British claim, Monson reminded Hanotaux of the Grey 1895 declaration which had stated that a French advance on the Nile would be considered an "unfriendly act." Hanotaux, of course, never accepted the policy implied in the Grey declaration. Reminded about this declaration, Hanotaux denied its asserted validity. In his answer to Monson, he reviewed the debate. Unfortunately, nothing was done, and each side clung to its own theories.[18]

Throughout the debate about West Africa the French had several important objectives. First, the Quai d'Orsay wanted to rectify to its own advantage what it considered excessive concessions made in favor of Great Britain in 1890. The French therefore refused to accept the British thesis that by extension the 1890 agreement should prolong the Lagos-Dahomey frontier from its terminal point on the ninth degree of latitude north to Say. Elements of the same Anglo-French difference included opposing theories about the rights of powers occupying territories along the coast with respect to the areas in the hinterlands. The British thought claims backed by treaties were enough. The French countered that claimed territories had to be effectively occupied. Representatives of Paris soon put the French claim into practice, sending missions to occupy Boussa, Say, and many other centers in disputed areas. Having carefully reconsidered the 1890 agreement, the Quai d'Orsay became convinced that it could legitimately occupy such points. Downing Street, of course, combatted the French interpretations of past agreements. The most important competition took place in the Niger bend where the British in 1898 practiced the same policy of strength and occupation that France had practiced with few interruptions from late 1895 until 1898.[19] In the Niger bend the French wanted territorial control of some point on the lower navigable portion of the Niger below the Boussa rapids. The British were convinced they had a perfectly good case about Boussa and doggedly held to what they considered their own.

The British, with Salisbury as prime minister and foreign secretary, were willing enough to let the French use the Niger freely and would even have accepted a compromise which would have granted the French the right to cross British territories so that they might avail themselves of free navigation of the Niger. But London was unwilling to have armed French personnel cross these same British territories.[20] To be able to reach its Dahomean hinterland and more central African regions easily with military effectives was, of course, the reason why the French wanted territorial control of some portion of the lower Niger. This control they did not get, though in other respects, the French received by far the largest portion of disputed territories.

The Convention of June 14, 1898,[21] gave France Nikki and a large area east of Say on the left bank of the Niger. Say, of course, was supposed to be the starting point of the dividing line which was to go to Baruwa, south of which all territories were to be dominated by the British. That France got Say and territories one hundred kilometers east of that center must be accounted a great success for the Quai d'Orsay. The French also took the Mossi and Gourma kingdoms over which the British had had some claims. Thereby, the British Gold Coast went the way of German Togo and became another enclave in a vastness of French territories.

In the Niger bend, however, the French were frustrated. They did not get territorial control of areas on the right bank of the Niger below the Boussa rapids. Although the British granted France a lease on two four-hundred-meter-long properties on the right bank of the Niger (one being in the Niger estuary, the other between Leaba and Badjibo below Boussa), the French could not reach the lower Niger without crossing foreign territories. French colonialists criticized Hanotaux rather bitterly on this point, and generally complained that British concessions had been niggardly.[22] Though French colonialists demurred, the Anglo-French Convention of June 14, 1898, was a masterly diplomatic accomplishment, one of which Hanotaux was rightfully proud.

Conclusion

Chapter 10

Gabriel Hanotaux was foreign minister of France from May 30, 1894 to
November 1, 1895, and again from April 29, 1896 to June 15, 1898. A historian, he turned to the colonial history of his nation for inspiration and
often based his African policies on the past. In attempting to enforce what
he considered to be the imperial rights of France, he used legal and historical precedents effectively. Above all else, he was an opportunist who
always operated pragmatically. His primary objective was to unite all
French holdings in Africa into a huge continuous empire. Ferry, Hanotaux believed, had laid the foundation for such a program. It was Hanotaux's self-appointed task to complete the work of earlier colonialists. Although his policies were not original, the methods he used to achieve his
ends were ingenious; therein lay his principal contribution.

As master of the Quai d'Orsay Hanotaux became immediately involved
in diplomatic conflicts concerning Africa. The Moroccan question was
the first to arise, precipitated by the death of the Sultan at a time when
France was unprepared. Hanotaux sent a vice-consul to Fez in a unprecedented move that strengthened the French position in Morocco; he then
secured an agreement by the other European powers to shelve Moroccan
conflicts. This status quo was retained until France was able to secure the
largest share of Morocco for herself.

The Congo and the East African issues erupted next. The British had
made treaties with the Congo Free State and Italy that threatened French
designs in Central Africa. On the Congo question Hanotaux intimidated
the weaker party to the Anglo-Congolese treaty and obtained a cancellation of clauses that would have blocked the French access to the Upper
Nile Valley. In East Africa, the effect of the Anglo-Italian treaty was nullified when Emperor Menelik, using weapons and ammunition provided by
the French, routed the Italians at Adowa.

The Madagascar question presented still another colonial problem to
test Hanotaux's abilities. Here, as later in Tunisia, Hanotaux completed
the work of earlier colonialists. He rid these two countries of "foreign"
interference and brought them effectively under the sway of France. Madagascar became a French colony when a proposal advanced by Hanotaux

was passed into law in May 1896. He would have preferred to retain for the great African island the status of a protectorate, but the Radical politicians who were in power during Hanotaux's short absence from the Quai d'Orsay (November 1, 1895–April 29, 1896), had made his original program impossible. On the Tunisian question Hanotaux had his way. He negotiated twelve conventions with European powers that cancelled existing capitulations treaties and left France to deal freely with the protectorate. The deputies ratified Hanotaux's diplomatic success and Tunisia, unlike Madagascar which passed to the Colonial Ministry, continued to be administered by the Quai d'Orsay.

There remained the Sudan, an extension of the Egyptian question. This was, in a way, the French Alsace-Lorraine of Africa, a question overladen with conflicts of national pride. Throughout his forty-four months in office Hanotaux was involved in Anglo-French differences and arguments about the Sudan. In 1895 an agreement carefully composed by Hanotaux and Phipps during the preceding year was rejected by their respective governments. Failing to secure approval for renewed talks on the Sudan, Hanotaux agreed to negotiate Anglo-French differences about West Africa. But the unspoken question of the Sudan and Upper Nile Valley loomed threateningly over the West African talks. Indeed, both parties to these negotiations considered West African problems in relation to the Sudan question which was thought to be far more important. In the end, Hanotaux's greatest diplomatic and colonial success was marred by a disaster: the Franco-British West African agreement of June 14, 1898, was partially cancelled by the Fashoda crisis two months later. Yet the French domain in Africa was unified by the time Hanotaux retired from the Foreign Ministry.

Franco-Italian agreement about Tunisia soon led to a rapprochement between the two powers. The improvement in Franco-Spanish relations had begun with Hanotaux's understanding on Morocco. Only the Fashoda crisis prevented a continuation of Hanotaux's drive to eliminate Franco-British colonial differences, a policy intended to lead to friendlier diplomatic relations between France and Great Britain. Until 1902 Delcassé did not work for an Anglo-French entente. Even then it was Hanotaux who had laid the foundations upon which Delcassé built; it was Hanotaux who had eliminated colonial disputes in Morocco, Madagascar, Tunisia, and West Africa.

Because of the Fashoda crisis Hanotaux has been accused of Anglophobia. Actually, he was far less anti-British than his successor, Delcassé. During his four years at the Quai d'Orsay, Hanotaux moderated the anti-British demands of such colonialists as Delcassé and Eugène Etienne.[1] The latter was the recognized leader of the *groupe coloniale*, of the imperial activists in and around the French government who usually were dissatisfied because of Hanotaux's moderation. After the Fashoda incident, these imperialists changed their mind: instead of continuing on an aggressive course, they wished to give up French demands in Egypt in return for a British promise to let France have a free hand in Morocco.[2] In a way, Delcassé's relations with his fellow imperialist Hanotaux reflected this changing attitude. As Minister of Colonies, Delcassé pushed Hanotaux to more aggressive colonial policies. After 1898 when Delcassé became foreign minister, Hanotaux urged his replacement to a more aggressive policy. Eventually, Etienne and his group convinced Delcassé to carry into policy the Egypt for Morocco barter which in turn became the basis of the talks that eventually led to the entente cordiale. All other African differences had been settled by Hanotaux by the middle of June 1898.

The Egyptian question was, during Hanotaux's tenure at the Quai d'Orsay, the one problem that was never mentioned in diplomatic talks, but that was always on everyone's mind. It was the one question Hanotaux did not solve. That he dared challenge the British on this question, even though he did not himself order the Fashoda expedition, must remain the biggest blot on Hanotaux's career at the Quai d'Orsay. In any colonial war the French could not compete with the British because of the latter's domination of the seas, including the Mediterranean Sea. British superiority was particularly noticeable in 1895 during the Madagascar crisis, when Hanotaux worried lest a British declaration of neutrality deprive the expeditionary forces of the use of British bottoms for the transport of needed supplies.[3] Although he was in charge of French foreign policy and knew the dangers of an aggressive imperial policy, Hanotaux did not insist on the necessary moderation.

Hanotaux was forced out of office in the summer of 1898, and it is impossible to guess how he would have handled the Fashoda crisis, although he would probably have proceeded pragmatically. Delcassé did change his mind about African conflicts with Great Britain. Between 1894–95 and 1898, he became convinced that even with Russian help France could not win a naval war against England.[4] It was Hanotaux who had implemented the policy of confrontation. But he may have been too much of an opportunist. When he returned to the Quai d'Orsay in 1896 and found that the Radicals had changed his Madagascar policy, for example, he accepted the change; Hanotaux refused to fight on for his own system. Initially he fought against the policy which sent Marchand to Fashoda. But when he returned to the Foreign Ministry after the fall of the Bourgeois government, he did not insist on the recall of the Marchand expedition to the Upper Nile.[5] He displayed the same kind of attitude on internal questions. Although he was not at all convinced of Dreyfus' guilt, for example, Hanotaux did not become a dreyfusard.[6] Somehow, he wished that he could ignore the problem and thereby avoid embarrassing the government. He may also have toyed too long with the idea that the Germans might help France in Egypt. But he remained silent in November 1898 when challenged to say he would have sought German help against the British in Egypt. As for the Russians, he quickly lost faith in these allies and was actually referring to them as "traitors" in cabinet meetings by early 1898.[7]

In spite of what appears to have been glaring weaknesses in his African policies—France did not have the naval establishment to resist a decided British refusal or the solid diplomatic backing needed to fight them effectively on major issues such as the Egyptian question—Hanotaux did manage to unify practically all French territories in Africa. In the process, he eliminated a number of Anglo-French disputes, leaving only the Egyptian question to be solved by his successor. He did create the situation which enabled Delcassé in 1902 to begin negotiations for better relations between France and Great Britain.

On June 14, 1898, the very day Hanotaux signed the Anglo-French West African Agreement, politics gave Hanotaux back to history. Although he remained "available" (*en disponibilité*), Hanotaux was never again master of the Quai d'Orsay. Until he died in 1944, he wrote and edited historical studies, most of which were about the history of his own times. He also wrote many tracts demonstrating the virtues of colonial expansion. He waited for the day his country would again need his services in the Foreign Ministry. The call never came although he served as a member of the French delegations at Versailles and in the League of Nations.

Explanation to the Notes

For the documents from the *Archives de l'Ancien Ministère d'Outre-Mer*, a name followed by a Roman numeral identifies the file and the following Arabic numeral refers to the specific box used. Afrique VI, 129a is an example of a typical entry.

With reference to the documents found at the *Archives Nationales*, F^{80} refers to the Algerian collection while the number which immediately follows this refers to a particular box. Thus, F^{80}, 1283, is a typical example.

The documents of the *Archives Diplomatiques* are bound in volumes to which titles have been assigned. This presented no problem, the title followed by a volume number being given throughout. *Correspondance Politique: Maroc,* 70:38, is an example of a first entry. Late entries are abbreviated to *C.P.: Maroc,* 70:38.

Documents from the British Foreign Office are identified by file numbers such as F.O. 403 (which is the African file) followed by a slash (/) and a volume number.

Abbreviations for French documents:

FRANCE, ANCIEN MINISTÈRE DES COLONIES:

ABBREVIATION USED	FULL TITLE
Afrique III, 19a	*Correspondance Officielle: Afrique* (numbers that follow indicate particular files and boxes)
Madagascar 382 ^{1034}	*Correspondance Officielle: Madagascar* (_____._____)
Somalis 17	*Correspondance Officielle: Somalis* (one file number after title is a box number)

FRANCE, ARCHIVES DIPLOMATIQUES: (MINISTÈRE DES AFFAIRES ETRANGÈRES)

ABBREVIATION USED	FULL TITLE
Abyssinie 5	Mémoires et Documents: Afrique: Abyssinie.
C.P.: Angleterre	Correspondance Politique: Angleterre
C.P.: Belgique	Correspondance Politique: Belgique
C.P.: Espagne	Correspondance Politique: Espagne
C.P.: Italie	Correspondance Politique: Italie
C.P.: Maroc	Correspondance Politique: Maroc
C.P.: Angleterre: Aden (1885–1895)	Correspondance Politique: Angleterre: Aden (1885–1895)
Empire Britannique	Grande Bretagne, Possessions d'Outre-Mer: Empire Britannique: Dossier Général 1897–1901.
Grande Bretagne: 1897–1898	Grande Bretagne: Politique Etrangère, Relations avec la France: 1897–1898.

FRANCE, ARCHIVES NATIONALES

ABBREVIATION USED	FULL TITLE
F^{80}, 1684	F^{80} is the Algerian collection (the number that follows indicates particular boxes)

Abbreviations for foreign documents

F.O.	Great Britain, Foreign Office, *Confidential Prints* and *Diplomatic Correspondance* found at the Public Records Office in London.
J.C.	University of Birmingham, *The Joseph Chamberlain Papers*.

Abbreviations for printed documents

Archives diplomatiques	Renault, Louis, editor, *Archives diplomatiques: 1894–1898*.
Débats, députés	France, *Annales de la Chambre des députés, Débats parlementaires* (1894–1898)
Débats, Sénat	France, *Annales du Sénat, Débats parlementaires* (1894–1898)
D.D.F.	France, Ministère des Affaires Etrangères, *Documents diplomatiques français*, 1st series (1871–1901)
Documenti	Italy, Ministero Degli Affari Esteri, *I Documenti Diplomatici Italiani*, Terza Serie (1896–1907)

Mad.   France, Ministère des Affaires Etrangères, *Documents diplomatiques: l'affaire de Madagascar, 1885–1895* (Paris 1895)

State Papers   Great Britain, *British and Foreign State Papers,* 1889–1897

Tunisiens   France, Ministère des affaires Etrangères, *Documents diplomatiques: Révision des traités tunisiens, 1881–1897* (Paris 1897)

Notes

Chapter One

1. Baron Pierre de Coubertin, "The Chancellor of the French Republic—Gabriel Hanotaux," *The Review of Reviews*, 15 (1897), 546; M. Epstein, ed., *The Annual Register* (New Series; London, New York, and Toronto, 1945), p. 437; Franchet d'Esperey, "Du Directoire à la guerre de 1914," in Gabriel Hanotaux, ed., *Histoire de la nation française* 15 vols. (Paris, 1927), 8:471   *2.* Thomas M. Iiams, Jr., *Dreyfus Diplomatists and the Dual Alliance* (Geneva and Paris, 1962), p. 22.   *3.* Iiams, *Dreyfus Diplomatists and the Dual Alliance*, p. 20.   *4.* Vesta Sweitzer Vetter, "Gabriel Hanotaux" in Bernadotte E. Schmitt, ed., *Some Historians of Modern Europe* (Chicago, 1941), p. 173.   *5.* Stephen H. Roberts, *History of French Colonial Policy*, 2 vols. (London, 1929), 1:12–13.   *6.* Herbert Ingram Priestly, *France Overseas* (New York and London, 1938), p. 118; Louis Gillet, *Gabriel Hanotaux* (Paris, 1933), pp. 51–52; Albéric Neton, *Delcassé* (Paris, 1952), p. 132.   *7.* "M. Hanotaux," *The Fortnightly Review*, 69 (January to June 1898), 175–76.   *8.* Iiams, *Dreyfus Diplomatists and the Dual Alliance*, p. 22.   *9.* Ibid., pp. 23–24.

10. Gillet, *Gabriel Hanotaux*, p. 64.   *11.* "M. Hanotaux," *Fortnightly Review*, 69:177–180; Nath Imbert, ed., *Dictionnaire national des comtemporains* (Paris, 1939), 3:335; *Review of Reviews*, 15 (1897):545–46; Cardinal Dominique Ferrata, *Memoires*, 2nd ed. (Paris, 1922), p. 425.   *12.* *Fortnightly Review*, 61:177.   *13.* Gillet, *Hanotaux*, p. 110; *Who Was Who: 1941–1950* (London, 1952), p. 497.   *14.* See Monteil to Minister for Colonies, Paris, March 7, 1894, in Afrique III, 10 a, and "Convention franco-congolaise du 14 Aôut 1894," in *Revue Française* (September, 1894), p. 538.   *15.* Hanotaux, *Pour l'empire colonial* (Paris, 1933), 2:241, 245.   *16.* Jacques Stern, *The French Colonies Past and Present*, translated from the French by Norbert Guterman (New York, 1944), p. 22.

17. Sir Thomas Barclay, *Thirty Years* (Boston and New York, 1914), pp. 152–53; E. Bourgeois et G. Pagès, *Origines et résponsabilités de la grande guerre* (Paris, 1922), p. 246; A. F. Pribram, *England and the International Policy of European Great Powers* (Oxford, 1931), pp. 54–57.   *18.* Pierre Renouvin, "Introduction," in Ch.-A. Julien, J. Bruhat, et al., *Les politiques d'expansion imperialiste*, Colonies et empire, deuxième série; Etudes coloniales (Paris, 1949), 5:4; Charles Maurras, *De la paix de Francfort à la conference d'Algésiras* (Paris, 1909), p. 47 and Dimnet, *France Herself Again* (New York and London, 1914, p. 80. See also: Ch. V. Langlois, "Histoire" in Baillaud, Boutroux, Chailley et al., *Un demi-siècle de civilisation française* (Paris, 1916), p. 119.   *19.* William Langer, *European Alliances and Alignments*, (New York, 1931), pp. 297–98.

20. Gabriel Hanotaux, *Fachoda* (Paris, 1909), p. 57.   *21.* A.P.P. 5th Earl of Rosebery, *The Foreign Policy of Lord Rosebery* (London, 1901), pp. 71, 78; Langer, *The Diplomacy of Imperialism*, pp. 77–78; Giffen, *Fashoda* (Chicago, 1931), pp. 120–21.   *22.* A. J. P. Taylor, *The Struggle for Mastery in Europe, 1848–1918* (Oxford, 1954), p. 353.   *23.* Graham H. Stuart, *French Foreign Policy* (New York, 1921), pp. 12–13; Giffen, *Fashoda*, pp. 146–47.   *24.* Pierre Renouvin, *Le XIXᵉ siècle*, in *Histoire des relations internationales*, Pierre Renouvin, ed., 8 vols. (Paris, 1953–1957), 6:170–71.   *25.* A. J. P. Taylor, "Prelude to Fashoda: The Question of the Upper Nile, 1894–5," *English Historical Review*, 65 (1950), 80.   *26.* Ibid., and Hanotaux, *Fachoda*, pp. 90–91.   *27.* France, Ministère des Affaires Etrangères, *Documents Diplomatiques Française (1871–1914)*, 1st Series, Vol. 11, 1947, No. 286, p. 430; No. 335, p. 523; and No. 340, p. 530. Henceforth cited as *D.D.F.*   *28.* Gillet, *Hanotaux*, pp. 80, 84.

29. Hanotaux in "Carnets" as quoted in Iiams, *Dreyfus Diplomatists and the Dual Alliance*, pp. 24–25.   30. "Note du Ministre," Paris, June 2, 1894, *D.D.F.*, 11, 192–94. Compare this to Dufferin to Kimberley, Paris, June 7, 1894, F.O. 403/201, p. 85. Hanotaux exaggerated the role he played in the discussion.

Chapter Two

1. D'Aubigny to Hanotaux, June 10, 1894, France, *Archives diplomatiques, Correspondance politique: Maroc,* 70:38. Henceforth cited as *C.P.: Maroc.* Henri de la Martinière, *Souvenirs du Maroc* (Paris, 1919), p. 49.   2. See Baron von Marschall to Bernard von Bulow, January 13, 1895, E.T.S. Dugdale, ed.; *German Diplomatic Documents 1871– 1914,* 4 vols. (New York and London, 1929), 2:276–77; Henri Brunschwig, *L'expansion allemande outremer* (Paris, 1957), pp. 139–40, 146.   3. Mary Evelyn Townsend, *The Rise and Fall of Germany's Colonial Empire: 1884–1918* (New York, 1930), pp. 308– 9, and Melvin M. Knight, *Morocco as a French Economic Venture* (New York and London, 1937), p. 7.   4. Taylor, *The Struggle for Mastery*, pp. 404, 412; René Pinon, *L'empire de la Méditerranée,* 3rd ed. (Paris, 1912), p. 119; E.D. Morel, *Morocco in Diplomacy* (London, 1912), p. 3.   5. R. Robinson and J. Gallagher, *Africa and the Victorians* (New York, 1961), p. 95; Usborne, *The Conquest of Morocco,* p. 55. D'Aubigny to Hanotaux, July 10, 1894, *C.P.: Maroc,* 70:197–98.   6. Thomas Palamenghi-Crispi, *The Memoirs of Francesco Crispi,* trans., by Mary Prichard-Agnetti (London, 1914), p. 82; James Linus Glanville, *Italy's Relations with England,* (Baltimore, 1934), p. 27. 7. "The French in Africa," clipping from *The Observer,* n.d., annexed to D'Estournelle to Hanotaux, London, September 17, 1894, *C.P.: Angleterre,* 897:118.   8. François Charles-Roux, "La mort de Mouley Hassan" in *Revue d'Histoire diplomatique,* 69 (July–December, 1947), 193; De la Martinière, *Souvenirs du Maroc,* p. 49; Henri Terrasse, *Histoire du Maroc* (Casablanca, 1950), p. 381; Hanotaux to d'Aubigny, June 11, 1894, *C.P.: Maroc,* 70:39–40.   9. Hanotaux to Roustan, June 11, 1894, *C.P.: Espagne,* 924:194; Hanotaux to d'Aubigny, June 11, 1894, *C.P.: Maroc,* 70:39–40; "Avant propos," *D.D.F.,* 11:viii; Roustan to Hanotaux, June 11, 1894, *C.P.: Espagne,* 924:192, 197–99, 200.

10. Decrais to Hanotaux, London, June 12, 1894, *C.P.: Angleterre,* 824:152, and Hanotaux to Roustan, June 11, 1894, *C.P.: Espagne,* 924:201–3.   11. Hanotaux to Decrais, June 11, 1894, *C.P.: Angleterre,* 894:132; "Avant propos," *D.D.F.,* 11:viii. 12. Debidour, *Histoire diplomatique,* 1:280; Terrasse, *Histoire du Maroc,* 1:384–85; Hanotaux, *La paix latine,* pp. 45–47 et passim.   13. Hanotaux to d'Aubigny, June 11, 1894, *C.P.: Maroc,* 70:39–40; Hanotaux to Decrais, June 11, 1894, *C.P.: Angleterre,* 824:132; Jules Cambon, *Le gouvernement général de l'Algérie* (Paris and Algiers, 1918), p. 413.   14. Paul Leroy-Beaulieu, *De la colonisation chez les peuples modernes,* 3rd ed. (Paris, 1886), p. vii.   15. Hanotaux to Decrais, June 11, 1894, *C.P.: Angleterre,* 894:132; Hanotaux to d'Aubigny, June 11, 1894, *C.P.: Maroc,* 70:39–40. 16. Cambon, *Le gouvernement général de l'Algérie,* p. 413.   17. See Baron Von Marshall to Bernard Von Bulow, January 13, 1895, in Dugdale, *German Diplomatic Documents,* 2:276–77.   18. Hanotaux to d'Aubigny, June 11, 1894, *C.P.: Maroc,* 70:39–40. 19. Geneviève Tabouis, *The Life of Jules Cambon,* trans. from the French by C. F. Atkinson (London, 1938), pp. 46–47, and Marquis d'Ormesson, "Deux grandes figures de la diplomaties française: Paul et Jules Cambon," in *Revue d'histoire diplomatiques,* 57 (1943–45):33–71.

20. Charles-Roux, "La mort de Mouley Hassan," p. 191; Henri Brunschwig, *La colonisation française* (Paris, 1949), p. 235.   21. Tabouis, *The Life of Jules Cambon,* pp. 75–77; Cambon, *Le gouvernement général de l'Algérie,* pp. 412–14.   22. D'Aubigny to Hanotaux, July 24, 1894, *C.P.: Maroc,* 70:236–40. See also: Miège, *Le Maroc,* pp. 38– 39.   23. Gabriel Esquer, *Histoire de l'Algérie: 1830–1960* (Paris, 1960), pp. 44–45; Hanotaux to d'Aubigny, June 11, 1894, *C.P.: Maroc,* 70:39–40.   24. De la Martinière, *Souvenirs du Maroc,* p. 47; E. F. Cruickshank, *Morocco at the Parting of the Ways* (Phila-

delphia, 1935), p. xvii.   *25.* Cambon to Hanotaux, Paris, July 21, 1896, Archives Nationales, *F⁸⁰ 1684*, Dispatch 2057. Henceforth cited as *F⁸⁰*. See also Phipps to Kimberley, September 18, 1894, F.O. 413/22, p. 101. Documents from the British Foreign Office are henceforth cited as F.O. followed by a file number, a slash, and a volume number.
26. Roustan to Hanotaux, June 15, 1894, *C.P.: Espagne*, 924:223; D'Aubigny to Hanotaux, June 13, 1894, and June 14, 1894, *C.P.: Maroc*, 70:53–54, 61, 71.   *27.* D'Aubigny to Hanotaux, June 14, 1894, and June 17, 1894, and Hanotaux to d'Aubigny, June 16, 1894, *C.P.: Maroc*, 70:64–65, 68–69, 71.   *28.* Count Hatzfeldt to the German Foreign Office, June 12, 1894, Dugdale, *German Diplomatic Documents*, 2:314–15; Bernhard von Bulow to the German Foreign Office, Rome, June 17, 1894, Ibid, 2:318; Crispi, *Memoirs*, pp. 82–83.   *29.* D'Aubigny to Hanotaux, June 14, 1894, and Hanotaux-Mission française à Tanger, June 18, 1894, *C.P.: Maroc*, 70:64, 74.

30. D'Aubigny to Hanotaux, June 21, 1894, *C.P.: Maroc*, 70:115, 123–24.
31. Souhart (Chargé d'affaires) to Hanotaux, August 13, 1894, *C.P.: Maroc*, 70:304–308; Si Mohammed Gharnit to Her Majesty Queen Victoria, August 16, 1894, FO 413/22, pp. 68–69; Henri Cambon, *Histoire du Maroc* (Paris, 1952), pp. 93–94.   *32.* Ford to Kimberley, Rome, July 7, 1894, "Replies to Questions in the Italian Chamber of Deputies," FO 403/22, p. 9; Souhart to Hanotaux, August 24, 1894, *C.P.: Maroc*, 70:340; Defrance (Chargé d'affaires) to Hanotaux, Madrid, August 20, 1894, *C.P.: Espagne*, 925 (August–December, 1894):52; Jeronimo Becker, *España y Marruecos*, (Madrid, 1903), p. 287; Brunschwig, *La colonisation française*, pp. 235–36.   *33.* Souhart to Hanotaux, August 22, 1894, *C.P.: Maroc*, 70:324; Rodolfo Gil Benumerja (pseud. of Rodolfo Gil Torres), *España y el Mundo Arabe* (Madrid, 1955), p. 103.   *34.* Hanotaux to d'Aubigny, June 18, 1894, and d'Aubigny to Hanotaux, July 6, 1894, *C.P.: Maroc*, 70:85, 175–77.
35. Moret to Potestad, Madrid, June 20, 1894, Annex II in d'Aubigny to Hanotaux, Tangiers, July 6, 1894, *C.P.: Maroc*, 70:175–77; Defrance to Hanotaux, Madrid, August 13, 1894, *C.P.: Espagne*, 925:44–45.   *36.* D'Aubigny to Hanotaux, July 9, 1894, and Souhart to Hanotaux, August 10, 1894, and August 13, 1894, *C.P.: Maroc*, 70:191–92, 283–85, 286–88 and 300–303; Monbel to Hanotaux, September 15, 1894, *C.P.: Maroc*, 71 (September–December, 1894): 63; Defrance to Hanotaux, August 7, 1894, *C.P.: Espagne*, 925: 27–28; Satow to Kimberley, Tangiers, July 7, 1894, F.O. 413/22, p. 22.   *37.* Hanotaux to d'Aubigny, June 21, 1894, and July 6, 1894, Souhart to Hanotaux, August 19, 1894, and August 24, 1894; and Nisard (Directeur) to Tangiers Legation, August 22, 1894, *C.P.: Maroc*, 70:114, 169, 314, 340, 323.   *38.* Hanotaux to Souhart, August 13, 1894, *C.P.: Maroc*, 70:298–99; Defrance to Hanotaux, July 31, 1894, *C.P.: Espagne*, 824:354–59; and Souhart to Hanotaux, August 13, 1894, *C.P.: Maroc*, 70:300–303.   *39.* Hanotaux to Monbel, September 14, 1894, *C.P.: Maroc*, 71:58; Directeur to d'Aubigny, July 18, 1894, *C.P.: Maroc*, 70:230, 236–40.

40. Hanotaux to d'Aubigny, July 13, 1894, *C.P.: Maroc*, 70:205–6, 207–9; Hanotaux to Monbel, December 3, 1894, *C.P.: Maroc*, 71:350–354.   *41.* Hanotaux to d'Aubigny, July 30, 1894, and Souhart to Hanotaux, August 13, 1894, *C.P.: Maroc*, 70:260, 343–45.   *42.* "Sa confiance dans l'agent anglais n'est-elle pas un peu excessive?" reads the marginal comments on Souhart to Hanotaux, August 24, 1894, *C.P.: Maroc*, 70:341–42.
43. Monbel to Hanotaux, September 14, 1894, and Hanotaux to Monbel, September 16, 1894, *C.P.: Maroc*, 71:56, 67; Hanotaux to Legation in Madrid, October 8, 1894, *C.P.: Espagne*, 925:191–92.   *44.* Monbel to Hanotaux, September 30, 1894, *C.P.: Maroc*, 71:120.   *45.* Reverseaux to Hanotaux, Madrid, July 25, 1894, in *C.P.: Espagne*, 934: 349–351.   *46.* Hanotaux to d'Aubigny, June 13, 1894, d'Aubigny to Hanotaux, June 19, 1894, and June 20, 1894, and Monbel to Hanotaux, October 23, 1894, *C.P.: Maroc*, 70:52, 103, 109–13, 212–14. See also Pierre Dumas, *Le Maroc* (Grenoble, 1928), p. 45.
47. D'Aubigny to Hanotaux, August 3, 1894, and Abd el Aziz to Casimir Perier, August 13, 1894, *C.P.: Maroc*, 70:217, 275, 304–6; Satow to Kimberley, Tangiers, August 16, 1894, and Phipps to Kimberley, Paris, September 28, 1894, F.O. 413/22, pp. 58–59, 111–12.
48. Satow to Kimberley, Tangiers, August 27, 1894, F.O. 413/22, p. 78.   *49.* Monbel to Hanotaux, September 16, 1894, *C.P.: Maroc* 71:72.

50. D'Aubigny to Hanotaux, July 6, 1894, Souhart to Hanotaux, August 10, 1894, Monbel to Hanotaux, September 19, 1894, *C.P.: Maroc:* 71:86–91, 184, 283–85.
51. Hanotaux to d'Aubigny, July 5, 1894, in *C.P.: Maroc,* 70:163; Monbel to Hanotaux, September 7, 1894, *C.P.: Maroc,* 71:38; Kimberley to Phipps, September 25, 1894, F.O. 413/22, p. 113.

Chapter Three

1. Note sur le différend franco-belge, February 28, 1894, and Hanotaux to Nisard, Brussels, April 17, 1894, *Afrique* IV, 120a, June 1894, p. 329; Kimberley to Cromer, London, March 16, 1894, F.O. 633/7 (The Cromer Papers), p. 93; Edward Marbeau, "L'Accord Anglo-Congolais et les résponsabilities," in *Revue française,* June 1894, p. 329. *2. The Foreign Policy of Lord Rosebery,* p. 34; Gooch, *History of Modern Europe,* p. 209; Kimberley to Cromer, March 1894, F.O. 633/7, p. 96. *3.* "Note du Ministre," June 20, 1894, *D.D.F.,* 11:241–43; Dufferin to Kimberley, July 5, 1894, F.O. 403/202, pp. 14–15; M. Rouire, "La France et l'état du Congo," in *Revue bleue,* 4, 1 (June 2, 1894): 685; Comte Louis de Lichtervelde, *Leopold of the Belgians* trans. by Thomas H. Reed and H. Russell Reed (New York and London, 1929), p. 215. *4.* France, *Debats Parlementaires, Chambre des Députés, Session ordinaire de 1894* (Paris, 1894), 2: 278–314. Cited henceforth as *Débats, députés.* Perier to Bourée, May 26, 1894, *D.D.F.,* 11:169–170. *5.* A. Soulier, *L'instabilité ministerielle sous la Troisième République* (Paris, 1939), p. 419; Daniel, *L'année politique 1894,* pp. 144–45. *6. Débats, députés,* 1894, 2:325–36. *7.* Iiams, *Dreyfus Diplomatists and the Dual Alliance,* p. 25. *8. Fortnightly Review,* 69:179. *9.* Iiams, *Dreyfus Diplomatists and the Dual Alliance,* pp. 25–26.

10. Ibid., quoting André Siegfried, *Discours de M. André Siegfried* (Paris, n.d.), p. 5, and Hanotaux, "Carnets," February 13, 1895. *11.* Hanotaux to Montebello, June 1, 1894, *D.D.F.,* 11:190–92; Plunkett to Kimberley, Brussels, June 2, 1894, and Dufferin to Kimberley, Paris, June 13, 1894, F.O. 403/201, pp. 71, 113. *12.* Carroll, *French Public Opinion,* pp. 166–67; Sir James Rennell Rodd, *Social and Diplomatic Memories* (London, 1923), 2:132; René Millet, *Notre politique extérieur de 1898 à 1905* (Paris, 1905), p. 5; and *The Foreign Policy of Lord Rosebery,* p. 34. *13.* P. L. Monteil, *Quelques feuillets de l'histoire coloniale* (Paris, 1914), pp. 66–67; Monteil to Delcassé, Paris, March 7, 1894, *Afrique* III, 19a. *14.* Monteil to Minister for Colonies, Paris, May 30, 1894, *Afrique* III, 19a. *15.* Monteil to Guieysse, Grand-Labou (French Congo), November 6, 1894, *Afrique* III, 19a; Phipps to Dufferin, Paris, June 6, 1894, F.O. 403/201, p. 82; Dufferin to Kimberley, July 5, 1894, F.O. 403/202, p. 14. *16.* Hanotaux to Delcassé, August 8, 1894, *Afrique* III, 19c. "Rapport presenté au nom de la commission d'enquête sur les operations de la colonne de Kong," March 14, 1893, p. 10, *Afrique* III, 21d; Dufferin to Kimberley, June 11, 1894, "Affaires Coloniales," F.O. 403/201, p. 105. *17.* Phipps to Kimberley, Paris, June 6, 1894, F.O. 403/201, p. 82. *18.* Decrais to Hanotaux, June 1, 1894, *D.D.F.,* 11:186–190. *19.* Note du Ministre, June 2, 1894, *D.D.F.,* 11:192–94.

20. Dufferin to Kimberley, June 7, 1894, F.O. 403/201, p. 82. *21.* Dufferin to Kimberley, June 13, 1894, F.O. 403/201, p. 115. *22.* Charles E. Drummond Black, *The Marquess of Dufferin and Ava* (Toronto, 1903), pp. 362–63, 388; Sir Alfred Lyall, *The Life of the Marquis of Dufferin and Ava,* 2 vols. (London, 1905), 2:276–77. *23.* Note du Ministre, June 2, 1894, *D.D.F.,* 11:192–94; Dufferin to Kimberley, June 7, 1894, F.O. 403/201, p. 85. Carroll, *French Public Opinion,* p. 166; Henri Blet, *France d'Outre-Mer* (Paris, 1950), p. 25. *24.* E. L. Guernier, *L'Afrique* (Paris, 1933), p. 71. *25. Débats, députés,* 184, 2:401–5; Gooch, *Franco-German Relations,* p. 35. *26.* Daniel, *L'année, politique, 1894,* p. 160. "Le nouveau ministre des affaires etrangères, M. Hanotaux, fit un lumineux exposé de la question de notre politique. . . ." pp. 160–175. *27.* Sontag, *Germany and England,* p. 292; Dufferin to Kimberley, June 13, 1894, FO 403/201, pp. 112–15. *28. Débats, députés,* 1894, 2:410–414. *29.* Hanotaux aux Représentants Diplomatiques . . . , June 7, 1894, *D.D.F.,* 11:205–6.

30. Fortnightly Review, 69:169; Daniel, *L'année politique,* 1894, p. 176. *31.* Dufferin to Hanotaux, June 6, 1894, and Note du Ministre, June 11, 1894, *D.D.F.,* 11:204–5, 209–12; Dufferin to Kimberley, June 13, 1894, F.O. 403/201, p. 114. *32.* Hatzfeld to Caprivi, June 1, 1894, Dugdale, *German Diplomatic Documents,* 2:292–94. *33. British and Foreign State Papers,* 82 (1889–1890):35–47. Henceforth cited as *State Papers.* Dufferin to Kimberley, June 13, 1894, F.O. 403/201, p. 115; Decrais to Hanotaux, June 15, 1894, *C.P.: Angleterre,* 894:217–18. *34.* Herbette to Hanotaux, Berlin, June 5, 1894, June 13, 1894, *D.D.F.,* 11:200–201, 215–16; Hanotaux to Herbette, June 17, 1894, Ibid., pp. 226–29. *35. The Foreign Policy of Lord Rosebery,* p. 35; Sontag, *Germany and England,* p. 294. *36.* Hanotaux to Decrais, June 15, 1894, and Hanotaux to Herbette, June 17, 1894, *D.D.F.,* 11:218, 226–29. *37.* Note du Ministre, June 20, 1894, *D.D.F.,* 11:241–43. *38.* Bourée to Hanotaux, June 1, June 9, and June 14, 1894, *C. P.: Belgique,* 91:10–13, 56–57, 97; M. Louis Renault, ed., *Archives diplomatiques* (Paris, 1894), 2nd series, 49:22. Henceforth cited as *Archives diplomatiques.* *39.* Gooch, *History of Modern Europe,* pp. 272–73; Bourée to Hanotaux, June 9, and June 20, 1894, *C.P.: Belgique,* 91:56–57 and 113–14.

40. Bourée to Hanotaux, June 22, and July 6, 1894, *C.P.: Belgique,* 91:122, 159–169; Currie to Kimberley, Constantinople, June 6, 1894, F.O. 403/201, p. 80; Cambon to Hanotaux, Pera, June 4, 1894, Therapia, June 6, and June 18, 1894, and others, *D.D.F.,* 11: Nos. 127, 131, 155, 156. *41.* Plunkett to Kimberley, Brussels, June 2, and June 10, 1894, F.O. 403/201, pp. 70–71, 96. *42.* Bourée to Hanotaux, June 1, June 3, 1894, *C.P.: Belgique,* 91:10–13, 30; Hanotaux to Bourée, June 22, 1894, Ibid., pp. 118–19. *43.* Bourée to Hanotaux, July 17, 1894, Hanotaux to Bourée, July 17, 1894; Bourée to Hanotaux, July 20, 1894, *C.P.: Belgique,* 91:180, 181–82, 185–190. *44.* Plunkett to Kimberley, Brussels, June 10, 1894, Dufferin to Kimberley, Paris, June 13, 1894, F.O. 403/201, pp. 96, 115; Phipps to Kimberley, Paris, August 2, 1894, F.O. 403/202, p. 39; Hanotaux to Bourée, June 5, and July 31, 1894, *C.P.: Belgique,* 91:36 and 199; Bourée to Hanotaux, Brussels, June 14, and June 18, 1894, Ibid., pp. 97, 104. *45. Archives diplomatiques,* 2nd series, 51:306–7; Plunkett to Kimberley, Brussels, August 8, 1894, F.O. 403/202, pp. 59–60; *The Foreign Policy of Lord Rosebery,* p. 36. *46.* Delcassé to Monteil, Paris, August 14, September 22, and September 24, 1894, *Afrique* III, 19b.

Chapter Four

1. State Papers, 83:19–21, 86:55. *2. State Papers,* 83:672–75. *3.* Note pour le gouvernement britannique, London, May 28, 1894, *D.D.F.,* 11:174; Note pour le gouvernement italien, Rome, May 29, 1894, *D.D.F.,* 11:181. *4.* Ernest Lavisse, *La Revue de Paris,* February 1, 1894, passim; Langer, *The Diplomacy of Imperialism,* p. 181. *5.* Hanotaux, *Fachoda,* pp. 84–85; Monteil, *Quelques feuillets de l'histoire coloniale,* p. 65; Gustave Schlumberger, *Mes Souvenirs,* 2 vols. (Paris, 1934), 2:74. *6.* Pierre Renouvin, "Les Origines de l'expedition de Fachoda," in *Revue Historique,* 200 (October–December 1948), 183. *7.* Marlow, *A History of Modern Egypt,* pp. 152–53; Lord Lugard, *National Review,* 25:609, 622. *8.* Decrais to Hanotaux, London, June 5, 1894, *D.D.F.,* 11:201–2. *9.* Hanotaux, *Fachoda,* p. 80.

10. Hanotaux to Dufferin, June 9, 1894, Hanotaux to Decrais, June 19, 1894, and Delcassé to Monteil, July 13, 1894, *D.D.F.,* 11:207, 236–38; 275–78; Taylor, *The Struggle for Mastery in Europe,* p. 353. *11.* Decrais to Hanotaux, June 8, 1894, *C.P.: Angleterre,* 894:103; De Saint Aymour, *Fachoda,* p. 14. *12.* France, *Débats Parlementaires, Sénat, Session ordinaire de 1895* (Paris, 1895), 1:470. Cited henceforth as *Débats, Sénat.* *13.* Renouvin, *Le XIXᵉ siècle,* p. 194; Keith Eubanks, *Paul Cambon* (Norman, Oklahoma, 1960), p. 66. *14.* Lord Lugard, *National Review,* 25:617; André Lebon, "La mission Marchand et le cabinet Méline," *Revue des deux mondes,* 163 (March–April, 1900): 276; Victor Prompt, "Le Soudan nilotique," *Bulletin de l'institut égyptien,* Series III, No. 4, as quoted by Langer, *The Diplomacy of Imperialism,* p. 127; *State Papers,* 82:35–47, 82:19–21, 86:55. *15.* Note de l'Ambassade d'Italie, May 31, 1894, *D.D.F.,* 11:184–85. *16.* Decrais to Hanotaux, June 1, 1894, *C.P.: Angleterre,* 894:10.

17. State Papers, 76:4–20.   *18.* Czeslaw Jesman, *The Russians in Ethiopia* (London, 1958), p. 69.   *19.* Menelik to Carnot, Addis Ababa, February 27, 1893, France, *Archives Diplomatiques, Mémoires et Documents: Afrique: Abyssinie 5*, 138:340–41. Cited henceforth as *Abyssinie 5*. L. J. Morié, *Histoire de l'Ethiopie*, 2 vols. (Paris, 1904), 2:425–26.

20. Note pour le Ministre, Djibouti, March 9, 1894, and Note sommaire personnelle pour M. le Ministre, June 1, 1894, *Abyssinie 5*, 138:420, 432; Lebon, "La mission Marchand . . . ," p. 285.   *21.* Francis Charmes, "Chronique de la quinzaine," *Revue des deux mondes*, September 15, 1894, pp. 472–73.   *22.* "Note pour M. Delcassé," Affaires Etrangères, June 6, 1894, *Abyssinie 5*, 138:437; Ernest Lavisse, "France et Angleterre," *La Revue de Paris*, February 1, 1899, p. 469.   *23. Débats, députés, 1894*, 2:404–5. *24.* John Marlow, *A History of Modern Egypt* (New York, 1954), p. 154.   *25.* Ernest Lavisse, *La Revue de Paris*, February 1, 1899, p. 479.   *26.* Renouvin, *Le XIXᵉ siècle*, p. 194.   *27.* Decrais to Hanotaux, July 24, 1894, *C.P.: Angleterre*, 895:256; *Débats, députés, 1894*, 2:401–414; Sorel, *Histoire de France et d'Angleterre* (Amsterdam et Paris, 1950), p. 389; Stephen H. Longrigg, *A Short History of Eritrea* (Oxford, 1945), p. 125. *28.* Lord Lugard, "England and France in the Nile Valley," *National Review*, 25 (1895): 609–622.   *29. Débats, députés, 1894*, 2:406; Hanotaux, *Fachoda*, pp. 82–83.

30. Hanotaux, *Fachoda*, p. 111.   *31. Débats, députés*, 1894, 2:410; Hanotaux to Montebello, June 1, 1894, *D.D.F.*, 11:190–92, particularly n. 1, p. 192.   *32.* Jean Darcy, *Cent années de rivalité coloniale* (Paris, 1904), p. 369.   *33.* Hanotaux, *Fachoda*, pp. 82–83.   *34.* De Montebello to Hanotaux, June 10, 1894, *D.D.F.*, 11:208–209.
35. De Montebello to Hanotaux, June 14, 1894, June 21, 1894, and June 26, 1894, *D.D.F.*, 11:216–17, 248–49 and 255–57.   *36.* Prince A. Lobanov-Rostovsky, *Russia and Asia* (New York, 1933), p. 211; Taylor, *The Struggle for Mastery in Europe*, p. 345; Czeslaw Jesman, *The Russians in Ethiopia*, pp. 9, 19, 99.   *37.* Hanotaux to the French Legations in London, Brussels, St. Petersburg, Vienna, and Constantinople, July 10, 1894, and Decrais to Hanotaux, July 30, 1894, in *C.P.: Angleterre*, 895:92, 313.   *38.* Note sommaire pour M. le Ministre: Affaires d'Ethiopie, June, 1894, Delcassé to Hanotaux, September 17, 1894, and Hanotaux to Lagarde, October 6, 1894, *Abyssinie 5*, 138:436, 451, 455–56.   *39.* G. Dethan, "Le rapprochement franco-italien . . ." *Revue d'histoire diplomatique*, 70 (1956):325; cf. Count Julius Andrassy, *Bismarck, Andrassy and Their Successors*, (London, 1927), p. 258.

40. J. Bourgin, "Francesco Crispi", in *Les politiques d'expansion impérialiste* (Paris, 1949), p. 145; Edward Ullendroff, *The Ethiopians* (London, New York, Toronto, 1960), p. 93; Richard Pankhurst, "L 'indépendance de l'Ethiopie et son importation d'armes au XIXᵉ siècle," in *Présence Africaine*, 32–33 (June–September, 1960):100–101.
41. Billot to Hanotaux, January 19, and 20, 1895, *C.P.: Italie*, 116:130, 136–140.   *42.* J. L. Garvin, *The Life of Joseph Chamberlain* (London, 1934), 3:168–69; Cromer to Salisbury, Cairo, December 18, 1895, F.O., 633/6, p. 256; D'Estournelle to Hanotaux, September 5, 1894, *C.P.: Angleterre*, 897:20; André Lebon, *Revue des deux mondes*, March 15, 1900, p. 287.   *43.* De Saint Aymour, *Fachoda*. p. 131.   *44.* Billot, *La France et l'Italie*, 2 vols. (Paris, 1905), 2:267.   *45.* Monteil, *Quelques feuillets de l'histoire coloniale*, p. 116; A. Ménier, ed.; "Lettres du Commandant Marchand à Guillaume Grandidier," *Revue d'histoire des colonies*, 45 (1958):61–108.   *46.* MM. Bonvalot, Clochett, and Bonchamp, were in charge of Nile expeditions from Djibouti. See Lebon to Lagarde, January 19, 1897, and Lebon to Hanotaux, October 6, 1897, *Somalis 17*.   *47.* Hanotaux, *Fachoda*, p. 133; Darcy, *Cent années*, p. 376.   *48.* Jean Doresse, *Ethiopia*, trans. Elsa Coult. (London and New York, 1959), pp. 202–3; Note sommaire personnelle pour M. le Ministre: Affaires d'Ethiopie, June 1, 1894, Lagarde to Hanotaux, Vichy, June 4, 1895, and Ménélik to Faure, Addis Ababa, September 24, 1894, *Abyssinie 5*, 138:432–36, 485, 507.

Chapter Five

1. Hanotaux, *L'Histoire de la France contemporaine*, Vol. 4, *La république parlementaire* (Paris, 1908), p. 385; Langer, *The Diplomacy of Imperialism*, p. 125; Sanderson,

England, Europe and the Upper Nile, pp. 12–13; James Rennell Rodd, *Social and Diplomatic Memories*, 2 vols. (London, 1923), 2:221, passim.   *2.* James W. Lowther, "Some Anglo-French Problems," *National Review*, 25 (March–August, 1895):306 *passim;* F.D. Lugard, "England and France in the Nile Valley," ibid., p. 609 passim, particularly the map facing p. 622; Francis Charmes, "Chronique de la quinzaine," *Revue des deux mondes*, 5 (1894):237; The Marquess of Crewe, *Lord Rosebery* (New York and London, 1931), p. 367; Taylor, *The Struggle for Mastery in Europe*, p. 349, n. 5.   *3.* Montholon to Hanotaux, Brussels, October 22, 1896, in *C.P.: Belgique*, 94:322–23.   *4.* Langer, *The Diplomacy of Imperialism*, pp. 109 and 264.   *5.* Taylor, "Prelude to Fashoda," p. 57; Daniel, *L'année politique, 1894*, pp. 252 and 422–23; Hanotaux to Decrais, August 17, 1894, *D.D.F.*, 11:319–321; Decrais to Hanotaux, August 15, 1894, *C.P.: Angleterre*, 896:134.   *6.* Monteil in Ménier, "Lettres du commandant Marchand," Paris, March 7, 1894, pp. 65–67; Monteil to Lebon, *D.D.F.*, 11:96–100; Delcassé to Monteil, July 13, 1894, *D.D.F.*, 11:275–78; Taylor, *The Struggle for Mastery in Europe*, p. 342; Charles W. Porter, *The Career of Théophile Delcassé* (Philadelphia, 1936), pp. 88–90.   *7.* Note du Ministre, October 30, 1894, *D.D.F.*, 11:393; Taylor, "Prelude to Fashoda," pp. 59, 64.   *8.* Blet, *France d'outre-mer*, 3:166; Millet, *Notre politique exterieure*, p. 150; August Terrier, *Afrique équatoriale*, Vol. 4 of Gabriel Hanotaux and Alfred Martineau, eds., *Histoire des colonies françaises et de l'expansion de la France dans le monde* (Paris, 1931), pp. 518–19; Saint-Aymour, *Fachoda*, pp. 126–27.   *9.* Dufferin to Hanotaux, Paris, June 6, 1894, *D.D.F.*, 11:204–5.

10. Decrais to Hanotaux, London, June 5, 1894, *D.D.F.*, 11:201–2; See also marginalia in Hanotaux's hand on Decrais to Hanotaux, London, July 12, 1894, *C.P.: Angleterre*, 895:114–17.   *11.* Note du Ministre, June 29, 1894, *D.D.F.*, 11:257–261.   *12.* Note du Ministre, June 11, 1894, June 20, 1894 (two notes), *D.D.F.*, 11:209–212, 241–43, 257–261.   *13.* Decrais to Hanotaux, London, June 17, 1894, *D.D.F.*, 11:287–88; A.G. Gardiner, *The Life of Sir William Harcourt*, 2 vols. (New York, [1904?]), 2:319.   *14.* Hanotaux to Decrais, August 17, 1894, *D.D.F.*, 11:319–321. *The Foreign Policy of Lord Rosebery*, p. 36; A.B. Keith, *The Belgian Congo and the Berlin Act* (Oxford, 1919), pp. 109–11.   *15.* Taylor, "Prelude to Fashoda," passim; J.D. Hargreaves, "Entente Manquée; Anglo-French Relations, 1895–1896," *Cambridge Historical Journal*, 11 (1953–55):66; Hanotaux, *Fachoda*, pp. 71, 80; Note du Ministre, October 30, 1894, *D.D.F.*, 11:393.   *16.* Gabriel Hanotaux, *Pour l'empire colonial française*, passim; *L'affaire de Madagascar*, passim; *Fachoda*, passim; *Mon Temps*, 2:97, 438, passim; see also Schuman, *War and Diplomacy in the French Republic*, p. 165; Taylor, "Prelude to Fashoda," pp. 59, 64; Charles Maurras, *Kiel et Tanger, 1895–1905*, 3rd ed., (Paris, 1921), p. 58; and Hargreaves, "Entente Manquée," p. 66.   *17.* Monteil in Ménier, "Lettres du Commandant Marchand . . . ," p. 67; Delcassé to Monteil, July 13, 1894, *D.D.F.*, 11:275–78; Taylor, "Prelude to Fashoda," p. 74.   *18.* Note du Ministre, October 30, 1894, and no date (November 17, 1894), *D.D.F.*, 11:393, 429; Hanotaux to Delcassé, December 5, 1894, *D.D.F.*, 11:468–69; and Taylor, "Prelude to Fashoda," p. 74.   *19.* Hanotaux, "Carnets," February 13, 1895, as quoted in Iiams, *Dreyfus Diplomatists and the Dual Alliance*, p. 25.

20. Note du Capitaine Marchand, Paris, November 10, 1895, *D.D.F.*, 12:278–80; Note pour le Ministre, Paris, November 13, 1895, *D.D.F.*, 21:288–89.   *21.* Berthelot to Guieysse, Paris, November 30, 1895, *D.D.F.*, 12:322–23; Terrier, *Afrique équatoriale*, pp. 518–19; Félix Faure, "Le Ministère Léon Bourgeois et la politique étrangère de Marcellin Berthelot au Quai d'Orsay," *Revue d'Histoire diplomatique*, 71 (1957):108; Vizetelly, *Republican France*, p. 437. Félix Faure erroneously attributes the whole scheme to Hanotaux. See Félix Faure, "Fashoda," *Revue d'histoire diplomatique*, 59 (1955):30.   *22.* Note du Capitaine Marchand, Paris, November 10, 1895, *D.D.F.*, 12:278–280.   *23.* Wilfrid Scawen Blunt, *My Diaries, Being a Personal Narrative of Events, 1888–1914*, 2 vols. (New York, 1921), 2:303.   *24.* R.W. Seton-Watson, *Britain in Europe, 1789–1914* (London, 1937), p. 571; Léon Cahen, "Les embarras de l'Angleterre en Afrique et Orient proche," Part IV, Chapter II of Henri Hauser, ed., *Histoire diplomatique de l'Europe, 1871–1914*, 2 vols. (Paris, 1929), 1:366; and Gardiner, *Life of Harcourt*, 2:322, 323.   *25.* Taylor, "Prelude to Fashoda," pp. 56, 60; Crewe, *Lord Rosebery*, p. 366.   *26.* Hanotaux to Dufferin, June 9, 1894, *D.D.F.*, 11:207, Langer, *The Diplomacy of Imperialism*, pp. 135, 260; Barclay, *Thirty Years*, p. 123; *Débats, députés, 1894*, 2:410–414; Daniel, *L'année politique, 1894*, pp. 160–175; Taylor, "Prelude to Fashoda," p. 61; Saint-Aymour, *Fachoda*, p. 116.   *27.* Hanotaux to Herbette, June 17, 1894, and Note addressée au Gouvernement britannique, London, August 6, 1894, *D.D.F.*, 226–29, 305; Taylor, *Struggle for Mastery in Europe*, p. 353; E. Malcolm Carroll, *French Public Opinion and Foreign Affairs* (New York and London, 1831), pp. 166–67.   *28.* Decrais to Hanotaux, London, July 17, 1894, and August 9, 1894, and Hanotaux to Decrais, Paris, August 7, 1894, *D.D.F.*, 11:287–88, 312, 306–7; Taylor, "Prelude to Fashoda," p. 67.   *29.* Hanotaux to Decrais, August 17, 1894, *D.D.F.*, 11:319–321.

    30. Ibid.   *31.* *State Papers*, 82:35–47; 83:19–21.   *32.* Crewe, *Lord Rosebery*, p. 366.   *33.* Decrais to Hanotaux, June 5, 1894, and Hanotaux to Dufferin, June 9, 1894, *D.D.F.*, 11:201–2, 207.   *34.* Taylor, "Prelude to Fashoda," pp. 73, 80; Taylor, *Struggle for Mastery in Europe*, p. 353; Langer, *The Diplomacy of Imperialism*, p. 260; Hanotaux to Decrais, August 17, 1894, *D.D.F.*, 11:319–321.   *35.* Note du Ministre, September 5, 1894, *D.D.F.*, 11:348–350.   *36.* Hanotaux to Decrais, August 17, and Note du Ministre, September 5, 1894, *D.D.F.*, 11:348–350.   *37.* Gardiner, *Life of Harcourt*, 2:322.
38. Note du Ministre, September 5, 1894, *D.D.F.*, 11:348–350; Taylor, "Prelude to Fashoda," p. 70, particularly n. 4; Crewe, *Lord Rosebery*, p. 367.   *39.* Note du Ministre, September 29, 1894, and Hanotaux to d'Estournelle, October 28, 1894, *D.D.F.*, 11:353–54, 382–89.

    40. October 10, 1894, *D.D.F.*, 11:357, 363–64. Hanotaux tried to put this formula off on Phipps. Phipps, however, protested that Hanotaux had first used the term *"clause de desinteresement"* which the Britisher understood as "one self-denying agreement." See Phipps to Hanotaux, October 10, 1894, *D.D.F.*, 11:364–65; see also: Taylor, *Struggle for Mastery in Europe*, p. 353; Taylor, "Prelude to Fashoda," p. 70, 72.   *41.* Hanotaux to d'Estournelle, Paris, October 28, 1894, and Note du Ministre, Paris, October 30, 1894, *D.D.F.*, 11:388–89, 393, *D.D.F.*, 11:393.   *42.* D'Estournelle to Hanotaux, October 31, 1894, *D.D.F.*, 11:396–97.   *43.* Hanotaux to d'Estournelle, October 28, 1894 and d'Estournelle to Hanotaux, November 22, 1894, *D.D.F.*, 11:386, 437–38; Hargreaves, "Entente Manquée," pp. 82–83; Sir Lewis Michell, *The Life of the Rt. Hon. Cecil J. Rhodes, 1853–1902*, 2 vols. (London, 1910), 2:48.   *44.* Hanotaux to Dufferin, July 12, 1894, De Montebello to Hanotaux, Saint Petersburg, July 25, 1894, and De Vauvineux to Hanotaux, Saint Petersburg, October 9, 1894, *D.D.F.*, 11:273, 299–300, 358; Paul Cambon to his mother, December 23, 1895, in Henri Cambon, ed., *Paul Cambon, Correspondence, 1870–1924*, 3 vols. (Paris, 1940–1946), 1:397.   *45.* Hanotaux to Vauvineux, April 9, 1895, and De Courcel to Hanotaux, April 10, 1895, *D.D.F.* 11:530–535; A.F. Pribram, *England and the International Policy of European Great Powers, 1871–1914* (Oxford, 1931), pp. 57, 130; Stuart, *French Foreign Policy*, p. 108.   *46.* Note du Ministre, November 1, 1894, *D.D.F.*, 11:397–98.   *47.* Note du Ministre, November 17, 1894, and Hanotaux to Delcassé, December 5, 1894, *D.D.F.*, 11:429, 468–69; C.W. Newbury, "The Development of French Policy in West Africa," *Journal of Modern History*, 31 (1959):25, passim.
48. Hanotaux, *Fachoda*, p. 90; Terrier, *Afrique équatoriale*, p. 515; Hargreaves, "Entente Manquée," p. 60, passim; Usborne, *The Conquest of Morocco*, pp. 60–61.   *49.* Pinon, *France et Allemagne, 1870–1913*, p. 129: Landau, *Moroccan Drama*, pp. 60–61; Cruickshank, *Morocco*, pp. xii-xiii; Walter B. Harris, *France, Spain and the Rif* (London, 1927), pp. 1–3.

    50. Newbury, "The Development of French Policy . . . ," passim; Marcel Dubois et August Terrier, *Les colonies françaises: un siècle d'expansion coloniale* (Paris, 1902), p. 550; Margery Perham, *Lugard, the Years of Adventure, 1858–1898* (London, 1956), p. 626; H.L. Hoskins, *European Imperialism in Africa* (New York, 1930), pp. 56–57.
51. F.A. Edwards, "The French on the Niger," *Fortnightly Review*, 69 (1898):576–77, 591; Diplomaticus, "Where Lord Salisbury Has Failed," ibid., p. 518.   *52.* Hargreaves, "Entente Manquée," p. 66, passim.

Chapter Six
1. Taylor, *The English Historical Review*, 65:64, n. 5, gives a complete account of the

ultimatum incident.   *2.* Trans. by Norbert Guterman (New York, 1944), p. 46.
3. France, *Documents Diplomatiques, Affaires de Madagascar, 1885–1895* (Paris, 1895), pp. 1–8. Cited henceforth as *Mad.*; Marshall to Herbette, Berlin, November 17, 1890, in Ibid., p. 10.   *4.* Priestly, *France Overseas*, p. 309.   *5.* Larrouy to Develle, Tananarive, November 6, 1893, and Larrouy to Hanotaux, Tananarive, June 25, and 30, 1894, *Mad.*, pp. 25, 30–31, 32–34.   *6.* Daniel, *L'année politique, 1894*, pp. 20–21.   *7.* Casimir Perier to Larrouy, Paris, March 29, 1894, *Mad.*, p. 30.   *8.* D'Estournelle to Hanotaux, London, October 5, and November 13, 1894, *C.P.: Angleterre*, 898:71 and 899:60.   *9.* "Madagascar: L'Hostilité des missionnaires étrangers" in *Revue française*, 22 (October 1896): 580; Sonia E. Howe, *The Drama of Madagascar* (London, 1938), p. 285.

10. Hanotaux to Larrouy, Paris, July 20, August 1, August 12, and September 9, 1894, and Larrouy to Hanotaux, Tananarive, July 27, 1894, *Mad.*, pp. 34–39. See also: Porter to Sauzier Tananarive, September 14, 1894, in Sauzier to Kimberley, Tananarive, October 8, 1894, F.O. 403/222, p. 7.   *11.* Hanotaux to de Vilers, September 12, 1894, *Mad.*, pp. 39–46.   *12.* *L'Affaire de Madagascar*, p. iii. See text of proposed treaty and of the more severe treaty which followed in *Mad.*, pp. 46, 65–67.   *13.* De Vilers to Hanotaux, Tamatave, October 8, 1894, Tananarive, October 26, 1894, Beforona, October 28, 1894, and Tamatave, November 5, 1894, all in ibid., pp. 47, 51–56.   *14.* Hanotaux to de Vilers, October 24, 1894, and de Vilers to Hanotaux, Tamatave, November 2, 1894, in ibid., pp. 51, 54; Dufferin to Kimberley, Paris, November 22, 1894, F.O. 403/222, p. 12A.   *15.* *Débats, députés, 1894*, 4:242–49.   *16.* *Débats, députés, 1894*, 4:413–17.   *17.* Cf. Ch.-A. Julien *et al., Les politiques d'expansion imperialiste,* (Paris, 1949), p. 70, and George Wormser, *La République de Clemenceau*, (Paris, 1901), p. 247.   *18.* Hildebert Isnard, *Madagascar*, (Paris, 1904), p. 99; Olivier Hatzfeld, *Madagascar*, (Paris, 1952), p. 39.   *19.* *Bulletin du Comité de Madagascar*, 2:2 (February 1896), pp. 90–101, gives a clear description of the "Tunisian" thesis.

20. De Vilers to Hanotaux, Tamatave, December 13, 1894, *Mad.*, p. 60; *Débats, députés, 1894*, 3:187–191, 196, 4:466; Emile Simond, *Histoire de la Troisième République* (Paris, 1921), pp. 327–28.   *21.* Hanotaux to Larrouy, August 12, 1894, *Mad.*, p. 37, and d'Estournelles to Hanotaux, London, September 14, 1894, *C.P.: Angleterre*, 897:95–96.   *22.* D'Estournelles to Hanotaux, September 7, September 14, and September 15, 1894, *C.P.: Angleterre*, 897:33–34, 95–96, 109–114; Note de M. Hanotaux, September 26, 1894, ibid., pp. 192–93.   *23.* Hanotaux to d'Estournelles, September 4, 1894, and d'Estournelles to Hanotaux, September 13, 1894, *C.P.: Angleterre*, 897:12, 72.   *24.* D'Estournelles to Hanotaux, September 17, September 22, and September 26, 1894, *C.P.: Angleterre*, 897:116–17, 167–170, 196–99; d'Estournelles to Hanotaux, London, October 4 and October 5, *C.P.: Angleterre*, 898:39, 68–70; Hanotaux to de Courcel, February 10, 1895, *C.P.: Angleterre*, 901:84–85.   *25.* Hanotaux to Decrais, June 8, 1894, *C.P.: Angleterre*, 894:109.   *26.* Kimberley to Dufferin, London, December 10, 1894, F.O. 403/222, p. 23; Hanotaux to d'Estournelles, December 19, 1894, *C.P.: Angleterre*, 899:394.   *27.* The Law Officers of the Crown to Kimberley, Royal Courts of Justice, February 12, 1895, and Bertie to Law Officers of the Crown, Foreign Office, February 8, 1895, F.O. 403/222, pp. 59–61; Kimberley to Dufferin, Foreign Office, February 13, 1895, ibid., pp. 60–62; de Courcel to Hanotaux, February 8, February 12, and February 15, 1895, and Hanotaux to de Courcel, February 10, 1895, *C.P.: Angleterre*, 901:80–83, 124–25, 174.   *28.* Rosebery to Cromer, London, April 22, 1894, F.O. 633/7, p. 89; Félix Faure, "Fachoda" in *Revue d'histoire diplomatique*, 69 (1955):34; Félix Faure, "Mars 1896" and "Le Ministère Bourgeois," Ibid., 71 (1957):118; and Christopher Andrew, *Théophile Delcassé* (New York, 1968), pp. 87–88.   *29.* Lagarde to Chautemps, Obock, April 9, 1895, *Abyssinie 5*, 138:482. Guez to Hanotaux, Aden, April 25, and October 9, 1895, and Hanotaux to Guez, July 20, 1895, *C.P.: Angleterre: Aden (1885–1895)*, 113:190–197, 304–6, 295.

30. Faure, *Revue d'histoire diplomatique*, 71:108–115.   *31.* Ferrata, *Mémoires*, pp. 574–75; Faure, "Fachoda," pp. 29–32; Faure, "Le Ministère Léon Bourgeois," p. 108.   *32.* Hanotaux, "Le traité de Tananarive," p. 12; Roberts, *History of French Colonial Policy*, pp. 386–87; Dwight L. Ling, *Tunisia*, (Bloomington, 1967). To compare Tunisian success to Algerian failure see Vincent Confer, *France and Algeria* (Syracuse, 1966).   *33.* Gabriel Hanotaux, "Madagascar et le régime du protectorat," *La revue de Paris*, 2

(March–April 1896):474, 481; Hanotaux, *L'affaire de Madagascar,* pp. ix, x, xiii; Marcel Dubois et August Terrier, *Les colonies françaises* (Paris, 1902), pp. 718–19; "Le livre jaune," in *Bulletin du Comité de Madagascar,* vol. 2, no. 2 (February 1896), p. 78. *34.* Diplomaticus, "Where Lord Salisbury Has Failed," p. 521; Blet, *France d'outre-mer,* 3: 185; Leblond, *Madagascar,* pp. 194–95.   *35.* André Lebon, *La pacification de Madagascar* (Paris, 1928), p. 7.   *36.* "Memorandum by Mr. Oakes," Foreign Office, April 2, 1896, in F.O. 403/240, pp. 16–18; Law Officers of the Crown to Salisbury, June 23, 1890, in F.O. 403/240, pp. 87–88.   *37.* Dufferin to Salisbury, Paris, March 31, 1896, Salisbury to Pauncefote, London, April 8, 1896, and Pauncefote to Salisbury, Washington, May 1, 1896, F.O. 403/240, pp. 48–49, 53, 74; Lebon, *La pacification de Madagascar,* p. 22; Robinson and Gallagher, *Africa and the Victorians,* pp. 342–43.   *38.* Salisbury to Dufferin, London, April 25, 1896, F.O. 403/240, pp. 63–66; Henri Mager, "Les exportations de Madagascar," in *La politique coloniale,* December 31, 1900, a press clipping in *Madagascar 382 1054;* cf. Galliéni to Decrais, Tananarive, November 9, 1900, in *Madagascar 382 1034.*   *39.* Salisbury to Dufferin, May 22, and September 14, and Salisbury to de Courcel, August 24, 1896, in F.O. 403/240, pp. 76–77, 115–16, 110.   *40.* Hanotaux to Lebon, Paris, April 22, 1897, *Madagascar 361 987.*

Chapter Seven

1. Hanotaux to de Courcel and to Billot, June 19, 1895, and Hanotaux to de Courcel, October 21, 1895, *C.P.: Angleterre,* 905:144, and Vol. 908, pp. 126–27; Haggard to Kimberley, Tunisia, May 25, 1895, F.O. 403/220, p. 21; and Arthur Marsden, "Britain and the End of the Tunis Treaties," *The English Historical Review,* Supplement I (London: Longmans, Green and Co. Ltd., 1965).   *2.* De Courcel to Hanotaux, August 18, 1895, and Hanotaux to de Courcel, August 26, 1895, *C.P.: Angleterre,* 906:129–132, 191; "Memorandum by Sir T. Sanderson," August 18, 1895, F.O. 403/204, p. 20.   *3.* Hanotaux to de Courcel, October 21, 1895, *C.P.: Angleterre,* 908:126–27.   *4.* Salisbury to Ford, July 15, 1896, F.O. 403/240, pp. 96–97; Foreign Office to Colonial Office, June 4, 1897, F.O. 403/254, pp. 32–33; Hanotaux to de Courcel and to Herbette, August 23, 1895, *C.P.: Angleterre,* 906:165.   *5.* Count Tornielli to Foreign Office, London, October 19, 1894, F.O. 403/304, p. 1; Haggard to Kimberley, Tunis, April 9, 1895, F.O. 403/204, pp. 7–8.   *6.* Kimberley to Tornielli, London, November 24, 1894, F.O. 403/204, p. 31; Salisbury to Edwardes, London, August 14, 1896, F.O. 403/204, p. 58; Billot to Hanotaux, Rome, March 9, 1895, *C.P.: Italie,* 117:44–48.   *7.* Billot to Hanotaux, Rome, February 19, and February 21, 1895, *C.P.: Italie,* 116:369–370, 390–92; Ezio F. Gray, *Italy and the Question of Tunis* (Milan, 1939), pp. 34–36, and Paolo d'Agostino Orsini, *Francia contro Italia in Africa da Tunisi a Suez* (Milan, 1939), passim.   *8.* Hanotaux to de Courcel, August 23, and August 28, 1895, *C.P.: Angleterre,* 906:165, 205; General Ferroro to Sir T. Sanderson, London, August 17, 1895, F.O. 403/204, p. 20.   *9.* "Memorandum by Sanderson," n.d. [probably August 17], F.O. 403/204, p. 20, and Hanotaux to de Courcel, October 21, 1895, *C.P.: Angleterre,* 908:126–27.

   10. De Courcel to Hanotaux, September 18, 1895, and Hanotaux to de Courcel, October 21, 1895, *C.P.: Angleterre,* 907:131–32, and 908:126–27; "Minutes by Sir T. Sanderson," London, October 24, 1895, F.O. 403/204, p. 25.   *11.* See Article 40 "Traité conclu avec l'Angleterre: 19 juillet 1875," in France, Ministère des affaires étrangères, *Documents diplomatiques: Revision des traités Tunisiens,* 1881–1897 (Paris, 1897), p. 39. Henceforth cited as *Tunisiens.* For the British reaction, see "Memorandum by Sir H. Bergne," October 25, 1895, F.O. 403/204, pp. 25–26.   *12.* Courtney Boyle to Sir Henry Bergne, Board of Trade, London, October 30, 1895, "Memorandum by Mr. Bateman," Board of Trade, London, October 28, 1895, "Memorandum by HGB," F.O. London, March 24, 1896, and "A minute by G.N.C. (Curzon)," n.d., F.O. 403/204, pp. 26–27, 46.   *13.* Hanotaux, *Fachoda,* p. 111; G. Hanotaux and A. Wolkenstein, "Déclaration," Paris, July 20, 1896, *Tunisiens,* p. 47; Howard to Salisbury, Paris, July 25, 1896, F.O. 403/204, p. 51.   *14.* Billot to Hanotaux, January 19, 1897, *Italie: Politique étrangère: Dossier général, 1897–1904,* 1:52–54, and Billot, *La France et l'Italie,* 2:333.   *15.* Tornielli to Caetani, Paris, May 4, 1896, in Italy, Ministero Degli Affari Esteri, Commissione per la Publicazione die Documenti Diplomatici, *I Documenti Diplomatici Italiani,* Terza Serie: 1896–1907 (Rome, 1953), 2:63–65. Henceforth cited as *Documenti.*   *16.* Caetani to Tornielli, May 19, 1896, *Documenti,* 2:69.   *17.* Tornielli to Caetani, May 22, 1896, *Documenti,* 2:71–75.   *18.* Caetani to Tornielli, June 1, 1896, *Documenti,* 2:74–75.   *19.* Tornielli to Caetani, May 22, 1896, *Documenti,* 2:71–72; Billot, *La France et l'Italie,* 2:332.

20. Billot, *La France et l'Italie,* 2:341; Ferrero to Sanderson, London, August 17, 1895, and Salisbury to Edwardes, August 14, 1896, F.O. 403/204, pp. 20, 58.   *21.* Billot to Hanotaux, June 1, 1896, Note du Ministre, June 5, 1896, and Hanotaux to de Sainte Fortunade (French chargé d'affaires in Rome), August 22, 1895, *D.D.F.,* 12:616, 616–621, 178.   *22.* Billot to Hanotaux, Rome, June 1, 1896, Note du Ministre, June 24 and July 1, 1896, *D.D.F.,* 12:619, 658–660, 671–72; Caetani to Tornielli, June 1, 1896, and Tornielli to Caetani, July 2, 1896, *Documenti,* 2:73–74, 84–85.   *23.* Billot to Hanotaux, June 25, 1896, *D.D.F.,* 12:666–69.   *24.* Billot to Hanotaux, July 3, 1896, *D.D.F.,* 12:680–82. *25.* Haggard to Salisbury, Tunisia, September 22, October 1, and 12, 1896, F.O. 403/204, pp. 67, 69–70, 84–85; Edwardes to Salisbury, Rome, September 18, and October 1, 1896, ibid., pp. 66–67, 69; "Convention de Commerce et de Navigation," "Convention Consulaire et d'Establissement," "Protocole," "Convention d'Extradition," and "Protocole," *Tunisiens,* pp. 47–51, 51–63, 64, 64–72; Billot, *La France et l'Italie,* 2:352–53.   *26.* Edwardes to Salisbury, October 7, 1896, F.O. 403/204, pp. 80–81; Note du Ministre, July 1, 1896, in *D.D.F.,* 12:671–72; Billot to Hanotaux, October 20, 1896, *D.D.F.,* 13:6–8. *27.* Salisbury to Edwardes, London, August 14, and Ford to Salisbury, Rome, December 3, 1896, F.O. 403/204, pp. 97–98.   *28.* Dufferin to Salisbury, October 2, 1896, F.O. 403/204, p. 70.   *29.* Ritchie to Giffen, London, n.d. (September 8, 1896), and Salisbury to de Courcel, London, September 12, 1896, F.O. 403/204, pp. 62, 63–66.

30. Vauvineux and Lamsdorff, "Déclaration," St. Petersburg, October 2, 14, 1896, and Hanotaux and Lardy, "Déclaration," Paris, October 14, 1894, *Tunisiens,* pp. 72–73. *31.* Noailles and Von Marshall, "Déclarations," Berlin, November 18, 1896, *Tunisiens,* pp. 73–74; Howard to Salisbury, Paris, August 15, 1895, and Minutes by Sir T. Sanderson, London, October 25, 1895, F.O. 403/204, pp. 18, 25.   *32.* Hanotaux to Herbette, July 5, 1895, *D.D.F.,* 12:107–8; Haggard to Salisbury, Tunis, March 19, 1895, Salisbury to de Courcel, London, September 12, 1896, F.O. 403/204, pp. 6–7, 63–66; *Tunisiens,* pp. 47–77.   *33.* De Courcel to Hanotaux, October 3, 1896, *D.D.F.,* 12:775.   *34.* Décret du 1ᵉʳ février 1897, and Décret du 30 août 1897, *Tunisiens,* pp. 83–85, 85–86.   *35.* Haggard to Kimberley, Tunis, April, 9, 1895, Howard to Salisbury, Paris, July 25, 1896, Dufferin to Salisbury, Paris, September 30, 1896, Monson to Salisbury, Vienna, October 2, 1896, Gosselin to Salisbury, Paris, November 20, 1896, F.O. 403/204, pp. 7, 51, 69, 72, 92; Haggard to Salisbury, Tunis, February 5, 1897, F.O. 403/254, pp. 2–3; Cambon to Hanotaux, October 3, 1896, *D.D.F.,* 12:775.   *36.* Sanderson to Board of Trade, London, February 15, 1897, and Memorandum by Sir H. Bergne, March 2, 1897, F.O. 403/254, pp. 3–4, 7; Hanotaux, *Fachoda,* p. 111.   *37.* Note du Ministre, March 26, 1897, *D.D.F.,* 13:291–95. See also Communication de M. le Baron de Courcel, Paris, March 26, 1897, *D.D.F.,* 13:-296–97.   *38.* Salisbury to Monson, March 5, 1897, and Memorandum forwarded to the French ambassador on April 22, 1897, F.O. 403/254, pp. 9, 20.   *39.* DeCourcel to Salisbury, April 29, 1897, F.O. 403/254, pp. 20–22.

40. Minute, London, April 30, 1897, F.O. 403/254, p. 22.   *41.* French Counter Proposal Communicated by M. de Courcel on May 19, 1897, Minute by H.G.B., Foreign Office, London, May 21, 1897, and Salisbury, Note, n.d. [May 21, 1897], F.O. 403/254, pp. 26, 27.   *42.* Salisbury to Monson, May 20, 1897, and Salisbury to Chamberlain, June 4, 1897, F.O. 403/254, pp. 28–29, 32–33.   *43.* Salisbury to Monson, London, July 28, 1897, and Monson to Salisbury, Paris, September 8, 1897, F.O. 403/254, pp. 45–47, 50–51. *44.* Colonial Office to Foreign Office, London, September 10, 1897, Salisbury to Monson, London, September 10, 17 and 19, 1897, Monson to Salisbury, Paris, September 12, and 13, 1897, F.O. 403/254, pp. 50–58.   *45.* Arrangement signed by Hanotaux and Monson at Paris on September 18, 1897, *Tunisiens,* pp. 78–79.   *46.* Monson to Salisbury, September 30, 1897, F.O. 403/254, p. 63.   *47.* Foreign Office to Board of Trade, December 6, 1897, and Board of Trade to Foreign Office, December 17, 1897, F.O. 403/254, pp. 89, 90.

Chapter Eight

1. "Arrangement entre la France et la Grande Bretagne fixant la frontière . . . de Sierra Leone" in France, Ministère des affaires étrangères, *Documents diplomatiques, Afrique: Arrangements, Actes, et Conventions concernant le nord, l'ouest et le centre de l'Afrique, 1881–1898* (Paris, 1898), pp. 219–221. *2.* "Délimitation Franco-Anglaise entre la Guinée française et le Sierra Léone: Extrait de la notice sur la Guinée," undated manuscript report by Fernand Rouget in *Afrique* VI, 133c; Lebon to Hanotaux, July 2, 1896, *Afrique* VI, 141b; *L'oeuvre coloniale, algérienne et politique de Eugène Etienne*, collected and edited by the "Depêche Coloniale" (Paris, 1907), p. 324; Belabre (acting vice-consul of France) to Lebon, Sierra Leone, June 6, 1896, *Afrique* VI, 133a; d'Estournelle de Constant to Hanotaux, January 24, 1895, *C.P.: Angleterre*, 900:150. *3.* Hanotaux to Lebon, June 25, 1896, *Afrique* VI, 133c. *4.* Lebon to Hanotaux, January 19, 1897, and F. Jourdier, "L'occupation de Boussa", in *La Depêche Coloniale*, April 10, 1897, *Afrique* VI, 142a; Delcassé to Hanotaux, Paris, November 15, 1894, *Afrique* VI, 115c; *Débats, Sénat, 1895,* 1:469–470. *5.* Robinson and Gallagher, *Africa and the Victorians*, pp. 343, 382–83, 405; Edwards, "The French on the Niger," *The Fortnightly Review*, 63, n.s. (January–June 1898):578–591. *6.* Glanville, *Italy's Relations with England*, pp. 21, 25, passim; Renouvin, *Histoire des relations internationales*, 6:195; Taylor, *The Struggle for Mastery in Europe*, p. 355; Maurice Crouzet, "Joseph Chamberlain", in Ch.-A. Julien, et al., *Les politiques d'expansion imperialiste* (Paris, 1949), p. 179. *7.* Berthelot to Guieysse, January 30, 1896, *Afrique* VI, 133b; "Déclaration" annexed to de Courcel to Berthelot, January 15, 1896, *D.D.F.*, 12:406–9. *8.* Cherry Gertzel, "Relations Between African and European Traders in the Niger Delta," *Journal of African History* 3, no. 1 (1962):361–66. *9.* August Terrier and Charles Mourey, *L'expansion française et la formation territoriale*, (Paris, 1910), pp. 286–290.

10. Ibid.; Delcassé to Hanotaux, November 19, 1894, *Afrique* VI, 115c; Hanotaux to Geoffray, November 13, 1896, *C.P.: Angleterre*, 920:88–89. *11.* Cf.: "L'opinion de Sir G. Goldie sur l'occupation de Boussa," and F. Jourdier, "L'occupation de Boussa" in *La Depêche Coloniale*, April 9, 1897, in *Afrique* VI, 142a. *12.* Hanotaux to de Courcel, August 23, 1895, *C.P.: Angleterre*, 906:166–67; De Courcel to Hanotaux, August 23, 1895, *C.P.: Angleterre*, 906:175–77; Note pour l'ambassade d'Angleterre, May 18, 1895, *C.P.: Angleterre*, 904:134–35; Lebon to Hanotaux, Paris, May 11, 1897, *Afrique* VI, 142a. *13.* Hanotaux to Delcassé, August 23, 1894, and Delcassé to Hanotaux, September 18, 1894, *Afrique* IV, 38a; Terrier and Mourey, *L'expansion française*, pp. 290–95. *14.* De Courcel to Hanotaux, December 17, 1896, and Lebon to Hanotaux, January 19, 1897, and May 11, 1897, *Afrique* VI, 142a; Hanotaux's marginal comments on Geoffray to Hanotaux, November 26, 1896, *C.P.: Angleterre*, 920:199–204; Hanotaux to de Courcel, Paris, December 12, 1896, in *C.P.: Angleterre*, 921:111–14. *15.* The evacuation was ordered by Chautemps, Hanotaux's colleague in the Ribot cabinet, not by Hanotaux. See Lebon to Hanotaux, May 11, 1897, *Afrique* VI, 142a. On Goldie's claims, see "L'opinion de Sir G. Goldie sur l'occupation de Boussa," *Afrique* VI, 142a. *16.* Toutée, "Régime Légal de Navigation du Bas Niger: 1895," Paris, July 16, 1895, *Afrique* VI, 124c. *17.* Hanotaux to Lebon, March 31, and May 3, 1897, and Lebon to Hanotaux, April 12, and May 11, 1897, *Afrique* VI, 142a. *18.* Lebon to Hanotaux, November 16, 1897, *Afrique* VI, 142a; Monson to Hanotaux, Paris, April 17, 1897, Goldie to Commandant of European expedition in Boussa, Ilorin, February 25, 1897, Bretonnet to Goldie, Boussa, February 23, 1897, and Hanotaux to Lebon, November 16, 1897, *Afrique* VI, 142a. *19.* "Déclaration" annexed to de Courcel to Berthelot, January 15, 1896, *D.D.F.*, 12:406–9.

20. Faure, "Le ministère Léon Bourgeois," pp. 120–21, 125. *21.* Berthelot to Montebello, March 16, 1896, *D.D.F.*, 12:496–97; Hanotaux, *Fachoda*, pp. 102–4, 112–13; Salisbury to Cromer, London, December 24, 1896, F.O. 633/7, pp. 118–19. *22.* Geoffray to Hanotaux, London, June 2, 1896, *C.P.: Angleterre*, 916:17–18; Hanotaux, *Fachoda*, pp. 110–11, 181; Robinson and Gallagher, *Africa and the Victorians*, p. 407. *23.* Note de M. Guieysse, Ministre des Colonies, November 21, 1895, Berthelot to Guieysse, Paris, November 30, 1895, and Lebon to Liotard, Paris, June 23, 1896, *D.D.F.*, 12:304, 322–23, 655. Also interesting are Hanotaux, *Fachoda*, pp. 108–9 and A. Vizetelly, *Republican France*, Boston, [1912], p. 435. *24.* Hanotaux, *Fachoda*, pp. 105, 109. *25.* Camille

Vergniol, "Fachoda: I," in *La revue de France,* 16th year, 4 (July–August 1936):639–640: "Fachoda: III," in *La revue de France,* 5 (September–October, 1936):112. *26.* Hanotaux in a 1931 speech to the Académie des Sciences Coloniales, as quoted in Vergniol, "Fachoda: II," p. 642. *27.* Hanotaux to de Courcel, October 21, 1895, *C.P.: Angleterre,* 908:127–28; Hanotaux to de Courcel, December 12, 1896, *C.P.: Angleterre,* 921:115–16. *28.* Herbette to Bourgeois, Berlin, April 1, 1896, *D.D.F.,* 12:551–52; De Noailles to Hanotaux, Berlin, May 16, 1897, *D.D.F.,* 13; Nos. 237, 399; Robinson and Gallagher, *Africa and the Victorians,* p. 403. *29.* Lebon to Hanotaux, January 19, 1897, and Salisbury to de Courcel, December 30, 1896, *Afrique* VI, 142a; see also Geoffray to Hanotaux, London, November 26, 1896, *C.P.: Angleterre,* 920:199–204, and Chamberlain to Salisbury, Highbury, June 6, 1897, *The Joseph Chamberlain Papers,* The University of Birmingham, J.C. 11/6. Henceforth cited as J.C. 11/6.

30. Chamberlain to Selborne, Interlakken, September 12, 1897, letter, secret, in J.C. 11/6. *13.* Pontarice (Lieutenant Colonel, Attaché Militaire à l'Ambassade) to M. le Ministre de la Guerre, London, May 10, 1898, *Afrique* VI, 149c; Geoffray to Hanotaux, November 25 and November 26, 1896, *C.P.: Angleterre,* 920:194, 199–204; De Courcel to Hanotaux, December 2, 1897, *Afrique* VI, 142a; Robinson and Gallagher, *Africa and the Victorians,* p. 406; Margery Perham and Mary Bull, eds., *The Diaries of Lord Lugard,* 4 vols. (Evanston, Ill., 1963), 4:11–12, 325–29, passim. *32.* Geoffray to Hanotaux, April 1, 1897, *Grande Bretagne: Possession d'Outre Mer: Empire Britannique. Dossier General: 1897–1901,* pp. 26–27. Henceforth cited as *Empire Britannique: 1897–1901.* *33.* De Courcel to Hanotaux, July 18, 1896, *C.P. Angleterre,* 917:190–92; Geoffray to Hanotaux, December 31, 1896, *C.P.: Angleterre,* 921:236–37; Geoffray to Hanotaux, October 12, 1897, *Afrique* VI, 142a. *34.* Hanotaux to de Courcel, July 4, 1897, *Grande Bretagne: Politique Etrangère, Relations avec la France: 1897–1898* (Archives Diplomatiques), p. 72. Henceforth cited as *Grande Bretagne: 1897–1898;* Hanotaux to Lebon, October 15, 1897, *Afrique* VI, 142a.

Chapter Nine

1. Note du Ministre, March 26, 1897, and Communication du Baron de Courcel, Paris, March 26, 1897, both in *Grande Bretagne: 1897–1898,* pp. 31–38 and 48–51. *2.* Note de l'ambassade d'Allemagne, Paris, May 16, 1894, annexed to Hanotaux to Delcassé, August 23, 1894, and Delcassé to Hanotaux, September 18, 1894, *Afrique* IV, 38a; Article paru dans la *Kolnische* et la *Kreutz Zeitung* du 2 Octobre 1895, *Afrique* VI, 127a; Lebon to Hanotaux, January 26, 1897, *Afrique* VI, 144a. *3.* Guieysse to Ballot, Paris, March 26, 1897, *Dahomey,* 1–17; Robert Cornevin, *Histoire du Togo* (Paris, 1959), pp. 154–58; Hanotaux to Lebon, June 3 and December 11, 1896, *Afrique* IV, 38b; Lebon to Hanotaux, July 15, 1897, *Dahomey,* 1–18. *4.* Lebon to Hanotaux, May 4, and June 17, 1897, and Hanotaux to Lebon, June 3, 1897, *Afrique* VI, 142a. *5.* Note pour la Commission du Niger: Février 1896, *Afrique* VI, 133c; *Afrique* VI, 142a; Delcassé to Hanotaux, September 24, 1894, *Afrique* VI, 115c. *6.* Chamberlain to Selborne, Interlaken, September 12, 1897, secret, in J.C., 11/6 and Salisbury to Chamberlain, Hatfield House, September 17, 1897, in J.C. 5/7. (Selborne had shown Salisbury Chamberlain's September 12 letter.) See also C.W. Newbury, *The Western Slave Coast and its Rulers* (Oxford, 1961), p. 141. *7.* France, Ministère des Affaires Etrangères, *Documents Diplomatiques: Convention relative à la délimitation des possessions françaises du Dahomey et du Soudan et des possessions allemandes du Togo* (Paris, 1897); Hanotaux to Lebon, March 12, 1898; Hanotaux to Lebon, November 4, 1897, *Afrique* VI, 152a. *8.* Lebon to Hanotaux, January 19, 1897, Hanotaux to Lebon, June 3, 1897, and Monson to Hanotaux, September 24, 1897, *Afrique* VI, 142a. See also Binger to Hanotaux, Paris, November 5, 1897, *Afrique* VI, 141a. *9.* De Courcel to Hanotaux, May 13, 1897, *Empire Britannique: 1897–1901,* pp. 28–31.

10. Hanotaux to Lebon, October 27, 1897, and Salisbury to Monson, London, September 16, 1897, communicated to Hanotaux on October 3, 1897, *Afrique* VI, 142a. *11.* Lebon to Hanotaux, October 3, 1897, and Hanotaux to Lebon, September 29, 1897,

Afrique VI, 142a. *12.* This and the material in the next few paragraphs is based on comptes-rendus of the sessions written and signed by the French delegates, G. Binger and René Lecomte and found in *Afrique* VI, 149a. *13.* Comptes-rendus of the 8th session, December 7, 1897. *14.* Comptes-rendus of the 12th session, December 23, 1897; Hanotaux to Lebon, n.d., *Afrique* VI, 142a. *15.* Cf. Monson to Hanotaux, Paris, December 10, 1897, and Hanotaux to Monson, December 24, 1897, France, *Documents Diplomatiques, affaires du Haut Nile et du Bahr-el-Ghazal: 1897–1898* (Paris, 1898), pp. 1–3. *16.* Robinson and Gallagher, *Africa and the Victorians*, pp. 406–8; Monson to Salisbury, Paris, March 6, 1898, *British Documents on the Origins of the War* . . . , 1:146–47. *17.* Hanotaux to Lebon, January 25, 1898, *Afrique* VI, 149c; Hanotaux to Lebon, April 26, 1898, *Afrique* IV, 57c; Balfour to Monson, London, March 28, 1898, *British Documents on the Origins of the War*, 1:148–49. *18.* See n. 15. *19.* Hanotaux to Lebon, September 23, 1897, and Lebon to Hanotaux, September 29, 1897, *Afrique* VI, 142a; Hanotaux to Lebon, April 26, 1898, *Afrique* IV, 57c; Balfour to Monson, London, March 28, 1898, *British Documents on the Origins of the War*, 1:148–49.

20. Salisbury to Monson, London, May 6, 1898, *British Documents on the Origins of the War*, 1:158–59. *21.* France, *Documents Diplomatiques: Convention entre la France et la Grande Bretagne fixant la délimitation des possessions françaises . . . signé à Paris le 14 Juin 1898* (Paris, 1898). *22.* Etienne: *Son oeuvre coloniale* . . . , 1:312–13, 324.

Chapter Ten

1. There is a published dissertation on Etienne in German. See Herward Sieberg, *Eugène Etienne und die Französische Kolonialpolitik: 1887–1904*, (Cologne, 1968). An even better, although still to be published dissertation, is James J. Cooke, "Eugène Etienne and New French Imperialism: 1880–1910" (University of Georgia, 1969). *2.* Christopher Andrew, *Théophile Delcassé and the Making of the Entente Cordiale* (London and New York, 1968), pp. 51–52, 103–4. *3.* See Chapter VI. *4.* Andrew, *Théophile Delcassé*, pp. 87ff., 119ff. *5.* Renouvin, "Les origines de l'expedition de Fachoda," p. 96. *6.* Iiams, *Dreyfus, Diplomatists and the Dual Alliance*, pp. 91 ff. *7.* Faure, "Fachoda (1898)," p. 31 and Félix Faure, Notes personnelles xxiii, xxv, March 16, 30, 1895, Faure MSS. as quoted in Andrew, *Théophile Delcassé*, pp. 94–96, 119.

Selected Bibliography

Manuscript Sources

France, Archives de l'Ancien Ministère des Colonies, Correspondance Officielle: [File number in Roman numerals, box number in Arabic.]

Afrique II, 5; III, 17, 19–21, 30, 32, 33, 37; IV, 29, 30, 33–39, 44, 47, 53, 57; VI, 114, 115, 117, 120, 124–131, 133, 134, 136, 137, 141–144, 146, 149–154, 157; XII, 2; XIII, 1.

Afrique Equatoriale Française, I, 1.

Côte d' Ivoire, VI, 3.

Côte des Somalis, 131, 136, 137, 142.

Dahomey, I, 17–19.

Gabon, VI, 19.

Guinée, VI, 1, 5.

Madagascar, 216^{448}, 216^{451}, 216^{452}, 314^{813}, 361^{987}, 382^{1034}.

Océan Indien, 18^{98}, 20^{107}, 21^{115}.

Somalis, 17.

Soudan, VI, 1.

France, Archives Diplomatiques, Correspondance Politique:

Allemagne, Questions Coloniales, vol. 1 (1897–1903).

Allemagne, Politique Etrangère, Dossier Général, vol. 1 (1897–1903).

Allemagne, Politique Etrangère, Relations avec la France, vol. 1 (1897–1900).

Angleterre, vols. 894 (June 1894)–921 (December 1896).

Angleterre, Aden, vol. 113 (1885–1895).

Angleterre, Zanzibar, vol. 19 (1894).

Autriche-Hongrie, Politique Etrangère, Relations avec la France, vol. 1 (1896–1901).

Belgique, vols. 91 (June–December 1894) – 94 (1896).

Belgique, Politique Etrangère, Dossier General, vol. 1 (1897–1914).

Belgique, Politique Etrangère, Relations avec la France, vol. 1 (1897–1907).

Espagne, vols. 924 (April–June 1894) – 929 (July–December 1896).

Espagne, Politique Etrangère, Dossier General, vol. 1 (1896–1906).

Espagne, Politique Etrangère, Relations avec la France, vol. 1 (1896–1904).

Grande Bretagne, Affaires Commerciales: Relations et Conventions avec la France, vol. 1 (1897–1908).

Grande Bretagne, Politique Etrangère, Dossier Général, vol. 1 (1897–1898).

Grande Bretagne, Politique Etrangère, Relations avec la France, vol. 1 (1897–1898).

Grand Bretagne, Possessions d'Outre-Mer, Empire Britannique, Dossier Général, vol. 1 (1897–1901).

Italie, vols. 116 (January–February 1895) – 118 (May–June 1895).

Italie, Colonies, vol. 1 (1897–1906).

Italie, Politique Etrangère, Dossier Général, vol. 1 (1897–1904).

Italie, Politique Etrangère, Relations avec la France, vol. 1 (1897–1898).

Maroc, vols. 70 (June–August 1894) – 74 (August–September 1895).

Russie, Politique Etrangère, Dossier Général, vol. 1 (March 1893–December 1894, and January 1897–September 1898).

Mémoires et Documents: Afrique, Abyssinie 5, vol. 138 (1887–1895).

Mémoires et Documents: Afrique Australe 2, vol. 140 (1888–1895).

Mémoires et Documents: Congo et Gabon, vol. 14 (1894–1898).

Mémoires et Documents: Possessions Allemandes de l'Afrique Occidentales, vol. 134 (1884–1895).

Mémoires et Documents: Possessions Anglaises de la Côte Occidentales, vol. 131 (1893–1894).

France, Archives de l'ex-government général de l'Algérie, Aix en Provence: A sampling to check information found at the Archives Nationales and in the Archives Diplomatiques was made.

France, Archives du Ministère de la Guerre; Section Moderne: Various boxes were read on a sampling basis to cross-check information from other manuscript sources.

France, Archives Nationales, F.[80] (Algeria), 1684, 1686–1690, 1693, 1695–1698, 1709, 1710, 1715, 1727, 1733, 1744, 1773, 1784–1786, 1794, 1860, and F.[80*] (Algeria: maps), 2037, 2040.

Great Britain, Foreign Office, Confidential Prints, F. O. 403 (Africa), vols. 201, 202, 218, 219, 236, 237, 252, (Congo); 222, 240, 256 (Madagascar); 235, 251, (Niger); 204, 205, 220, 238, 253, 254, 272, 273 (Tunisia).

Great Britain, Foreign Office, Confidential Prints, F.O. 413 (Morocco), vols. 22–29.

Great Britain, Foreign Office, Confidential Prints, F.O. 633 (The Cromer Papers), vols. 5–8, 11.

Great Britain, Foreign Office, *Diplomatic Correspondence,* F.O. 146 (Paris), vols. 3415, 3422.

University of Birmingham, *The Joseph Chamberlain Papers.*

Published Documents

De Clercq, Jules, ed. *Recueil des traités de la France.* Paris, 1900.

Dugdale, E. T. S., ed. *German Diplomatic Documents: 1871–1914.* 4 volumes. New York, 1923–1931.

France, *Annales de la Chambre des deputés, Débats parlementaires.* 1894–1898.

France, *Annales du Sénat, Débats parlementaires,* 1894–1898.

France, Ministére des Affaires Etrangères, *Documents diplomatiques:*

L'affaire de Madagascar: 1885–1895. Paris, 1895.
Affaires du Haut Nil et du Bahr el Ghazal: 1897–1898. Paris, 1898.

Afrique: Arrangements, actes et conventions concernant le nord, l'ouest et le centre de l'Afrique, 1881–1898, Paris, 1898.

Convention entre la France et la Grande Bretagne fixant la délimitation des possessions françaises . . . signé à Paris le 14 juin 1898. Paris, 1898.

Convention relative à la délimitation des possessions françaises du Dahomey et du Soudan et des possessions allemandes du Togo. Paris, 1897.

Correspondance et documents relatif à la convention franco-anglaise du 14 juin 1898: 1890–98. Paris, 1898.

Délimitation des possessions françaises à la côte occidentale d'Afrique: 1889–1895. Paris, 1895.

Révision des traités Tunisiens: 1881–1897. Paris, 1897.

France, Ministère des Affaires Etrangères, *Documents diplomatiques français.* 1st series (1871–1901), vols. 11–14. Paris, 1947–1951.

Hertslet, Sir Edward. *The Map of Africa by Treaty.* 3d ed. 3 volumes. London, 1909.

Great Britain. *British and Foreign State Papers, 1889–1897.* vols. 82–89. London, 1890–1900.

Great Britain. *British Documents on the Origins of the War.* vol. 1. London, 1922.

Italy. Ministero Degli Affari Esteri. *I Documenti Diplomatici Italiani.* Terza Serie (1896–1907). vols. 1, 2. Rome, 1953.

Renault, Louis, editor. *Archives diplomatiques: 1894–1898.* vols. 49–67. Paris, 1894–1899.

Biographies and Memoirs

Andrassy, Count Julius. *Bismarck, Andrassy and Their Successors.* London, 1927.

Andrew, Christopher. *Théophile Delcassé and the Making of the Entente Cordiale.* New York and London, 1968.

Barclay, Sir Thomas. *Thirty Years: Anglo-French Reminiscences (1876–1906).* Boston and New York, 1914.

Billot, A. *La France et l'Italie, Histoire des années troubles, 1881–1899.* 2 volumes. New York, 1921.

Black, Charles E. Drummond. *The Marquess of Dufferin and Ava.* Toronto, 1903.

Blunt, Wilfrid Scawen. *My Diaries: Being a Personal Narrative of Events, 1888–1914.* 2 volumes. New York, 1921.

Boulger, Demetrius C. *The Reign of Leopold II.* 2 volumes. London, 1925.

Bourgin, J. "Francesco Crispi" in *Les politiques d'expansion imperialiste.* Paris, 1949.

Braibant, C. editor. *Félix Faure à l'Elysée: Souvenirs De Louis Le Gall.* Paris, 1963.

Buckle, George Earle, editor. *The Letters of Queen Victoria.* 3d. series, 3 volumes. London, 1932.

Cambon, Henri, editor. *Paul Cambon, Correspondance, 1870–1924.* 3 volumes. Paris, 1940–1946.

Cecil, Lady Gwendolen. *Life of Robert Marquis of Salisbury.* 4 volumes. London, 1931–1932.

Cooke, James J. "Eugène Etienne and New French Imperialism: 1880–1910." Ph.D. dissertation, University of Georgia, 1969.

Crewe, Robert Offley Ashburton, 1st Marquis of. *Lord Rosebery.* New York, 1931.

Delabrousse, Lucien. *Joseph Magnin et son temps, 1824–1910.* 2 volumes. Paris. n.d. [1916.]

De Lichtervelde, Comte Louis. *Leopold of the Belgians.* Translated by Thomas H. Reed and H. Russell Reed. New York and London, 1929.

Deschamps, Hubert, et Paul Chauvet, eds. *Gallieni Pacificateur: Ecrits coloniaux de Gallieni.* Paris, 1949.

Deschanel, Paul. *Gambetta.* Paris, 1919.

Eubank, K. *Paul Cambon, Master Diplomatist.* Norman, Oklahoma, 1960.

Ferrata, Cardinal Dominique. *Mémoires: Ma nonciature en France.* 2d. ed. Paris, 1922.

Franqueville, Comte de. *Souvenirs, 1840–1919.* Paris. [1920].

Gardiner, A. G. *The Life of Sir William Harcourt.* 2 volumes. New York, 1923.

Garvin, J. L. *The Life of Joseph Chamberlain.* 3 volumes. London, 1933–1934.

Gillet, Louis. *Gabriel Hanotaux: 19 Novembre 1933.* Paris, 1933.

Grenville, J. A. S. *Lord Salisbury and Foreign Policy.* London, 1968.

Grey, Viscount Edward, of Fallodon. *Twenty-Five Years, 1892–1916.* 2 volumes. New York, 1925.

Hanotaux, Gabriel, "Carnets" (Selections edited by G. L. Jaray), *Revue des Deux Mondes,* April 1949, pp. 385–403, 573–588.

—————. *Mon Temps.* 4 volumes. Paris, 1933.

Hansen, Jules. *Ambassade à Paris du Baron de Mohrenheim (1884–1898).* Paris, n.d.

Hardinge, Sir Arthur. *A Diplomatist in Europe.* London, 1927.

Hardy, G. *Portrait de Lyautey.* Mayenne (France), 1949.

Iiams, T. M. Jr. *Dreyfus Diplomatists and the Dual Alliance: Gabriel Hanotaux at the Quai d'Orsay 1894–1898.* Geneva, 1962.

James, R. R. *Rosebery: A Biography of Archibald Philip, Fifth Earl of Rosebery.* London, 1963.

Julien, Ch.-A. "Lyautey" in Robert Delavignette et Ch.-A. Julien. *Les constructeurs de la France d'outre-mer.* Paris, 1946.

Julien, Ch.-A., J. Bruhat, G. Bourgin, M. Crouzet et P. Renouvin. *Les Politiques d'expansion imperialiste: J. Ferry—Léopold II—Fr. Crispi—J. Chamberlain —Th. Roosevelt.* Paris, 1949.

Julien, Ch.-A., et al. *Les Techniciens de la colonisation* (XIXᵉ—XXᵉ siècles). Paris, 1947.

Kennedy, A. L. *Salisbury 1830–1903: Portrait of a Statesman.* London: John Murray, 1953.

La Martinière, Henri de. *Souvenirs du Maroc.* Paris, 1919.

Legrand-Girard, Général. *Un Quart de siècle au service de la France.* Paris, 1954.

Lyall, Sir Alfred. *The Life of the Marquis of Dufferin and Ava.* 2 volumes. London, 1905.

Lyautey, Hubert. *Lettres du Tonkin et de Madagascar (1894–1899).* 2nd. ed. Paris, 1921.

Maurois, André. *Lyautey.* Translated by Hamish Miles. New York, 1931.

Michell, Sir Lewis. *The Life of the Rt. Hon. Cecil J. Rhodes, 1853–1902.* 2 volumes. London, 1910.

Monteil, P. L. *Quelques feuillets de l'histoire coloniale.* Paris, 1924.

Neton, Albéric. *Delcassé: 1852–1923.* Paris, 1952.

L'oeuvre colonial, algérienne et politique de Eugène Etienne; collected and edited by the "Depêche Coloniale." Paris, 1907.

Palamenghi-Crispi, ed. *The Memoirs of Francesco Crispi.* Translated by Mary Prichard-Agnetti. 3 volumes. London, 1914.

Paléologue, Maurice. *Journal de l'affaire Dreyfus, 1894–1899: L'affaire Dreyfus et le Quai d'Orsay.* Paris, 1955.

Paul-Boncour, Joseph. *Recollections of the Third Republic.* Translated by George Marion, Jr. New York, 1957.

Perham, Margery. *Lugard: The Years of Adventure 1858–1898.* London, 1956.

Perham, M., and Mary Bull. eds., *The Diaries of Lord Lugard.* Evanston, Ill., 1963.

Porter, Charles W. *The Career of Théophile Delcassé.* Philadelphia, 1936.

Power, Thomas F., Jr. *Jules Ferry and the Renaissance of French Imperialism.* New York, 1944.

Rambaud, Alfred. *Jules Ferry.* Paris, 1903.

Reclus, Maurice. *Jules Ferry, 1832–1893.* Paris, 1947.

Rodd, Sir James Rennell. *Social and Diplomatic Memories, 1884–1901.* 2 volumes. London, 1922.

Saint-Aulaire, Comte de. *Confession d'un vieux diplomate.* Paris, 1953.

Samné, George. *Raymond Poincaré, politique et personnel de la IIIe République.* Paris, 1933.

Sieberg, Herward, *Eugène Etienne und die Französische Kolonialpolitik: 1887–1904.* Cologne, 1968.

Siegfried, André. *Mes souvenirs de la IIIe République: Mon père et son temps, 1836–1922.* Paris, 1946.

Simon, Jules. *Le soir de ma journée.* Paris, n.d.

Steed, Henry Wickham. *Through Thirty Years, 1892–1922.* 2 volumes. New York, 1924.

Suarez, Georges. *La vie orgueilleuse de Clemenceau.* Paris, 1930.

Tabouis, Geneviève. *The Life of Jules Cambon.* Translated by C. F. Atkinson. London, 1938.

Trevelyan, George Macauley. *Grey of Fallodon: The Life and Letters of Sir Edward Grey, afterwards Viscount Grey of Fallodon.* Boston, 1937.

Un Diplomate. *Paul Cambon ambassadeur de France.* Paris, 1937.

Villot, Roland. *Eugène Etienne: 1844–1921*. Oran, 1951.

William II. *The Kaiser's Memoirs*. Translated by R. Ybarra. New York, 1922.

Willson, Beckles. *America's Ambassadors to France (1777–1929)*. New York, 1928.

Articles

Berger, François. "Le ministère Léon Bourgeois et la politique étrangère de Marcellin Berthelot au Quai d'Orsay." *Revue d'histoire diplomatique* 71 (1957):93–125.

Cambon, Paul. "Lettres au Président de la République Félix Faure (1895–1899)." *Revue d'histoire diplomatique* 68 (1954):189–201.

Charles-Roux, François. "La mort de Moulay Hassan." *Revue d'histoire diplomatique* 61 (1947):191–98.

Charmes, Francis. "Chronique de la quinzaine." *Revue des deux Mondes* 122–153 (April 1894–April 1900).

Comité de l'Afrique française. *Bulletin de l'Afrique française* (1893–1898).

"Convention franco-congolaise du 14 Août 1894." *Revue Française* (September 1894).

Coubertin, Baron Pierre de. "The Chancellor of the French Republic—Gabriel Hanotaux." *The Review of Reviews* (1897).

Dehéran, Henri. "L'Egypte et la province équatoriale." *Revue des deux Mondes* 121 (January–June 1894).

De la Martinière, M. H. "Le règne de Moulai-el-Hassen." *Revue des deux Mondes* 125 (September–October 1894):398–436.

Dethan, Georges. "Le rapprochement franco-italien après la chute de Crispi jusqu'aux accords Barrère-Visconti-Venosta sur le Maroc et la Tripolitaine (1896–1900)." *Revue d'histoire diplomatique* 70 (1956):323–339.

Diplomaticus. "Where Lord Salisbury Has Failed." *The Fortnightly Review* 63 (1898): 513–523.

Dollot, René. "Un ambassadeur de France sous la troisième République: Albert Decrais (1838–1915)." *Revue d'histoire diplomatique* 63 (1949):9–37.

_____ "Commémorations: Camille Barrère (1851–1940)." *Revue d'histoire diplomatique* 65 (1951):241–47.

_____ "Deux grands Lorrains Jules Ferry et Raymond Poincaré." *Revue d'histoire diplomatique* 62:172–214.

_____ "Diplomatie et Présidence de la République." *Revue d'histoire diplomatique* 68 (1954):208–230.

_____ "Un Triestin ambassadeur d'Italie à Paris: Constantin Ressman (1832–1899)." *Revue d'histoire diplomatique* 67 (1953):127–139, 227–250.

_____ "Sous les lambris de l'Elysée, La vie diplomatique au temps de Félix Faure." *Revue d'histoire diplomatique* 69 (1955):40–60.

_____ "Souvenirs diplomatiques." *Revue d'histoire diplomatique* 64 (1950):142–170.

Dupuis, Charles. "Le français langue diplomatique moderne." *Revue d'histoire diplomatique* 39 (1925): 103–130.

Edwards, F. A. "The French on the Niger." *The Fortnightly Review* 63, New Series (January–June 1898):578–591.

Estournelles de Constant, Paul d'. "Contre la représentation coloniale." *La Revue de Paris* 6, 1 (January–February 1899):203–213.

Faure, Félix. "Fachoda (1898)." *Revue d'histoire diplomatique* 69 (1955):29–39.

Filon, Augustin. "Lord Salisbury from a French Point of View." *The Fortnightly Review* 64 (December 1, 1895):803–812.

François, Auguste. "Exhumation des restes de Richelieu à la Sorbonne par M. Hanotaux, Ministre des Affaires Etrangères." *Revue d'histoire diplomatique* 70 (1956):151–55.

Gertzel, Cherry. "Relations Between African and European Traders in the Niger Delta: 1880–1896." *Journal of African History* 3 (1962):361–66.

"M. Hanotaux." *The Fortnightly Review* 63 New Series (January–June 1898): 173–188.

Hanotaux, Gabriel. "Madagascar et le régime du protectorat." *La Revue de Paris* 3, 2 (March–April 1896):474–487.

_____ "Le Partage de l'Afrique." *La Revue de Paris* 3, 2 (March–April 1896), 5–27.

_____ "Le Traité de Tananarive." *La Revue de Paris* 3, 1 (January–February 1896), 5–25.

Hargreaves, J. D. "Entente Manquée; Anglo-French Relations, 1895–1896." *The Cambridge Historical Journal* 11, no. 1 (1953):65–92.

Hornik, M. P. "The Anglo-Belgian Agreement of 12 May 1894." *The English Historical Review* 62 (April, 1942):227–243.

Hugodot, M. "L'opinion publique anglaise et l'Affaire de Fachoda." *Revue d'histoire des colonies* 44 (1957): 113–137.

Jourdier, F. "L'occupation de Boussa." *La Depêche Coloniale* (April 10, 1897).

Lavisse, Ernest. "France et Angleterre." *La Revue de Paris* 6 (January–February 1899): 453–482.

Leaman, Bertha R. "The Influence of Domestic Policy on Foreign Affairs in France, 1898–1905." *Journal of Modern History* 14 (1942):449–479.

Lebon, André. "La mission Marchand et le cabinet Méline." *Revue des deux mondes* 163 (March–April 1900):274–296.

LeGall, L. "Opinions de Paul Cambon sur le rôle, en politique étrangère de quelques Ministres et de divers Presidents de la République." *Revue d'histoire diplomatiques* 68 (1954): 202–7.

Le Myre, De Villers. "Le Traité Hova." *La Revue de Paris* 2, 6 (November–December 1895):225–241.

Lowther, James W. "Some Anglo-French Problems." *National Review* (March–August 1895), 306–317.

Lugard, F. D. "England and France in the Nile Valley." *National Review*: 25 (March–August 1895):609–622.

Lyautey, M. le lieutenant-colonel. "Du rôle colonial de l'armée." *Revue des deux mondes* 162 (January–February 1900):308–328.

Mackenzie, George S. "Uganda and the East African Protectorates." *The Fortnightly Review* 62 (December 1, 1894):882–894.

Marcus, Harold G. "Ethio-British Negotiations Concerning the Western Border with Sudan, 1896–1902." *Journal of African History* 4 (1963):81–94.

Marsden, Arthur. "Britain and the End of the Tunis Treaties, 1894–1897." *The English Historical Review* Supplement 1 (1965).

Menier, M. A., editor. "Letters du commandant Marchand à Guillaume Grandidier." *Revue d'histoire des colonies* 45 (1958):61–108.

Miller, T. B. "The Egyptian Question and British Foreign Policy, 1892–1894." *Journal of Modern History* 32 (March, 1960):1–15.

Newbury, C. W. "The Development of French Policy on the Lower and Upper Niger, 1880–98." *The Journal of Modern History* 31 (March 1959):16–26.

Ormesson, Marquis d'. "Deux grandes figures de la diplomatie française: Paul et Jules Cambon." *Revue d'histoire diplomatique* 62 (1943):37–71.

"The Progress of the World," *The Review of Reviews* 9–18 (1894–1898).

Rain, Pierre. "La Diplomatie Européenne à la fin du XIXᵉ siècle." *Revue d'histoire diplomatique* 54 (1960):271–281.

"The Record of the Rosebery Administration." *The Review of Reviews* 12 (August 1895):190–200.

Renouvin, P. "Les origine de l'expedition de Fachoda." *Revue Historique* 200 (1948):180–197.

Riker, T. W. "A Survey of British Policy in the Fashoda Crisis." *Political Science Quarterly* 44 (1929):54–78.

Saint Quentin, René de. "Le Comte de Saint-Aulaire." *Revue d'histoire diplomatique* 68 (1954):285–295.

Saint-René-Taillandier, Mᵐᵉ. "Silhouettes d'ambassadeurs." *Revue d'histoire diplomatique* 66 (1952):7–22, 189–206.

Sanderson, G. N. "Contribution from African Sources to the History of European Competition in the Upper Valley of the Nile." *Journal of African History* 3 (1962):69–90.

Siegfried, André. "Un Centenaire: Théophile Delcassé (1852–1923)." *Revue d'histoire diplomatique* 66 (1952):23–26.

Stengers, Jean. "La première tentative de reprise du Congo par la Belgique." *Bulletin de la société royale belge de géographie* 63 (1949):1–80.

Taylor, A. J. P. "Prelude to Fashoda: The question of the Nile, 1894–5." *The English Historical Review* 65 (January, 1950):52–80.

——————. "Les premières années de l'alliance russe (1892–1895)." *Revue historique* 204 (July–September 1950):62–76.

Vergniol, Camille. "Fachoda." *La Revue de France* 4 (July–August 1936):416–434, 630–645; 5 (September–October 1936): 112–128.

Selected Works

Abbas, Mekki. *The Sudan Question: The Dispute over the Anglo-Egyptian Condominium, 1884–1951*. London, 1952.

Baillaud, Boutroux, Chailley, et al. *Un demi-siècle de civilisation française*. Paris, 1916.

Barisien, Pierre. *Le Parlement et les Traités*. Paris, 1913.

Becker, Jeronimo. *España y Marruecos: Sus Relaciones Diplomaticas Durante el Siglo XIX*. Madrid, 1903.

Betts, Raymond F. *Assimilation and Association in French Colonial Theory: 1890–1914*. New York and London, 1961.

Blet, Henri. *France D'Outre-Mer*. Paris, 1950.

Bourgeois, E., et Pagès, G. *Origines et responsibilités de la grande guerre*. Paris, 1922.

Brunschwig, Henri. *La colonisation française*. Paris, 1949.

Brunschwig, Henri. *L'expansion allemande outre-mer: du XVᵉ siècle à nos jours*. Paris, 1957.

Brunschwig, Henri. *French Colonialism, 1871–1914: Myths and Realities*. Translated by W. G. Brown. London, 1964.

Buck, Philip W. and Martin B. Travis, Jr. *Control of Foreign Relations in Modern Nations*. New York, 1957.

Cambon, Henri. *Histoire du Maroc*. Paris, 1952.

Cambon, Jules. *Le gouvernement général de l'Algérie: 1891–1897*. Paris and Algiers, 1918.

Card, E. Rouard de. *Le Prince Bismarck et l'expansion de la France en Afrique*. Paris, 1918.

Carroll, E. Malcolm. *French Public Opinion and Foreign Affairs*. New York and London, 1931.

_____. *Germany and the Great Powers, 1866–1914: A Study in Public Opinion and Foreign Policy*. New York, 1938.

Chapman, Guy. *The Dreyfus Case*. London, 1955.

Charles-Roux, François et Jacques Caillé. *Missions diplomatiques françaises à Fez*. Paris, 1955.

Confer, Vincent. *France and Algeria: The Problem of Civil and Political Reform, 1870–1920*. Syracuse, 1966.

Cornevin, Robert. *Histoire de l'Afrique des origines à nos jours*. Paris, 1956.

_____. *Histoire du Togo*. Paris, 1959.

Cruickshank, Earl Fee. *Morocco at the Parting of the Ways*. Philadelphia, 1935.

Daniel, André. (Georges Bonnefous) *L'année politique, 1894–98*. Paris, 1895–99.

D'Anthouard, Baron, et al. *L'empire colonial français*. Paris, 1929.

Darcy, Jean. *Cent années de rivalité coloniale*. Paris, 1904.

Debidour, A. *Histoire diplomatique de l'Europe depuis le congrés de Berlin jusqu'à nos jours*. 2 volumes; Paris, 1919.

De Lanessan, J.L. *Histoire de l'entente cordiale franco-anglaise*. Paris, 1916.

Derry, T. K. and T. L. Jarman. *The European World, 1870–1945*. London, 1950.

De Saint Aymour, Robert Caix. *Fachoda: la France et l'Angleterre*. Paris, 1899.

Dhombres, Pierre. *Imperialismes et démocraties*. Paris, 1946.

Dimnet, Ernest. *France Herself Again*. New York and London, 1914.

Doresse, Jean. *Ethiopia*. Translated by Elsa Coult. London and New York, 1959.

Droz, Jacques. *Histoire diplomatique de 1648 à 1919*. Paris, 1952.

Dubois, Marcel et August Terrier. *Les colonies françaises: un siècle d'expansion coloniale*. Paris, 1902.

Duchêne, Albert. *La politique coloniale de la France*. Paris, 1928.

Dumas, Pierre. *Le Maroc*. Grenoble, 1928.

Ensor, R. C. K. *England, 1870–1914*. Volume 14 of *The Oxford History of England*. Oxford, 1952.

Epstein, M., ed. *The Annual Register: A Review of Public Events at Home and Abroad for the Year 1944*. New Series; London, New York, and Toronto, 1945.

Esquer, Gabriel. *Histoire de l'Algérie: 1830–1960*. Paris, 1960.

Gay, J. *Les deux Romes et l'opinion française: Les rapports franco-italien depuis 1815*. Paris, 1931.

Gibbons, Herbert Adams. *The New Map of Africa, 1900–1916*. New York, 1916.

Giffen, Morrison Beall. *Fashoda: The Incident and Its Diplomatic Setting*. Chicago, 1930.

Glanville, James Linus. *Italy's Relations with England: 1896–1905*. The Johns Hopkins University Studies in Historical and Political Science, vol 52, no. 1. Baltimore, 1934.

Gooch, G. P. *Franco-German Relations, 1871–1914*. New York, Toronto, 1923.

_____. *History of Modern Europe, 1878–1919*. New York, London, 1923.

Grant, A. J. and Harold Temperley. *Europe in the Nineteenth and Twentieth Centuries, 1789–1939*. London, 1940.

Gray, Ezio F. *Italy and the Question of Tunis*. Milan, 1939.

Guernier, E. L. *L'Afrique champ d'expansion de l'Europe*. Paris, 1933.

Hale, Oron James. *Publicity and Diplomacy: With Special Reference to England and Germany, 1890–1914*. New York, 1940.

Hamman, Otto. *The World Policy of Germany, 1890–1912*. Translated by Maude A. Huttman, New York, 1921.

Hanotaux, Gabriel. *L'Affaire de Madagascar*. Paris, 1896.

_____. *Fachoda*. Paris, 1909.

_____. *Histoire de la France contemporaine*. 4 volumes. Paris, 1908.

_____. *La paix latine*. Paris, 1903.

_____. *Pour l'empire colonial français*. Paris, 1933.

_____, and Alfred Martineau, eds. *Histoire des colonies françaises et de l'expansion de la France dans le monde*. 6 volumes. Paris, 1929–1934.

Hardy, Georges. *Vue générale de l'histoire d'Afrique*. Paris, 1922.

Hargreaves, J. D. *Prelude to the Partition of West Africa*. London, 1963.

Harris, Norman Dwight. *Europe and Africa*. Boston, 1927.

Harris, Walter B. *France, Spain and the Rif*. London, 1927.

Hauser, Henri, ed. *Histoire diplomatique de l'Europe, 1871–1914*. 2 volumes. Paris, 1929.

Herzog, Wilhelm. *From Dreyfus to Pétain*. Translated by Walter Sorell. New York, 1947.

Holt, P. M. *The Mahdist State in the Sudan, 1881–1898*. Oxford, 1958.

Horrabin, J. F. *An Atlas of Africa*. 2d ed.; New York, 1961.

Hoskins, H. L. *European Imperialism in Africa*. New York, 1930.

Hughes, John. *The New Face of Africa South of the Sahara*. New York, London, Toronto, 1961.

Imbert, Nath, ed. *Dictionnaire national des contemporains*. Paris, 1939.

Jesman, Czeslaw. *The Russians in Ethiopia*. London, 1958.

Jolly, Jean, et al. *Dictionnaire des parlementaires français*. Paris, 1960.

Julien, Ch.-A., J. Bruhat, et al. *Les politiques d'expansion imperialiste*. Colonies et empire, deuxième serie: Etudes coloniales. Paris, 1949.

Keith, A. B. *The Belgian Congo and the Berlin Act*. Oxford, 1919.

Keltie, J. Scott. *The Partition of Africa*. London, 1893.

Knight, Melvin M. *Morocco as a French Economic Venture*. New York and London, 1937.

Landau, Rom. *Moroccan Drama, 1900–1955*. London, 1956.

Langer, William L. *European Alliances and Alignments*. New York, 1931.
_____. *The Diplomacy of Imperialism*. 2d ed. New York, 1956.

Lebon, André. *La pacification de Madagascar: 1896–1898*. Paris, Plon, 1928.

Lémonon, Ernest. *L'Europe et la politique britannique, 1882–1911*. Paris, 1912.

Leroy-Beaulieu, Paul. *De la colonisation chez les peouples modernes*. 3d. ed. Paris, 1886.

Lewin, P. Evans. *The Germans and Africa*. London, Toronto, Melbourne, and Sydney, 1939.

Ling, Dwight L. *Tunisia from Protectorate to Republic*. Bloomington and London, 1967.

Lobanov-Rostovsky, Prince A. *Russia and Asia*. New York, 1933.

Longrigg, Stephen H. *A Short History of Eritrea*. Oxford, 1945.

Lucas, Sir Charles. *The Partition and Colonization of Africa*. Oxford, 1922.

Marlowe, John. *A History of Modern Egypt*. New York, 1954.

Martin, Claude. *Histoire de l'Algérie française: 1830–1962*. Paris, 1962.

Masoin, Fritz. *Histoire de l'Etat Independent du Congo*. Namu, 1913.

Maurras, Charles. *Kiel et Tanger, 1895–1905: La République française devant l'Europe*. 3d ed. Paris, 1921.

Mévil, André. *De la paix de Francfort à la conférence d'Algésiras*. Paris, 1909.

Michon, George. *L'Alliance franco-russe, 1871–1917*. Paris, 1927.

Miège, J. L. *Le Maroc*. Paris, 1962.

Millet, René. *Notre politique exterieur de 1898 à 1905*. Paris, 1905.

Moon, Parker T. *Imperialism and World Politics*. New York, 1947.

Morel, E. D. *Morocco in Diplomacy*. London, 1912.

Morié, L.-J. *Histoire de l'Ethiopie*. 2 volumes. Paris, 1904.

Newbury, C. W. *The Western Slave Coast and its Rulers*. Oxford, 1961.

Orsini, Paolo d'Agostino. *Francia contro Italia in Africa da Tunisi a Suez*. Milan, 1939.

Pedler, F. J. *Economic Geography of West Africa*. London, New York and Toronto, 1955.

Pinon, René. *L'Empire de la Mediterranée*. 3d ed. Paris, 1912.

_____. *France et Allemagne: 1870–1913*. Paris, 1913.

Pribram, A. F. *England and the International Policy of European Great Powers, 1871–1914*. Oxford, 1931.

Priestley, Herbert Ingram. *France Overseas*. New York and London, 1938.

Réclus, Maurice. *Grandeur de la Troisième République: De Gambetta à Poincaré*. Paris, 1948.

_____. *La Troisième République de 1870 à 1918*. Paris, 1945.

Renouvin, Pierre. *Le XIXᵉ siècle: De 1871 à 1914: l'apogée de l'Europe*. Volume 6. Pierre Renouvin, editor. *Histoire des relations internationales*. 8 volumes. Paris, 1953–1957.

Reynald, George. *La Diplomatie française: L'Oeuvre de M. Delcassé*. Paris, 1915.

Roberts, Stephen H. *History of French Colonial Policy*. 2 volumes. London, 1929.

Robinson, Ronald and John Gallagher. *Africa and the Victorians*. New York, 1961.

Rosebery, Archibald Philip Primrose. *The Foreign Policy of Lord Rosebery: Two Chapters in Recent Politics 1886 and 1892–5 With Extracts from Lord Rosebery's Speeches*. London, 1901.

Sanderson, G. N. *England, Europe and the Upper Nile, 1882–1899*. Edinburgh, 1965.

Schmitt, Bernadotte E., ed. *Some Historians of Modern Europe*. Chicago, 1941.

Schuman, Frederick L. *War and Diplomacy in the French Republic*. New York and London, 1931.

Seton-Watson, R. W. *Britain in Europe, 1789–1914*. London, 1937.

Shibeika, Mekki. *British Policy in the Sudan, 1882–1902*. London, New York, Toronto, 1952.

Simond, Emile. *Histoire de la Troisième République de 1897 à 1899*. Paris, 1921.

Sontag, Raymond James. *Germany and England, Background of Conflict, 1848–1894*. New York and London, 1938.

Sorel, Jean Albert. *Histoire de France et d'Angleterre*. Amsterdam et Paris, 1950.

Soulier, A. *L'instabilité ministérielle sous la Troisième République*. Paris, 1939.

Stern, Jacques. *The French Colonies Past and Present,* translated from the French by Norbert Guterman. New York, 1944.

Stuart, Graham H. *French Foreign Policy: From Fashoda to Serajevo, 1898–1914.* New York, 1921.

Taylor, A. J. P. *The Struggle for Mastery in Europe, 1848–1918.* Oxford, 1954.

Temperley, Harold and Lillian M. Penson. *Foundations of British Foreign Policy: From Pitt (1792) to Salisbury (1902).* London, 1938.

Terrasse, Henri. *Histoire du Maroc des origines à l'éstablissement du protectorat français.* Casablanca, 1950.

Terrier, August and Charles Mourey. *L'expansion française et la formation territoriale.* Paris, Larose, 1910.

Theobald, A. B. *The Mahdiya: A History of the Anglo-Egyptian Sudan, 1881–1899.* London, New York, Toronto, 1951.

Torres, Rodolfo Gil [Benumerji]. *España y el Mundo Arabe.* Madrid, 1955.

Townsend, Mary Evelyn. *The Rise and Fall of Germany's Colonial Empire, 1884–1918.* New York, 1930.

Ullendorff, Edward. *The Ethiopians.* London, New York, Toronto, 1960.

Usborne. *The Conquest of Morocco.* London, 1936.

Vizetelly, Ernest Alfred. *Republican France.* Boston. [1912?]

Zévaes, A. *Histoire de la Troisième République.* Paris, 1926.

Index